SECRETS
of the SEVEN
SMALLEST
STATES
of Europe

TRAVEL AND CULTURE GUIDES FROM HIPPOCRENE BOOKS

Language and Travel Guide to Ukraine, Fourth Edition

Poland's Jewish Landmarks: A Travel Guide

SECRETS
of the SEVEN
SMALLEST
STATES
of Europe

ANDORRA, LIECHTENSTEIN,
LUXEMBOURG, MALTA,
MONACO, SAN MARINO,
AND VATICAN CITY

Thomas M. Eccardt

HIPPOCRENE BOOKS, INC.
New York

© 2005 Thomas M. Eccardt

All rights reserved.

ISBN 0-7818-1032-9

For information, address:
Hippocrene Books, Inc.
171 Madison Avenue
New York, NY 10016

Book design and composition by Susan A. Ahlquist.

Cataloging-in-Publication data available from the Library of Congress.

Printed in the United States of America.

To my high school friend, Shep, whose 1983 microstate grand tour inspired this book.

Contents

Contents

Contents

A Short Introduction to Some Small Places

F ew people know much about microstates, though millions visit them each year. Many travelers to Rome have been in a microstate without realizing it: When you walk into St. Peter's Square, you enter the world's smallest country, Vatican City, population 890. People who travel by rail between Austria and Switzerland zip right through another microstate: most trains that pass through Liechtenstein do not stop there.

Not every microstate is in Europe. Nauru, a tiny island nation in the South Pacific, has 10,000 citizens, the next highest population after Vatican City. The most popular definition of a microstate limits its population to 300,000. That includes about thirty independent states. But if you have visited Bermuda, population 64,000, you were not in a microstate. Bermuda is a dependent territory of the United Kingdom. However, the seven dwarfs discussed in this book are full-fledged United Nations member states, except for the Vatican, which is an observer state.

These seven independent European countries have the smallest areas on that continent. Countries with small areas don't have room for a lot of people, and it is not surprising that these microstates also have the lowest populations. (Iceland's population of 284,300

1

would make it a microstate, but its area is forty times larger than Luxembourg, so Iceland is not covered here.) Relatively speaking, the biggest microstate, Luxembourg, is eight times smaller than the next larger country in Europe, Slovenia. And Luxembourg is six times the size of the second biggest microstate, Andorra. It is considered the biggest of the European microstates—and these countries do have a lot in common to distinguish themselves from other states.

The Microstates in Size Order

Luxembourg, the largest microstate, is the most similar to its geographically greater neighbors. It lies on the border between France, Germany, and Belgium. It is the third member of the Benelux group of small European countries, and it was a founding member of the UN and the European Union.

Andorra is a coprincipality located in the Pyrenees between France and Spain. Its "coprinces" are the bishop of Urgell in Spain and the president of France. Andorra is known a skier's vacationland.

Malta is a Mediterranean island off Sicily. Its warm, sunny climate may remind you of Sicily as well. But the Maltese language is related to Arabic, unlike Italian or any other European tongue.

Liechtenstein is a small principality on the border between Switzerland and Austria. It was founded by the Liechtenstein family and is still ruled by them.

San Marino, the oldest republic in the world, is in the northeastern region of Italy. It consists of Mount Titano in the Apennines, and some of the surrounding mountainous area. Like Andorra, San Marino has two heads of state at the same time, but they are elected every six months.

Monaco, famous for its casinos and high-profile princely family, is at the foot of the Alps and on the French Riviera coast of the Mediterranean Sea. Like Vatican City, Monaco is an exclusively urban state.

Vatican City is entirely surrounded not only by Italy, but also by the city of Rome. The home of the pope, the Vatican is also called the Holy See because it is the world headquarters of the Roman Catholic Church.

Micropatrology

Why learn more about these tiny countries? For one thing, it's easier to become well acquainted with a microstate, since there isn't as much to acquaint yourself with. The same thing goes for visiting a microstate—you can see most of it in a short time. But there are more serious reasons for engaging in "micropatrology," as it is now called—the study of small countries. The European microstates all have mature service economies, and most have very little heavy industry or agriculture. They may represent the future of bigger states. Additionally, the microstates are more like regions more than full countries. In today's political climate of the European Union, such regions are drawing more attention to themselves in the international arena than ever before. Another interesting aspect of these countries concerns the military—they have little or no armies. Hopefully, the microstates will lead the way to the future in this regard, too. Finally, Andorra has the world's highest life expectancy, and San Marino has the second highest. In fact, all the microstates of Europe sustain long average life spans, and they have the lowest levels of unemployment as well. Obviously, these positive qualities of life are worth looking into.

Do these tiny countries really have much in common? This book is dedicated to answering that question affirmatively. Part I is organized not by country, but by the various shared traits of the seven European microstates—such subjects as independence, economics, government, history, religion, and language and education. The second part deals with each microstate's individual history and with such cultural issues as art, cuisine, places of interest, and sport. Part III describes what you can do and see when you visit a European microstate. Any one of the seven microstates of Europe can be an ideal break from a vacation in a larger neighboring country, and a quick way to add to the list of countries you've visited in your lifetime.

PART I

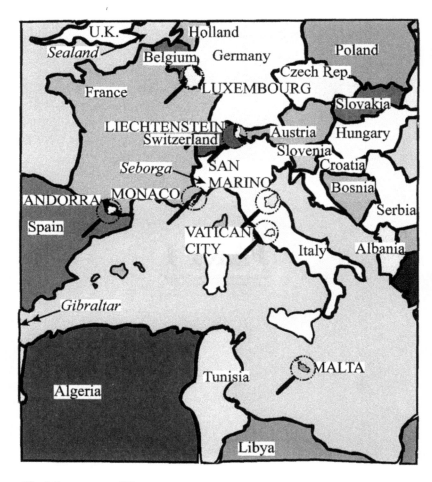

The Microstates of Europe.

THOMAS M. ECCARDT.

A Small World:
The Geography of
the Microstates

Locating the Microstates

The European microstates are so small it's hard to find them. They are hardly ever included on world maps, and if they are lucky enough to be shown on a map of Europe, they appear as cities or tiny regions. None of them is as big as the smallest American state, Rhode Island. If you look along the seacoasts on a map of Europe, you will find only one, Monaco, on the Mediterranean coast of France near Italy. But it's the size of a village, so you have to look closely. And apart from Malta, an island off southern Sicily, the rest of the microstates are landlocked.

If you follow the border between France and Spain, you will spot Andorra. Find the intersection of Germany, France and Belgium, and you will locate Luxembourg. Trace the border between Switzerland and Austria very carefully to pick out tiny Liechtenstein. Incidentally, Liechtenstein is "doubly landlocked," because its two neighbors are also landlocked.

Placing the other two microstates presents more of a challenge, since they are not located between countries, but entirely within one country, Italy. It's easy to find Rome, which entirely surrounds Vatican City, but this smallest of states is not always indicated on a map. San Marino is in northeastern Italy, near the Adriatic coastal city of Rimini. It has no coastline, although you can easily see the sea from its mountainous vantage point.

All of the European microstates are within a relatively small area, about the size of Bolivia. It's small enough that all seven are in the same time zone, one hour later than Greenwich time. The northernmost European microstate is Luxembourg, the western-most is Andorra, and Malta is both most southerly and most easterly. No microstate has a border with any other microstate. The closest two are San Marino and the Vatican, only about 150 miles away from each other. The furthest two are Malta and Luxembourg, a little more than 1,000 miles apart.

A Bird's-Eye View

The smallest microstate is the State of the Vatican City, also known as the Holy See, with 0.2 square miles. Containing only a few city blocks of area, Vatican City is the smallest country on earth, with less area than the world's biggest buildings have office space. The Vatican is surrounded by walls shaped like a backward D, which mark its international boundary with Italy. (A few churches outside the walls in various parts of Rome are also owned by the Vatican.) Dominated by St. Peter's Basilica, which takes up about an eighth of its territory in the southeast corner, the rest of the country is made up of gardens and buildings, most of which are off limits to visitors. There are no roads, but there are a few streets, and numerous walkways between buildings. There are about 890 Vatican citizens, but only about half that number live within the walled city. Incidentally, this is the only country in the world whose capital, also called Vatican City, occupies exactly the same territory as the whole country.

The Principality of Monaco, next in size, is six times larger than the Vatican. With about thirty-two thousand residents, it has the world's highest population density. Monaco is entirely urban, but nevertheless it is divided into towns, really no more than neighborhoods; Monaco-Ville is the country's capital. Monaco is a rifle-shaped area along the French Riviera. It is so narrow that you're never more than a few hundred yards from the sea. Monaco sits at the foot of the low French Mediterranean Alps, so as you walk away from the sea you walk upward as well. The hilltops and the high-rises offer spectacular views of the rest of the country in one eyeful.

The Most Serene Republic of San Marino, the world's oldest republic, is twenty times bigger than Monaco. Rising at the center of the nation, the triple-peaked Mount Titano dominates this flower-bud-shaped country. Up here is the capital, also called San Marino. Several rivers and streams run down the mountains, and there is even a tiny lake. Fewer people live in San Marino than in Monaco, and they are distributed among about fifteen tiny towns.

The Principality of Liechtenstein is twice as large as San Marino. Its population is only a little greater than San Marino's, which makes it much less crowded. Liechtenstein is shaped like a loose sack of potatoes, following the Rhine River on its western border with Switzerland. It is mountainous on its eastern side, and its capital, Vaduz, is located in the relatively flat Rhine valley on the western side. Only Liechtenstein, Monaco, and Luxembourg can claim to be on a major railway line, although most trains pass right through Liechtenstein without stopping.

The tiny, insular Republic of Malta is about twice the size of Liechtenstein. It actually consists of five islands, but only Malta, Gozo, and Comino are inhabited. Gozo is shaped like an inverted teardrop and Malta is a bigger teardrop hanging underneath. Malta has no rivers, no lakes, no mountains, and few trees. Its beautiful fortress capital, Valletta, is located on the southeast part of the northern shore on a peninsula within a small bay. Malta's

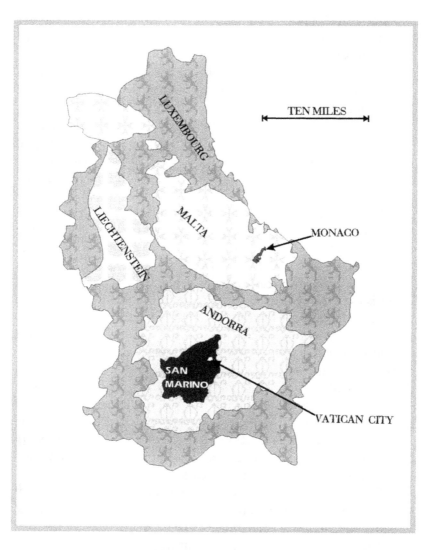

Comparative Sizes of the European Microstates.

THOMAS M. ECCARDT.

Many European Union institutions are housed in Luxembourg.
Luxembourg Tourist Board.

large population, 377,000, is second among the microstates, so there are sufficient people to populate many towns on the two main islands.

The Principality of Andorra is a little larger than Malta. An ink smudge in the rough shape of a right triangle, the map of Andorra has meandering rivers running through each of the angles. They join up in the center at Andorra la Vella, Europe's highest capital city. The main roads run along these rivers, and the major towns are found in the narrow river valleys as well. The rest of the country consists of steep mountains seemingly made for skiers.

The Grand Duchy of Luxembourg, the giant of the microstates, is six times bigger than Andorra, although it's still eight times smaller than Slovenia, Europe's smallest nonmicrostate. Its flower-bud shape is remarkably like a mirror image of San Marino, but of course it is much larger—so large that, its two main regions have slightly different climates. The Oesling in the north, covering the foothills and mountains of the Ardennes, is wetter and colder than Gutland, the industrial and agricultural region. Gutland (literally, "good land") contains the capital city, Luxembourg-Ville. Just outside Luxembourg's capital stand several government buildings for the European Union so, in a sense, Luxembourg-Ville is the capital of Europe as well. Luxembourg also has the highest population of the European microstates: 438,000. There are several rivers, but the best known is the Moselle, after which the wine variety is named.

Subdivisions

Some of the microstates are too small to need political subdivisions. Vatican City and Monaco do not have local governments, but Monaco is divided into five *quartiers* anyway: Monghetti, Fontvieille, La Condamine, Monaco-Ville, and Monte-Carlo. Until recently, Malta was run entirely by a central government.

San Marino is divided into nine *castelli* ("castles"): Acquaviva, Borgo Maggiore, Chiesanuova, Domagnano, Faetano, Fiorentino, Monte Giardino, San Marino, and Serravalle. Each of the four oldest of these *castelli* actually was founded on an ancient fortress or castle—today they correspond to most of the major towns. They are each governed by a castle captain, modeled on the two captains regent who rule the whole country.

Liechtenstein has two regions, the Oberland and the Unterland. The Oberland is also called Vaduz, and consists of the communes of Vaduz, Balzers, Planken, Schaan, Triesen, and Triesenberg. The Unterland is also called Schellenberg, and consists of the communes Eschen, Gamprin, Mauren, Ruggell, and Schellenberg. These two regions correspond to the two parcels of real estate that an ancient prince of Liechtenstein purchased to give himself a title. In doing so, he also founded the principality.

In order to join the European Union, Malta had to comply with the European Charter of Local Self-Government, so it divided itself into three regions and 68 local councils. On Malta, the Majjistral ("Northwest wind") consists of 29 councils, and the Xlokk ("Southeast wind") has 35 councils. The Gozo region has 14 councils. The councils correspond to small towns, with a mayor, deputy mayor, and council members.

For hundreds of years, Andorra was divided into six parishes, which corresponded to Catholic parishes: Andorra la Vella, Canillo, Encamp, La Massana, Ordino, and Sant Julià de Lòria. Each would send two representatives to the General Council of Andorra. Recently, when Andorra became more democratic and the General Council got real power, a seventh parish, Escaldes-Engordany, was added to even out the representation. Each parish is run by an elected council and a mayor, and some of the parishes are further subdivided as well.

In Luxembourg are three administrative regions: the Oesling is called Diekirch, and Gutland is divided into Luxembourg and Grevenmacher. They are headed by a commissioner appointed by the head of the country, the grand duke. The regions are divided into a total of twelve cantons, which are subdivided into communes. The communes are run by locally elected councils. But the cantons are not real administrative divisions; they are a remnant from Napoleon's occupation of Luxembourg.

Other Characteristics

The microstates of Europe are very poor in natural resources. In fact, their apparent worthlessness might have contributed to their being left alone by bigger countries—and to their survival. Whatever resources they had, however, they used. For example, San Marino was blessed with abundant sandstone, and many buildings and statues are made from it. Malta has limestone, and practically all buildings there make use of it. Andorra had iron mines, and you will come across fancy ironwork decorating the oldest stone buildings there. Luxembourg had iron mines, too. But in Luxembourg, an iron and steel industry developed in the late nineteenth and early twentieth centuries, and that transformed the country.

Being in Europe, the seven microstates are blessed with mild climates. Malta, Monaco, and the Vatican are Mediterranean, and have hot and dry summers and wetter but mild winters. Summer sea breezes bring relief to Malta and Monaco. Andorra and San Marino aren't as hot in summer because they are at a higher altitude. Liechtenstein's and Luxembourg's summers also are wetter and cooler. And it snows or rains in mountainous Andorra and Liechtenstein during the winter.

Only the Vatican and Malta are completely flat—the other microstates mostly consist of mountains, and these mountains may have saved them from invading neighbors. It is said that the Moors did not remain in Andorra very long because they were not accustomed to the high altitudes of that country. Many Sammarinese are convinced that their mountaintop fortification gave them the advantage they needed to keep others out.

Andorra has no fortifications, only because castle building was prohibited by treaty between its corulers. But the capital cities of Luxembourg, Malta, Monaco, and San Marino all have old fortifications, and even the Vatican is walled up. This is not surprising because, to remain independent, a small state must defend its territory against big neighbors. The struggle was not always successful, and at least two of the microstates used to be a lot bigger.

Territorial Changes

Until sixty years before there was a Vatican City, popes ruled large portions of central Italy. This territory was called the Papal

States. Over the centuries, the Papal States gained and lost territory until 1870, when Italy became an independent country and abolished them completely. In 1929, Italy gave what it considered to be the smallest possible territory to the Holy See and created Vatican City.

Long before Luxembourg became independent, it was under the control of Spain. Then the French defeated the Spaniards, and in 1659 Luxembourg it lost its southern part to France. Almost two hundred years later, King William I of the Netherlands ruled Luxembourg and Belgium. They both revolted against this king, and the dispute was settled by the great powers of Europe in 1831: the French-speaking part of Luxembourg was awarded to Belgium, and the remainder of Luxembourg remained under Dutch rule. When Luxembourg later became independent, most of its French-speaking territory remained part of Belgium. Today, Belgium is a small state containing a province called Luxembourg, while Luxembourg-the-country was born a microstate.

In 1346, Monaco purchased the cities of Monton and Roquebrune and added them to its territory. Almost exactly five hundred years later, they declared themselves free cities and then were annexed to France. A few years after that, Monaco accepted this loss in exchange for a guarantee of recognition and independence from France. The inclusion of Monton and Roquebrune would not have raised Monaco above the level of microstate; however, very recently, Monaco increased its territory by one-fifth via the implementation of landfill projects.

In 1463, San Marino joined an alliance against the lord of Rimini. The spoils of the victory were the neighboring towns of Fiorentino, Montegiardino, and Serravalle. Three hundred years later, Napoleon suggested expanding the borders again, but San Marino declined the offer.

Throughout the ages, the borders of these nations have been remarkably stable compared with those of their bigger neighbors.

While other European countries were taking turns conquering and dominating the continent, the microstates, without territorial ambitions, were able to maintain their borders mostly by minding their own business.

A Short Tether:
How Independent Are
the Microstates?

If a microstate qualifies as one, then just what is a state? Unfortunately, there is no universally accepted definition of statehood. But generally there are five things that most experts feel a country needs in order to be counted as such: control of territory, permanent population, government, independence, and diplomatic recognition. A single race, language, or culture is not considered a criterion, because most states have several of each—and many states share a language and culture with other countries.

Is a microstate a kind of minimalist country? Could you even create your own? Maybe you don't need any of the five criteria to declare a state. Indeed, some such amateur countries have actually acquired a few of the standard qualifications for statehood, and therefore some acceptance.

It is relatively easy to get a following of people who are willing to apply for citizenship, especially through the Internet, so now you have your "population." And you can name yourself as the government, and create your own postage stamps and currency. The other three qualifications are not so easy: You need to control a specific amount of territory, preferably not claimed by any other country. You need independence, presumably from the country from which you are now a former citizen. And you need recognition.

The Five Criteria in Practice

Membership in international organizations implies recognition, but is very difficult to obtain, even for the microstates of Europe. United Nations membership is prestigious, and it can lead to acceptance by other organizations. After Andorra became a member of the United Nations in 1993, it was accepted immediately into ITU, UNESCO, EUTELSAT, and WIPO. The other microstates, which had applied first to these lesser international organizations before they were UN members, had to wait years for their UN applications to be accepted. Liechtenstein is willing to pay the highest per capita dues for its membership in the UN in exchange for the platform it uses to make its views known to the world community. Luxembourg pays the second highest per capita UN dues. Membership in the United Nations also gives countries a certain kind of indirect recognition by other members with whom they may or may not have diplomatic relations and/or an embassy. But many aspiring countries like the "Republic of Texas" have been turned down for membership in the United Nations.

There are two ways of looking at the problem of determining what is a state. One theory says that the five criteria intrinsically show which entities pass muster. Advocates of international law support this theory, and they would have some world judicial body decide each case, based on the criteria. The other theory considers the criteria to be only guidelines, which the countries of the world can use at their discretion to recognize or not recognize other entities as states. So the second theory relies on de facto recognition as the criterion for statehood. But there is a kind of circular reasoning in both theories, since both use recognition itself to some degree in determining whether a country should be

Liechtenstein was admitted to the United Nations in September, 1990.

LIECHTENSTEIN TOURISM.

recognized. It is also ironic that signing an international convention or treaty provides recognition but often requires surrender of some amount of sovereignty, a reduction of independence.

There are ambiguities in the other four criteria as well. Control of territory may seem like an obvious necessity for a state. But when the Luxembourg government fled a World War II invasion, the government in exile in London continued to be recognized by many countries. It seems that a country is more likely to be recognized if it has *had* control of its territory—a government in exile, for example—than if potential leaders simply *intend* or *promise* to control the territory—a liberation movement, for instance. And what exactly does "independence" mean? Every country on earth is somewhat dependent on other countries, but at what point does too much dependence disqualify the state from the community of nations? Nobody knows for sure.

Other entities, in Europe and elsewhere, qualify as independent states to a lesser degree than the microstates. First, there are several "dependencies." The Faeroe Islands, owned by Denmark, recently began negotiating for independence—unsuccessfully. Gibraltar, a dependency of Britain's, is stuck between its desire for independence and its fear of Spain's claims on its territory. The Faeroes and Gibraltar are countries with territory, population, and government but without independence or recognition. If any of these dependencies are ever given their independence, then recognition will follow, and they will easily qualify as microstates.

Sealand, an abandoned military platform in the North Sea, was declared by an English court to be outside British territory. But the head of this "principality" has also had some unsuccessful court struggles, one of which declined to recognize Sealand's independence, finding that it has no real communal life, and therefore no permanent population. So far, no government has recognized Sealand's independence.

Seborga is a tiny Italian town, not far from Monaco. Since the 1960s the people of this "ancient principality" have claimed to be independent, and Italy has done little to actively suppress their wishes. But Italy has done nothing to grant them independence, either, and no government will recognize them. Seborga fulfills all of the criteria for statehood, except independence or recognition.

International Organizations

There is an entity that has no territory, but that has diplomatic relations with forty-nine states—including six of the seven European microstates—namely, the Sovereign Military Order of Malta, also known as the Knights of Malta. Today they are only a "lay religious order," but for 270 years they also ruled Malta, now a microstate. After Napoleon expelled them from their island, the Knights were left with no territory but with the trappings of government, much like the Holy See after 1870. The popes had better luck than the Knights: sixty years after the Holy See lost all its territory, Mussolini gave it the tiny Vatican area in order to insure that it would remain a political entity in the minds of those who think territory is a prerequisite to statehood. Unlike the Vatican, the Knights of Malta never recovered any territory. Incidentally, one of the duties of every Knight is to defend the Roman Catholic faith, which makes members of the Order great friends of the Vatican. The pope set them up in Rome in a building with a courtyard, but Italy considers this headquarters to be Italian territory. The Knights of Malta issue their own passports, stamps, and coins, but it is unclear to what these items entitle their owners.

There is another entity that has diplomatic relations with as many countries as just about any other entity. It, too, issues stamps and passports, and it also controls a small amount of territory. It is the United Nations, whose New York headquarters are considered an international zone, technically outside the United States. Actually, any embassy is considered to be the sovereign territory of the country it represents, and the purpose of the United Nations is strictly diplomatic. But the UN's budget of $10 billion per year is fifty times bigger than the Vatican's. One major contradiction to the claim that the UN is a country, however, would be its lack of a stable population. Nobody lives at UN headquarters, not even its hardest-working employees, nor has anyone been born there since New York ceded its territory to create the place. (Vatican City's population is not permanent either, because a complicated set of regulations rules out a second generation.) For all intents and purposes, the United Nations is not a microstate simply because it doesn't claim to be one.

The microstates of Europe have never found it easy to join such international organizations as the UN. The League of Nations was the precursor to the United Nations. Founded just after World War I, in 1920, it failed in its mission to prevent another world war, partly because Republicans in the Senate would not pass President Wilson's proposal for the United States to join. When the League was created, there was no Vatican City territory, there was only a Holy See government. Because the Holy See did not control any territory, it was not considered a state, and the League would not admit it as a member. Malta, too, was not yet an independent country, and as a colony it could not apply for membership. France handled most of Andorra's international relations until 1993, and as France did not consider Andorra to be a state under international law, it decided not to apply for membership for Andorra. Monaco did apply for membership, but the British refused to allow it to join because they felt it would give France two votes at the League of Nations. One reason that Liechtenstein was refused membership in the League was its lack of an army. You can see that the definition of statehood has changed considerably since then. The League promised to consider a kind of associate membership for Liechtenstein, San Marino, and Monaco, but never got around to it. In the end, Luxembourg was the only microstate to get into the League of Nations.

On April 18, 1946, the League transferred all its assets to the United Nations. Luxembourg, of course, was admitted as a founding member of the UN when the Second World War ended. Secretary General U Thant attempted to revive the idea of associate

Liechtenstein's last soldier died in 1939.

membership for the microstates of Liechtenstein, San Marino, and Monaco, but in the 1950s they had to settle for observer status. One reason for this was the fear of vote dilution among the big members of the UN. Tiny Monaco would have the same power as the United States and the other big victors of the war, at least in the General Assembly. There was also fear of fragmentation of colonial powers: if Liechtenstein could have a vote, why couldn't the dozens of colonies that were much bigger? When most of these colonies, including Malta, became independent and joined the United Nations in the 1950s and '60s, that became a moot point. The great powers could take comfort in the fact that the Security Council gives them a bigger voice, and some of them have a veto. Still, the microstates' UN applications languished until the early 1990s. After the breakup of the Soviet Union and the admission of another huge block of members, it seemed silly to quibble about the microstates, and they finally took their place among the nations of the world—all except the Vatican, which desired to remain an observer.

Membership in the UN has erased just about any doubt about whether the microstates are real countries. Today, the delegates of its six European microstates consult and meet with each other in New York. Although the Holy See once considered full membership in the UN, it is now satisfied with its observer status, partly because membership in the UN would give it certain obligations it is not prepared to fulfill. There is a small movement in the UN that would strip the Holy See of its observer status and expel it from certain international organizations. This might be partly due to the Holy See's choice of name—if they called themselves Vatican City, they might appear more like a country and less like a religion. The semantic difference between these two entities is discussed in greater detail in the chapter on the Vatican.

Customs, Monetary, and Postal Unions

Every European microstate except Malta has at least one larger neighbor, a "big sister," with which it has had to contend for its independence. Sometimes this has meant loss of territory, as when Luxembourg lost most of its land to Belgium. Other times it has meant loss of certain rights, such as the Italian ban on San Marino operating a radio station, which lasted for many years. Still other times it has meant a real struggle between two states, as when the French banned the importing of pharmaceuticals from Monaco. On the other hand, it can be handy having a big sister to take care of some of the government services which are harder to do on a small scale. Two countries using the same such services are said to be in a "union," such as a monetary union (same money), postal union (same postal service), and customs union (same import duties). The only microstate not in some kind of union is isolated Malta.

It is notoriously difficult to manage a small currency, but the Maltese lira, the only totally independent currency of the European microstates, is unexpectedly one of the strongest in the world. All the other microstates are in some kind of monetary union or other. That means they use the currency of their neighbors, although most of them are allowed to make coins with their own national emblems. Before the advent of the euro, San Marino and the Vatican were in monetary union with Italy, and Monaco was in monetary union with France. From their multiple neighbors,

The Plenary Hall of the European Union.
LUXEMBOURG TOURIST BOARD.

Luxembourg and Liechtenstein chose Belgium and Switzerland, respectively, as their big sisters in currency matters. As Andorra's two heads of state are from Spain and France, it has often depended on both of these countries, so until January 2002, Andorrans used both French francs and Spanish pesetas, and were not allowed to mint their own version of these currencies. From 2002 on, all the microstates but Malta and Liechtenstein began using the euro, because that became the new currency of their big sisters.

Strangely, this puts Andorra, Monaco, and San Marino inside the "euro zone" but outside the European Union. Luxembourg was a founding member of the European Union. Of the other microstates, only Malta applied for membership in the EU and joined it, but it twice changed its mind about joining. As for Andorra and San Marino, they have simply run up against same representation problem they had with the UN: allowing them to join the EU would give them an undesirably equal vote with their big sisters. Liechtenstein is happy to remain in the European Free Trade Association with its big sister, Switzerland. Monaco and the Vatican will not be able to join the EU unless and until they become more democratic. Although it is now approaching a kind of political federation, the European Union was originally just a customs union. Before that time, most of the microstates were already in customs unions with their big sisters. As the big sisters entered the EU, the microstates had to sign new customs agreements with the EU. That is their current status today.

Although they all have their own customized postage stamps, Andorra, Liechtenstein, Monaco, San Marino, and the Vatican are in postal unions with their neighbors. In some cases, this means that the big sister provides all the postal services; in others, only the postage rates are the same as big sister's. Liechtenstein owns its postal equipment and processing plant, but Switzerland provides all the services. Every microstate but the Vatican has its own telephone country code, but most are in some kind of telephonic union with their big sisters.

Letting Your Big Sister Do It

Diplomacy can be a costly undertaking for a microstate—just staffing embassies in almost two hundred countries could make a serious dent in a population, not to mention the costs. So the diplomatic staff of the microstates is limited, and they often rely on their big sisters for consular services and the like. For example, Liechtenstein has only four accredited embassies, located in Austria, Belgium, the Holy See, and Switzerland. Yet Liechtensteiners around the world can seek help in Swiss embassies. And Sammarinese can go to Italian embassies. Vatican City never needs the diplomatic help of other countries, because its chief function is already diplomacy. Andorra often lets Spain or France represent it at international conferences. Sometimes the microstates have difficulty fulfilling their obligations in international organizations, and they may call on the help of other nations, as when a Canadian was appointed to be a "Liechtenstein" judge in the European Court of Human Rights.

Four of the seven microstates of Europe have no annual defense budget. Liechtenstein and Andorra have proclaimed themselves neutral—presumably their isolation and good relations with neighbors will keep them secure. The Vatican is obliged to be neutral by the treaty that created it. The Vatican's Swiss Guards are really a police force, partly an ornamental one, but they do indeed come from Switzerland. Perhaps for lack of resources, St. Peter's Square, officially Vatican territory, comes under Italian police protection when it is open to the public. Malta is neutral, but every Maltese citizen contributes on average five hundred dollars in taxes each year for the defense of the island. Luxembourg is not neutral, since it participates in NATO. Monaco is not neutral either, but it has no defense budget. By treaty, its foreign policy must be aligned with its neighbor's, and the French Republic assumes all responsibility for the defense of Monaco. Because Monaco is not *allowed* to handle its own defense or foreign policy, its independence is limited by this treaty.

Limits to Sovereignty

Over the years, Monaco has signed several treaties with France, which promised to guarantee its sovereignty. Unfortunately, most of the treaties have limited Monaco's independence at the same time. In 1918, the prince of Monaco agreed to exercise his rights of sovereignty in "perfect conformity with the naval and economic interests of France." Another treaty, of 1930, requires the two most important ministers of four to be French nationals. The French government proposes several candidates and then Monaco's prince chooses among them. Although his family is officially in charge of succession, the French government must approve the next ruling prince or princess. There is even a stipulation that, should there be a vacancy in the throne, Monaco will revert to a French protectorate. At least in theory, the French could legally put an end to Monaco's statehood by refusing to approve a successor. It doesn't seem likely that a member state of the United Nations would be allowed to disappear, but all these legal limitations to Monaco's sovereignty make it the least independent of the seven microstates of Europe.

Liechtenstein's independence is limited somewhat by its monetary and customs union with Switzerland. The Swiss National Bank exercises the same rights over Liechtenstein banks as it does over Swiss ones. And Switzerland has the right to appoint and dismiss customs officers and border guards in Liechtenstein.

Before 1993, when its new constitution was approved and it entered the United Nations, Andorra had outstripped Monaco as the least independent of the microstates. Originally, the coprinces from France and Spain were much more than ceremonial rulers, and France handled all of Andorra's international relations. Even now, the coprinces can participate in international treaty negotiations. Though the coprinces have much less power today, Andorrans are permitted absolutely no input concerning their appointment. The president of France, of course, is elected by the French people, and the bishop of Urgell is appointed by the head of another microstate, the pope. However, the Vatican claims that it gives no instructions to the bishop of Urgell regarding Andorra. (At one time, Spain had input on the appointment of that bishop.)

Radio transmission has been a bone of contention in a few of the microstates over the years. Until 1987, San Marino was not allowed to have its own media: no radio, no television, no newspapers. Now that the ban is lifted, it has all three. In 1935, when Andorra was still a vassal state, its local government gave a Frenchman a license for a radio station. Although the French government radio system was not very happy with the competition, it tolerated the new Radio Andorra, which was broadcasting into France as well as Spain and Andorra. During World War II, this station was able to transmit freely despite the Nazi occupation of France. In 1947, the French began jamming the transmission, until a lawsuit in the French courts forced them to stop. Radio Andorra continued broadcasting under private French ownership until Andorra nationalized it in 1981. In the early twenty-first century, powerful Vatican radio transmitters became the concern of Italians living in a Roman suburb, who suspected that they caused cancer. Some Italian government officials even threatened to cut off electricity unless the transmission power was reduced. After months of negotiations, the microstate and its big sister finally agreed that Italy would pay to have the transmitters moved elsewhere.

A microstate may be willing to accept the kind of legal limitations described here but may also have to put up with a certain amount of downright bullying as well. If a big sister is unhappy with a tiny nation's policies, there is little the latter can do to defend against any backlash. Big sister, after all, is holding all the cards. Such was the case for Monaco, San Marino, and Andorra, described more fully in their respective chapters.

Staying Independent

Despite bullying, all seven microstates have maintained their independence. How did they do it? Mostly, they didn't. They never had much control of their own destiny, and they owe their survival to factors beyond their control, such as their geography. For example, mountains may have protected San Marino and Andorra; Liechtenstein, too, has mountains, and may have survived in part because of its isolation.

Another factor that may have kept some microstates independent is their central location between competing countries. Being situated right between Spain and France, and being politically controlled by both kept Andorra from being pulled into either of its big sisters. If France wanted to absorb Andorra, for example, it would have to answer to Spain. So Andorra has been left alone. Much of Luxembourg's territory was taken away from it by neighbors before it became the independent grand duchy it is today. Even just before independence, in 1867, several countries were in competition to possess it. Fortunately, the dispute was settled peacefully, and a multination treaty made Luxembourg a neutral independent country. So Luxembourg's central position both created and preserved it.

Malta has been a possession of other countries throughout most of recorded history. It only became independent in 1964. The microstate's position in the midst of Mediterranean trade routes had made it susceptible to invasion until then. Vatican City was created in 1929, sixty years after the demise of the Papal States. Yet the power and influence of the Catholic Church convinced Italy to give the Church its own territory and to guarantee that territory by treaty.

Finally, two of the microstates seem to have survived at least partly through their own clever policies. The Grimaldi family has ruled Monaco from the beginning, and under their management Monaco still survives today. A few centuries after they took over, they came under Spanish protection. When that did not work out so well, they made a deal with the French and drove the Spanish out. After ill treatment by Napoleon, the Grimaldi family participated in the Congress of Vienna, was restored, and got the protection of the Italian kingdom of Sicily. Eventually they came back to the French, giving up their rights to a couple of cities in exchange for a promise of protection. After the First World War, they had their independence written into the Treaty of Versailles.

San Marino seems to have anticipated events and made the right friends at the right time. After being attacked by its neighbors during the thirteenth century, San Marino had made an alliance with the dukes of Urbino for protection. Urbino was the popes' enemy, but just thirty years before the last of the dukes died, San Marino signed a treaty of recognition with the popes. When the dukes were gone, the popes seized most of the dukes' lands, but not San Marino. This also came in handy when Cardinal Alberoni took over the lands in 1739, and the people of San Marino successfully appealed to the pope to have the cardinal release their republic. Perhaps because San Marino was founded by a saintly stonecutter, popes have had a soft spot in their hearts for it. But in the nineteenth century, when Italy was fighting for its own unification, San Marino must have seen the writing on the wall, and gave shelter to one of the heroes of Italy's Risorgimento. When the Italians took the Papal States—which surrounded San Marino—they let this microstate remain independent as a reward, perhaps to the chagrin of the pope.

Microeconomics:
The Economies of the Microstates

If a family expanded to have 28,800 members, would its economy resemble that of microstate San Marino? Probably not. On the other hand, San Marino's economy is not a miniaturization of Italy's, either. Microstate economies are somewhere in between their big sisters' and that of a large household. They have some of the problems of each.

Agricultural Beginnings

For many years most of the European microstates had economies similar to those of their neighboring regions. That meant they were mostly poor agricultural economies. Today, despite modern agricultural methods, the microstates are far from self-sufficient, and they import most of their food. The Vatican and Monaco are completely urban today, and the areas they occupy today were never very agricultural—all they have is a few vegetable gardens. All the other microstates in Europe still have some land used for agriculture, but even this is often rocky and mountainous, and hard to farm. Like their bigger neighbors, these microstates have fewer and larger farms than in the past. Due to their small size,

Maltese farmers terrace their land to prevent topsoil erosion.
MALTA TOURIST OFFICE, NEW YORK.

however, the microstates have lost a bigger proportion of their land to urbanization than have their neighbors, leaving much less for agriculture. As one's house expands, the less one has room for a garden.

Some of the grain produced by the nonurban microstates is used as feed for cattle. Liechtenstein and Andorra retain the quaint annual tradition of ceremoniously driving the cattle down from grazing areas in the mountains to warmer places for the winter. The cows produce milk, sometimes made into cheese. These dairy items are consumed locally and hardly ever exported. Only Malta is known for its agricultural produce, potatoes and onions, which it exports to Holland.

Moselle wine harvest.
LUXEMBOURG TOURIST BOARD.

By coincidence, all of the European microstates are situated in areas that can produce grapes, and all have long traditions of wine production and consumption. On a trip to these countries, you may want to sample some of the local wine, especially in Luxembourg, where Moselle wines are famous. Incidentally, Luxembourg dedicates about half of its land to agriculture, making it by far the largest food producer of the microstates.

In four of the five agricultural microstates of Europe river fishing is popular. For Malta, sea fishing from the Mediterranean is a major industry, with the constant problem of overfishing. On the other hand, Malta's tiny size and isolation have deprived it of much animal wildlife: whereas hunting is popular in the other agricultural microstates, it is unheard of in Malta, except for annual bird shooting. In most other microstates, however, you can order a meal featuring local fish or wildlife.

In the 1800s, Andorrans found that tobacco was becoming a profitable commodity, and farmers began to devote more and more of their land to raising tobacco. When France and Spain imposed large import duties on tobacco, smuggling it in became a very popular way to make a living—so popular, in fact, that Andorra started transforming itself into a unique economic zone, distinct from Pyrenees France or Spain. The idea of using Andorra as a routing station to save on taxes spread to other goods as well. Eventually the legal "transshipment of goods" became Andorra's major industry—especially since the 1930s, when roads to France and Spain were opened. Today, this business continues, with visitors coming to Andorra specifically for its duty-free shopping. The value-added tax in Andorra is sufficiently low to attract millions of tourists per year, yet high enough to generate plenty of income for the government.

Transformations

Andorra's economic transformation has been shared by all of the European microstates in one form or another. For centuries, people knew that Luxembourg was blessed with an abundance of iron ore. But the ore was considered of poor quality, because it contained too much phosphorus. In the late 1800s, a process to remove the phosphorus was invented, as well as a new method of producing rolled steel beams. Within a few decades, Luxembourg had exploited these methods and transformed itself from an agricultural society into an industrial economy. Several iron and steel companies later merged into ARBED, the giant industrial consortium that is still profitable. Luxembourg became a great exporter of steel beams, some of which may be supporting the buildings you use today.

Minette steel rails. Luxembourg's steel industry supplies the world's builders with extra-strong iron.

For centuries, Monaco had been a backwater fluke of a principality. Then in 1865, the clever Prince Charles III opened Monaco's first casino. The attraction of gambling plus the beautiful Mediterranean beaches led in flocks of tourists, including some of the world's richest people. Monaco offered tax havens and residency—though not citizenship—to these people, transforming itself into a prosperous playground for the wealthy almost overnight. The marriage of Prince Rainier to the glamorous actress Grace Kelly, and the subsequent adventures and scandals of the Grimaldi family kept the tourists coming through the end of the twentieth century.

Although Malta was disputed and ruled by different empires for many years, it never developed economically, even during the two hundred years of the Knights Hospitallers. Only when the British came in, in 1814, and started using Malta as a naval base, was the country slowly transformed. The famous dockyard was opened, and thousands of Maltese found jobs there repairing and dry-docking ships. The money spent by the British navy also helped keep up Malta's tiny economy.

Liechtenstein was a poor fiefdom for its first century of independence, when it was ruled from a distance by the princes of Liechtenstein, who lived in Austria. In 1938 Prince Franz Josef II moved to Liechtenstein and made his home there. He actively encouraged industrialization, but avoided heavy industry, making sure that the plants did not spoil the beauty of his principality. He also kept them from concentrating in any one area, and so avoided urban sprawl. So Liechtenstein had a rather rapid industrialization period just after the Second World War, but it always remained diversified.

Diversification

If the breadwinner in a household strikes it rich, the whole family benefits. If not, the family may remain poor. The same can be said of the microstates. Most of them found a single profitable

Charles Garnier designed this building in 1878. Currently it houses the world-famous Monte-Carlo Casino.

MONACO GOVERNMENT TOURIST OFFICE.

industry and transformed themselves into modern countries. Large countries tend to be more diversified, and their transformations more gradual. Not wishing to be subject to the risks of being a one-industry nation, most of the microstates have attempted to diversify as well, with varying degrees of success.

Andorra has built several auditoriums and meeting places, to attract conventions and congresses. In 1993, they passed a new law guaranteeing secrecy in banking, as in Switzerland, to get foreign investors who may need this kind of account. But Andorra is still known mainly for its skiing and duty-free shopping.

The 1970s brought a worldwide recession in the steel industry, and many workers were laid off. The downturn struck Luxembourg particularly hard, because 26 percent of the gross national product came from this industry, falling eventually to only 10 percent. But the country adjusted well by making the steel industry more efficient with fewer workers and by diversifying. Luxembourg became a bigger producer of stone, glass, and ceramics than ever before. The government encouraged development of the financial sector. And foreign companies were encouraged to build factories in Luxembourg.

In the 1960s, Prince Rainier set up the Monaco Economic Development Corporation (MEDEC), which encouraged businesses to incorporate there by imposing lighter regulation than in France. This caused a disastrous dispute with French president Charles de Gaulle, in which Monaco had to back down. Then in the 1980s, a scandal in the company that ran the casinos convinced the prince to limit the government's income from gaming to a maximum of 4 percent. Since then Monaco's chemical, pharmaceutical, and cosmetics industries have greatly expanded.

Malta depended on the British dockyards for much of the twentieth century. When it became independent of the UK and expelled the British from their base, serious economic problems arose. Malta is attempting solve these problems by expanding tourism and marine support services, and by joining the European

Union. Like Malta, San Marino has moved out of its traditional industry, stonecutting, and moved more heavily into tourism. Liechtenstein's industrialization was always rather diverse but, just in case, the prince encouraged the banking and financial sectors, keeping the economy running without interruption.

Microstate Industries

All of the microstates, except Liechtenstein, are heavily dependent on tourism. But the tourism industry, like so many other industries, is different from that of other countries. Perhaps most dramatically, every day thousands of tourists enter St. Peter's Square to view the Vatican but, after spending a few hours there, they go right back out to their hotels in Rome. The only people who eat and sleep in the Vatican are its few residents, mainly the clergy. The Vatican is happy to have a rapid throughput of visitors, but the other microstates are not: Though seven million people visit Andorra per year, their average stay is only two hours. San Marino can count its tourists in the millions as well, but less than a fifth of them stay overnight, even while they contribute at least half of the GDP of this tiny republic. Because of its isolated situation at sea, only Malta can be assured that most of its visitors will stay overnight and spend money on hotels and restaurants. Daytrippers can pop in and out of all the other microstates, where there are perennial campaigns to convince them to stay.

Most people come to Andorra and San Marino for duty-free shopping. The vast majority of these bargain-hunters come from the big sister countries of France, Spain, and Italy. Now, if the Andorra and San Marino were not independent countries, but only regions of the big sisters, these shoppers would not be able to enjoy this tax advantage. For these two microstates, the mere fact of their being independent created an "industry." Malta, too, participates in transshipment of goods, but by other means than tourism.

A selection of Liechtenstein postage stamps.
LIECHTENSTEIN TOURISM.

Other industries are well served by independent statehood—the printing and sale of postage stamps, for example. Liechtenstein, Monaco, San Marino, and the Vatican are famous for their beautiful postage stamps. Many collectors around the world buy these philatelic works of art but do not use them for postage, partly for fear of marring them by the cancellation, but also because they have no mail to send from the microstates where the stamps are valid. Getting paid for an unused service is almost always profitable, thus issuing postage stamps is a major source of income for these microstates. Unfortunately, prior to its recent independence, Andorra's post office was always run by France and Spain, so Andorra was never able to build the printing of postage stamps into an industry.

Traffic jam in Andorra la Vella.
MINISTRY OF TOURISM OF THE GOVERNMENT OF ANDORRA.

Gambling or "gaming" is another industry made possible by flocks of eager customers from outside the country. Andorra and San Marino have both tried to set up casinos, but they were stopped by their big sisters. Monaco is the only microstate with a casino, and of course the casino is its claim to fame. Interestingly, citizens of Monaco are not allowed to gamble but, needless to say, people from big-sister France and from all over the world come to Monaco to throw their money away.

A spin-off of the tourist industry and the tax advantages is the building industry, booming as it tries to keep up with demand for hotels, restaurants, and housing for permanent residents. A quarter of Andorra's workforce is engaged in building. As a matter of fact, Andorra's capital and surrounding areas are over-built, with modern housing overshadowing the more traditional Romanesque architecture. A similar thing happened in Monaco, where multistory hotels replaced beautiful old villas. On the other hand, San Marino, Malta, and Liechtenstein have been blessed with natural building stone, and their building industries have had the advantage of indigenous materials that, quite apart from archi-tects' modern visions, blend well into their respective landscape.

All those tourists need souvenirs to bring back with them, and there is no shortage of native crafts to buy in most of the microstates. After the steel recession, Luxembourg increased its output of Villeroy and Boch brand ceramics. In Malta, the city of Mdina is famous for its colored glassware, carpets, and other handmade crafts. Even in flashy Monaco, Princess Grace estab-lished a foundation to help local artisans and opened nonprofit shops to help them sell their wares. Liechtenstein and San Marino have strong craftmaking traditions as well. The only European microstate that does not make some income from craftsmanship is Vatican City, although the Vatican employs plenty of art restorers, art conservators, and tailors for its fabulous art museums and ceremonial vestments.

Several microstates offer tax breaks to industries that move or simply incorporate there. But taxes in general are low in the microstates: There is no income tax in Monaco and Andorra. The highest income tax rate in Liechtenstein is 16 percent. Italians who work in the Vatican have only their retirement insurance withheld from their paychecks, and pay no income tax.

Low business taxes are responsible for another trademark industry of the microstates: so-called "letter-box" companies. With easy rules for incorporation added to the mix, Liechtenstein has attracted almost seventy-five thousand companies registered there but without headquarters there. Although the taxes are very low, the large number of these companies provides 30 percent of Liechtenstein's government budget. Andorra, Luxembourg, Malta, San Marino, and especially Monaco also benefit from "letter-box" companies, but not to such a large extent. France has been putting pressure on Monaco to make stricter their rules on incorporation. It seems that big sisters are always trying to force "reform" on the microstates to eliminate the special industries that arise from the fact of being a small state. But whenever one such industry is eliminated, another always seems to pop up in its place.

The tiny nations of Europe are so small that their native populations usually do not provide a market large enough for their own industries' products. Like a doctor who cannot make a living by treating only his own household, a microstate must look elsewhere for customers. So their major products are usually their major exports as well. Liechtenstein, Luxembourg, and Malta export specialty machinery. Malta and Monaco export glassware. Andorra exports tobacco and furniture. Liechtenstein exports dental products, especially false teeth. Luxembourg exports steel products. Monaco exports cosmetics and pharmaceuticals. And San Marino exports building stone and wood. Only Vatican City is prohibited by law from exporting any goods. The Vatican is too small to manufacture anything on its own. Anything that could be exported would be "transshipped" imported goods from Italy, and since goods coming into the Vatican from Italy are not taxed, but goods sold in Italy are, reselling them could easily be profitable. Precisely to prevent this, when Italy signed the treaty establishing the Vatican, all exportation was prohibited except by special permission. Needless to say, Vatican City must import all products consumed there. Similarly, except for the few products that they can export, all the other microstates import the rest of the items they consume.

Fuzzy Financial Figures

People tend to avoid talking about their exact income. Similarly, many of the European microstates like to keep their economic figures unpublicized. For example, Liechtenstein, Monaco, and Vatican City have assets at home and abroad that are huge in comparison to their size, but no hard figures are available concerning these assets. Wealthy citizens of the other microstates may help to make their countries creditor nations as well, but nobody's telling. The only confirmable P/L figure on public record is that Malta has an external debt of some $130 million. On the other extreme, because San Marino and Monaco are in customs unions with Italy and France, they do not even keep track of their net imports and exports. Sometimes it doesn't even make sense to analyze microstates' economic figures, as they reflect circumstances unique to their geographic size.

Liechtenstein is the only microstate to show a trade surplus on paper. Andorra's trade deficit is a billion dollars per year. This may seem high for such a small state, but it is probably just a reflection of Andorra's specialization in tourism and transshipment of goods. It is true that Andorra imports most of the things it consumes and exports very little. Yet Andorra's citizens, employed in the service industries of tourism and retail sales, have prospered for generations. A symbiotic relationship exists: French and Spanish visitors come in droves and spend their euros in Andorra, then Andorrans use the profits from these transactions to import the goods they need from Spain and France. If Andorra had its own currency, it would simply get in the way. But the fact that Andorra doesn't simply run out of euros proves that the trade deficit in goods is counterbalanced by a trade surplus in services.

You can get a good idea of the financial health of some of the European microstates by looking at which ones are members of the European Bank for Reconstruction and Development (EBRD) and why. Liechtenstein and Luxembourg are in it for the purpose of giving aid to other countries. Malta is an aid recipient member of ERBD, and as such it is the only European microstate that accepts foreign aid. Vatican City and Monaco could probably afford to be contributor members of ERBD, but they choose to donate money not to countries but in other ways. The Vatican Bank manages the assets of Catholic religious orders and is the clearinghouse for money donated to missions around the world. Monaco's annual Red Cross charity ball is well known. Andorra and San Marino are probably not sufficiently wealthy to be large-scale benefactors.

Another area of unreliable statistics is GDP/GNP. Gross Domestic Product is simply the value of all the goods and services produced per year physically within a country (in other words, excluding any income earned abroad). Dividing the GDP by the population gives some idea of the amount that the average person has access to, and this is the per capita GDP. Luxembourg and Liechtenstein are probably the richest countries per capita in the world. Unfortunately, the statistics on economic output are unreliable. For Liechtenstein, for example, the CIA's *The World Factbook, 2003* (http://www.cia.gov/ cia/publications/factbook) gives $23,000 and the *Encyclopaedia Britannica* gives $37,000. These discrepancies probably cannot be explained by the difference between GDP and GNP (Gross National Product, the value of all goods and services produced by the country's residents, here and abroad), or by the purchasing power parity adjustment. The larger figure would make Liechtensteiners the richest people in the world. The smaller would make them the nineteenth richest. Besides being unreliable, these figures are difficult to interpret. A full 38 percent of Liechtenstein's labor force commutes daily into the country from Switzerland and Austria. Should these nonresident commuters figure into the calculation of the per capita GDP? As no large countries have to deal with such high percentages of commuters, few economists are interested in this problem. However their GDPs are calculated, the microstates of Europe are among the most affluent in the world—the lowest ranking, Malta, is only about forty-ninth among the 190 nations of the world. Closely after Luxembourg and Liechtenstein comes Monaco, the third or fourth richest country in the world. After Monaco come San Marino and Andorra, near number thirty.

Estimating the per capita GDP of the Vatican is particularly difficult. Less than a thousand people live within the walls of the city, yet another three thousand people work there. The per capita

GDP is either $49,500 or $243,542, depending on whether you count the commuters or not. Of course, either way, this would make the Vatican the richest country in the world. But although the Vatican has plenty of opulent buildings, few of its occupants can be said to live in the lap of luxury. Where did these figures come from? The Vatican does not issue GDP figures, and only recently have they begun to issue budget figures. Because the Vatican has a "noncommercial" economy, all economic activity is ordered and paid for by the government—and so the Vatican's national budget is really the same as its GDP. Dividing the $200 million dollar budget by the eight hundred-plus residents comes to about one-quarter of a million dollars per person. Where does all this money go? We must bear in mind that Vatican City is not an ordinary country, dedicated to the welfare of its citizens. It is the headquarters of the Roman Catholic Church, so the budget is spent on church administration, diplomatic missions, and Vatican radio, TV, and newspaper operations. Most of its workers live outside the Vatican and take their income away with them, the majority of the media is located in Italy-proper, and all the diplomatic missions are also outside the Vatican walls. So, in effect, most of the money that comes in goes right out the door. Where does the money come from? The microstate's income comes from interest on investments, profits from banking operations, and Peter's Pence, named for Peter, the first pope. The word "pence" comes from the pence (pennies) collected in medieval England, where the fund got its start. Today it is a voluntary collection taken up in Catholic churches worldwide, clearly understood to be for the Vatican.

Despite its ideological struggles with godless communism over the years, the Vatican is the closest country in history to approach ideal communism, where no private economic activity is allowed by the state. If you divide the government budget of any country by its GDP, you can come up with a handy index of socialism versus capitalism. According to this index, of course, the Vatican is the most socialist, with an index equal to 1. That is why we can assume that the government's budget is equal to its

GDP. San Marino is next, with 0.64, making it 64 percent socialist. Then comes Monaco, 59 percent socialist. Next are Malta, Luxembourg, and Liechtenstein each about 33 percent socialist. Apparently the most capitalist, laissez-faire microstate in Europe is Andorra, which spends only 29 percent of its GDP on government. Malta's government budget may be relatively low, but it should be noted that one-third of workers are employed in the public sector. In any case, all these percentages are quite high compared with those of larger countries, which typically are about 20 percent.

Another means of determining the nature of a country's economy is the percentage of the labor force employed in services. If all jobs not in agriculture, industry, or construction are considered service jobs, then of course the Vatican is again at the top of the list, with 100 percent service-sector employees. Next is Monaco, with almost 90 percent service workers; then Andorra at 78 percent; next Luxembourg and Malta, at about 70 percent; and last are Liechtenstein (61 percent) and San Marino (57 percent), the most industrialized microstates in Europe. Interestingly, almost 70 percent of the big Western European countries' work-force were employed in service positions by the end of the twentieth century. So being small and successful does not always imply a service-type economy.

Banking

Banking is an important sector of the microstates' economies, but it has not been without trouble. Liechtenstein borders on Switzerland, and its banking system is similar—in fact, all its banks are members of the Swiss Bankers Association and abide by their rules. But this also means that strict secrecy is observed for their clients, and there is the potential for money laundering. Recently Liechtenstein has been cracking down on illegal financial transactions after being cited as being a safe harbor for dirty money. Monaco's banks have also had their share of scandal: The Banque

Industrial de Monaco was involved in fraud and collapsed in 1990, and for years foreigners have been allowed to open bank accounts using the names of Monégasque citizens. The Vatican Bank, too, has been involved in the collapse of a bank, the Italian Banco Ambrosiano. The Vatican agreed to pay $241 million to creditors after an Italo-Vatican commission published the results of its investigation. Perhaps the Vatican Bank's problems stem less from dishonesty than from backward thinking and adherence to outmoded traditions, such as requiring that all depositors be Christians.

On the other hand, in Luxembourg banking has been exemplary and quite successful—it's the second largest economic sector after the steel industry. Luxembourg has encouraged foreign banks to set up branches in the country as well. In addition, Luxembourg has become a leader in the securities industry, convincing foreigners to invest their pension money in funds set up there.

International Economic Organizations

Much of this cross-border activity was made possible by Luxembourg's membership in the European Union, which abolished tariffs, taxes, and legal roadblocks to commerce between European countries. In fact, several European Union government buildings are located near Luxembourg-Ville. This is neither a coincidence nor a kind of consolation prize for the tiny country. Luxembourg was a founding member of the European Union's predecessor, the European Economic Community, which had been inspired by Benelux, the free-trade organization between Luxembourg and the small countries of Belgium and the Netherlands. Before that, Luxembourg and Belgium had been in their own economic union, which had set common commercial policies, linked the two countries' currencies, and established a customs union. A customs union is an agreement to abolish taxes (tariffs) on goods flowing between countries, and to share a common tariff policy for goods from outside the union. Beginning in 1849, Luxembourg partici- pated in one of the world's earliest customs unions, the Zol- lverein, between what was then the still-independent German Confederation states.

The other microstates of Europe have not been so eager to join economic unions, possibly because they fear elimination of their unregulated industries. As of the end of 2003, no microstate other than Malta has joined the EU (apart from Luxembourg) or even applied for membership. But all of the other microstates are in customs unions of one kind or another, and have been in them for years. In 1939, San Marino signed a customs union treaty with Italy. There are no border guards or customs houses between the two countries, and Italy pays San Marino an annual amount esti- mated to be what San Marino would get if all the goods it imported from other countries came directly into the country. Andorra was in a customs union with France since 1967. The only microstate not in a customs union with a big sister was Malta, which has no big sister, and needs its own currency. The expan- sion of the European Union has disrupted these individual cus- toms unions. As each big sister joined up, it had to adapt its customs procedures to those of the entire EU, invalidating the regulations in their prior treaties with the microstates.

Liechtenstein's experience was particularly difficult. In 1992, Switzerland's government announced its intention to join the EU, and scheduled a referendum on joining the EEA as a first step. The European Economic Area is a kind of customs union between the EU and EFTA. Because of its close customs and monetary union with Switzerland, Liechtenstein followed suit, and their ref- erendum on joining the EEA passed by 55.8 percent. Unfortu- nately, the Swiss referendum failed. So Liechtenstein had to adjust its laws to make itself a kind of middle ground between Switzerland and the EU.

All the other microstates, except, of course, Malta, formally terminated the customs unions with their big sisters and signed customs union treaties directly with the EU. Though they don't have their own currencies, Monaco, San Marino, and Vatican City had been allowed by treaty to mint a small number of their own coins in francs or lire to be sold as souvenirs. These coins depicted their national symbols and were valid currency. The European Union agreed to allow this practice to continue with the euro coins when the lira and the franc were withdrawn from circulation.

Assets

A country's economic success often depends on its workforce, and the microstates have been blessed with well-educated, hard-working people. It seems there is always a lot of work to do, and most of these small nations have to import workers, who either commute from big-sister states or are permanent residents. Perhaps the abundance of work is due to the overhead in managing an independent country. In any case, unemployment is extremely low in the microstates, rarely over 4 percent. For example, in 1997 there were only thirty-five people without a job in Monaco. Nevertheless, Monaco gives priority of employment to its citizens over foreigners. The governments of San Marino and Malta have practiced full employment policies as well.

By now, all of the microstates have their own radio, television, and newspapers. As for full-time, working railroads, only Liechtenstein, Luxembourg, and Monaco have them, although a freight line from the Roman railroad is sometimes used in the Vatican. During the Second World War, both San Marino's and Malta's railroads were damaged, and they were not repaired. So they and Andorra, which never had a railroad, rely on automobiles, trucks, and buses. Bus service is usually very good in the European microstates. Only Luxembourg and Malta have enough flat land for an airport and both have official airlines. Every microstate imports most of its energy, but Andorra and Liechtenstein, and to a smaller extent Luxembourg, fill some of their own energy needs through hydroelectricity.

The seven microstates have generally done a good job of managing their natural environment. Perhaps their limited resources have led them to take exceptionally good care of what they have. Liechtensteiners, in particular, are to be commended for the clean, neat way they have industrialized—there are no polluting industries and all factories blend into the scenery. An early example of recycling was the use as fertilizer of the waste phosphorous from Luxembourg's steel industry. And Maltese farmers try to conserve topsoil by planting trees and terracing. These countries have to deal with pollution emanating from their big sisters, of course, and they also create some problems of their own. Andorra and Malta are feeling the pinch of dwindling natural areas and resources while Malta and Luxembourg have experienced some pollution in their urban areas. But because they are usually less industrial or agricultural than their neighbors, the microstates of Europe remain cleaner.

Street procession.
MALTA TOURIST OFFICE, NEW YORK.

Lilliputians:
The People of the Microstates

Origins

Europeans are genetically the most homogeneous people of any continent, so despite the geographical distance between the microstates, the people of the microstates of Europe may be more closely related than you'd expect. Only the Maltese may be a mixture of Asians and Africans, because of the occupation by the Phoenicians and Carthaginians. But actually the first people to reach Malta came from Europe, crossing over from Sicily as far back as 5000 BC.

For most of Europe, the Indo-European peoples are so important that you can start your anthropological analysis by classifying tribes as either Indo-European or non-Indo-European. Except for Malta, non-Indo-Europeans were there first, and then the Indo-Europeans invaded. However, it is difficult to know how much any invasion influenced the genetic makeup of a people, which depends on how many invaders stayed and colonized versus how many natives died or fled, details that were not often documented.

Some foreign influences came from regions south of the European continent. The seafaring Phoenicians, from the area

The Microstates Demographically

Microstate	Vatican City	Monaco	San Marino	Liechtenstein	Malta	Andorra	Luxembourg
Name of Native	—	Monégasque	Sammarinese	Liechtensteiner	Maltese	Andorran	Luxembourger
Year Women Got Vote	—	1962	1959	1984	1947	1970	1919
No. Tourists per Year	7,300,000	259,000	3,345,000	57,000	1,100,000	6,000,000	715,000
Population (Residents)	911	32,130	28,119	33,145	400,420	69,150	454,157
% Foreign Residents	40	84	33	34	3	67	38
Labor Force	4,000	30,540	17,922	29,000	160,000	33,000	262,300
Cross-border Commuters	3,000	26,700	4,324	9,741	0	1,880	101,621

Sources: U.S. Central Intelligence Agency: *The World Factbook, 2003; Liechtenstein in Figures, 2003; Scientific Report on the Mobility of Cross-border Workers within the EEA; Worldmark Encyclopedia of Nations; Europa World Yearbook.*

Internet Sources: Monster.lu (May 2004); www.vatican.va (May 2004); www.omniway.sm (May 2004).

now known as Syria and Lebanon, became associated with Carthage, just across the Mediterranean from Malta, and they traded and coexisted with the Romans for many years. The Phoenicians reached Malta in about 1000 BC, and three hundred years later they conquered Monaco. They may have passed through Andorra, too, centuries later in the Carthaginian battles with the Romans.

A little before 1000 BC, the Villanovans came from Central Europe to Bologna and then to where San Marino is located. They were followed by the Etruscans, who occupied much of Italy, including Rome and the Vatican Hill. The Etruscans may have been closely related to the Rhaetians, who occupied the land now called Liechtenstein. Before the Phoenicians arrived, the natives in the area of Monaco were known as Ligurians, and the tribe that lived there, the Monoïkos, may have been responsible for its name. Meanwhile, the Basques, one of the oldest and most genetically distinctive people of Europe, were probably the original inhabitants of Andorra. A tribe called the Andosinos probably is the origin of the name Andorra. The Ligurians and the Basques occupied Monaco and Andorra respectively from prehistoric times, and are closely related genetically to today's native inhabitants. In sum, the Phoenicians, the Ligurians, the Etruscans and the Rhaetians were the early non-Indo-European inhabitants of the microstates.

At first, various Indo-European groups occupied only a few of the microstate regions of Europe. The ancient Greeks were great traders and colonizers of southern Europe, and their blood must have mixed with that of the inhabitants of all the microstates except Liechtenstein and Luxembourg, which were too far north. Around 400 BC, another early Indo-European people, the Celts, took over those two remaining microstates in the north, and probably Andorra as well. The ancestors of the Luxembourgers, the Treveri, were probably a Celtic tribe.

Then, two other Indo-European peoples rose in importance and conquered all of the microstates, eventually giving their languages to all but Malta. These were the Romans and the Germans. The Romans fought the Celts, the Germans, and the Phoenicians for control of the other microstates. They defeated them all, and a particular group of Romans from Liguria (near Monaco) occupied Luxembourg as well. Although the Romans spread their culture all over Europe, they never completely conquered the Germanic peoples, and eventually the Franks and the Alemanni overran Luxembourg and Liechtenstein, respectively, whose natives now speak Germanic languages. Germanic tribes eventually conquered the other microstates as well, but did not leave their languages. Every microstate but Malta speaks a Romance or Germanic languages today.

The last important people to conquer and colonize the microstates were the Saracens, or Arabs. They took and held on to Malta for two hundred years, and formed the basis of the Maltese language. The other major influence on the Maltese came from Italy. The Arabs also conquered Monaco, but left little influence there.

Microstate Populations

As a matter of fact, one microstate has no native population at all, namely the Vatican. Few people live in the Vatican, but those who do are ultimately guests of the pope, even if they have Vatican citizenship. Periodically, the pope must sign a document to renew each resident's right to remain within the Vatican walls. There doesn't even seem to be a name for a Vatican national, for that matter: *Vaticaner? Vatican Citizen?* As far as population is concerned, the Vatican must be the most unusual country in the world. For one thing, at least 75 percent of its residents are in the clergy. As many of these clerics hold important positions within the patriarchal hierarchy of the Catholic Church, most of them are men, though there are a few nuns. A further 16 percent of the residents belong to the Swiss Guard, giving the Vatican an almost completely male population. Thus, there is no official birth rate of the Vatican, as almost anyone giving birth there would immediately create a scandal!

Although the microstates have small populations, their population densities are rather high compared with that of the average country. In fact, Monaco has the world's highest number of people per living space. That is mostly because Monaco is entirely urban. The Vatican is the only other country that is exclusively a city. In the other European microstates, much of the population is concentrated in the capital city and its immediate surroundings. For example, about half the population of Andorra is found in the Andorra la Vella / Les Escaldes area. The major exception to this is Liechtenstein, whose capital Vaduz has less than one-sixth of its population. In this microstate, the population is so spread out that the entire country seems to be only suburbs and rural areas.

Cultural Areas

The microstates that are situated on borders between bigger countries have developed transitional cultures, borrowing much from their big-sister neighbors. Only San Marino and the Vatican, which are both surrounded by Italy, have become cultural icons in themselves. When one thinks of Italy, one may think of Rome and the Vatican, and also of St. Peter's, the pope, and the Catholic Church. Although San Marino is not as important as the Vatican, it is another aspect of "holey" Italy, the laid-back country that doesn't seem to mind having two independent countries punched right out of it. Monaco may have a seacoast, but it borders only on France. And Monaco, too, seems to be just another pleasurable fixture of French Riviera life.

Whereas the other microstates and their people are not well known, Monaco and the Vatican are the most famous of the seven European microstates. Many people don't realize that they are independent states, but they certainly recognize a few famous personalities hailing from these lands. A pope is always an important figure, but John Paul II especially has been an essential player in late twentieth-century history. Prince Rainier III and Princess Grace of Monaco were constantly in the news until her fatal car accident. Monaco still seems to be able to have its cake and eat it too, as an unflagging watering hole for the wealthy, but also as a tourist attraction for the gawking masses. There do not seem to be many famous personalities who come from the other European microstates. One exception may be Robert Schuman, the Luxembourger who became a French diplomat. Schuman proposed the West European Coal and Steel Pool, which later became the European Union. It is fitting that Luxembourg-Ville is now one of the "capitals" of the new Europe, where many of its institutions are headquartered. Another somewhat famous microstate personality, Dom Mintoff of Malta, appears in the chapter on government.

Tourism is big business in all the microstates. Each sees between 1 and 7 million visitors per year, except for Liechtenstein. Even for "giant" Luxembourg, this means two foreign visitors per inhabitant per year. For the Vatican, it means one thousand visitors per resident each year. This amount of exposure to foreigners can take its toll on the native culture, and some of the microstates are beginning to worry about this erosion.

Foreigners

And then there are the foreigners who stay. Some of the things that make the microstates attractive places to visit also make them attractive as places to live. One reason to move there is the spectrum of industries that especially flourish in microstates, for example, tourism itself. Also, the influx of foreigners taking up residence in these tiny countries has helped transform them from rural backwaters to densely populated urban centers. Andorra went from only 226 foreigners in 1918 to almost 60,000 by the end of the century. Today only one in five residents of Andorra is a native. Needless to say, native Andorrans are particularly worried that foreigners are chipping away at their values.

Children hikers in a flower-filled Rialp Valley.
MINISTRY OF TOURISM OF THE GOVERNMENT OF ANDORRA.

All the microstates but Malta have a rather high percentage of foreigners living within their borders. Liechtenstein and San Marino have 16 percent; the Vatican and Luxembourg, about 35 percent; Andorra and Monaco each have more than 80 percent foreign residents. Where do all these immigrants come from? Surprisingly, the single largest foreign nationality in the microstates taken as a whole is the Portuguese: They are the greatest foreign group in Luxembourg, which has the highest population of the European microstates; also, they are the second biggest group in Andorra, after the Spanish. There aren't so many Portuguese in the other microstates, probably because only Luxembourg is in the EU, which gives the economically challenged Portuguese the legal right to seek their fortunes there. Not surprisingly, most other foreigners in the microstates come from neighboring lands.

Italy has the most microstate neighbors, and thus Italians account for sizable minorities in the majority of the microstates. The French and the Spanish also account for many émigrés to microstates. Interestingly, the British are the fifth biggest minority group in all the microstates, and not simply because Malta was formerly a British colony, but because of their presence in Luxembourg and Monaco as well. And speaking of Malta, nowadays most émigrés to this island nation are descendants of or native-born Maltese who once emigrated to other countries.

Like many modern European countries, the microstates have low birth rates, about half of the world average. This is one reason why they encourage foreigners to live and work within them. Another reason is the need for talent and skills that cannot be found in small populations. Sometimes microstate governments have problems finding people for specialized positions. With so few people to choose from, the likelihood of finding a person with training for an unusual task is simply too low. The microstates also have relatively low natural population increases, again about half the world average. Monaco would actually lose 0.3 percent of its population annually if it weren't for its 0.4 percent immigration rate.

Citizenship and Naturalization

High numbers of foreigners within their countries have not convinced the governments of the microstates to grant these people citizenship. Unlike such immigrant countries as the United States, Canada, or Australia, no microstate has a regular process of naturalization based on length of stay. It may even be difficult to get permission to stay, though it is sometimes possible to get a work permit if a particular talent is needed. Regulations vary by country: If you want to stay for more than three months in Monaco, you must get permission from the French government as well. You can live in Andorra as long as you like, provided you don't work. On the other hand, there are no restrictions on working in Andorra if you live outside the country. As microstates are so small, it is not difficult to commute to a job there, and large portions of the labor force of Liechtenstein and especially of the Vatican do not live in the same country they work in.

It is very difficult to become a citizen of a European microstate. In most of these countries, you are not a citizen simply by being born there. Typically, both your parents must be citizens as well. Also, if a male citizen marries a female foreigner, his wife automatically becomes a citizen—but this is not the case if the sexes are reversed. Some of these restrictions are being eased, but not very much. In Liechtenstein, your application for citizenship must be approved first by the commune (local citizens) where you want to live, and then by the prince, the head of the whole country. And only the prince of Monaco can bestow citizenship in his country.

Because Malta used to be a colony, citizenship had to be defined carefully. On the day Malta was granted independence from Britain, everyone who had been born in Malta was granted citizenship. Also, those people who had become British citizens while living in Malta were given the opportunity to become citizens.

In Vatican City, most people are not married and do not have children. The Swiss Guards are the exception. The Guard, known in Latin as Cohors Helvetica, really are Swiss, recruited from the Catholic cantons of that country. They must be bachelors, have a minimum height, and present a letter from their local bishop to prove they are good Catholics. Only the most dedicated ones— who get promoted to officer or senior sergeant—are permitted to marry. As they actually live within the Vatican walls, these men are the heads of the only families in the Vatican.

Their families may live in the Vatican with them until they leave the guard. A male child may stay only until he is twenty-five years of age; a female may stay until she marries. These regulations ensure that the Vatican will have no native population, which might clamor for a political voice.

Swiss Guard, Vatican City.

PHOTO COURTESY OF PHILIP GREENSPUN, http://philip.greenspun.com.

In August 1999, San Marino introduced a new law requiring that all female domestic staff be over fifty years of age. This anti–gold digger law was designed to prevent young women from frivolously acquiring San Marino citizenship by marrying rich elderly men. A referendum to equalize citizenship laws between males and females was rejected soon after.

In Monaco and Andorra, citizens are a privileged minority. Monégasque citizens are given priority in employment and housing. As with all countries, only citizens vote in the microstates. In Andorra, this unequal treatment of residents has sometimes caused dissension among noncitizen residents. And so Andorra has given complete economic rights to anyone who has lived there over twenty years. That is, they may start businesses, or own property and build on it. But they do not have the right to vote. Monaco, too, has made a concession to its massive foreign population, in the form of an Economic Council, elected by all residents, including noncitizens, and consulted by the prince on economic matters. But the fact that only citizens elect the officials who make the laws seems to guarantee that they will remain in charge.

When most of its residents do not have the right to vote, a country's leaders may have a hard time convincing people of the benefits of democracy. In the face of this, some of the microstates have been trying to figure out ways to encourage civic pride among their people. However, two of the microstates do not seem to have any interest in promoting democracy. Monaco and the Vatican are ultimately ruled by a single person, the prince and the pope, respectively. True, there are elections to the National Council in Monaco, but the prince has the power to block any and all legislation. And nearly the only element of democracy in Vatican City is the election of the pope, a lifetime office. Nevertheless, the residents and the citizens of these nations seem to be happy living in their "dictatorships." After all, as a tax haven, Monaco attracts more people than there is room for. Those who live in the Vatican are mostly clerics in the upper part of the hierarchy, who apparently consider it a privilege to live there. While the European Union has strict requirements on democracy for its government members, Monaco and the Vatican both claim no interest in joining the EU; if they were to change their mind, they would have to reform their governments considerably.

Emigration

Perhaps the residents of Monaco and the Vatican are happy, since these are the only microstates that have not experienced mass emigration. Of course, many other European countries have lost population to the New World and other places, but the microstates are particularly vulnerable—because they are so very small, a border is never very far away from anyone's home. The slightest dissatisfaction is liable to evoke a wave of emigration. For example, inheritance customs once created problems in both Andorra and Luxembourg, leading to emigration: In Andorra, the traditional practice of a farmer's leaving three-fourths of his land to his oldest son led the younger sons to emigrate to Spain and France. Today there are actually more people of Andorran descent in those two countries than in Andorra itself. Conversely, in the late nineteenth century, Luxembourg reformed its system to require that a farm be divided equally among all sons. Within a couple of generations, divided farms became so small that they could not support a family. Thousands of Luxembourgers emigrated, many to the United States, which was offering them land in the Midwest. They settled mostly in Minnesota, Iowa, and Illinois.

Liechtenstein also experienced emigration, in the days when it was ruled by an absentee prince in Austria. Liechtensteiners settled in Iowa and Indiana, and also in Canada and South America. The Sammarinese also emigrated in vast numbers to the United States, specifically, the Michigan cities of Troy and Detroit. There is such a large community of Maltese in Australia that they publish their own newspapers in Maltese. In short, there has been extensive emigration from all of the European microstates except the two smallest. Today, however, the microstates are so prosperous that there is little emigration.

In recent history, the microstates have sometimes called on their expatriates for help. During World War II, when Luxembourg was occupied and its government in exile, the son of the grand duchess, Grand Duke Jean, visited some American cities that had significant populations of Luxembourgers, and set up a national relief fund in Chicago. More recently, Malta has helped fill its needs in the public sector by searching for talent in the large Maltese communities of Australia, the United States, and Canada.

Refugees

If the European microstates are not generous bestowing citizenship, they have been generous in helping the citizens of their neighbors. Andorra remained neutral during the Spanish Civil War and, after that, during World War II. It became an escape route for refugees from Spain fleeing to France, and then vice versa. San Marino took in one hundred thousand refugees fleeing fascist Italy during the same period: there were more than four guests for every inhabitant. Seventy years before that, San Marino took in many refugees fleeing retribution during Italy's struggle for unification, including one of its heroes, Garibaldi. Malta was another important refuge for Italians during the Risorgimento.

Women

Despite years of exposure to foreign ways, the microstates of Europe are still very conservative and traditional. As noted, some of their laws on immigration are still not the same for men and for women. In Europe and America, the women's suffrage movement found success in the early part of the twentieth century, and by the late 1920s women already had the vote in many Western nations. By contrast, no microstate except Luxembourg allowed women to vote until the second half of the twentieth century. Liechtenstein waited the longest—until 1984—before allowing the female half of its population to vote.

Polyglots

Being small and perhaps on the border of bigger states has given the microstates a linguistic advantage—many of the people of the microstates can speak more than one language. The Vatican and Monaco each have an especially large segment of residents from the international community. Cardinals and other clergymen come from all over the world to participate in the administration of the Catholic Church from within the Vatican. When they arrive, most of them learn Italian and even Latin. A good deal of Monaco's residents are jet-setters from among the wealthiest people around the world. Andorra, too, can count on its many foreign residents to provide linguistic diversity. But Luxembourg gets the prize for linguistic talent: Everybody in Luxembourg is at least trilingual, since there are three national languages, all employed in its educational system. Perhaps this is why the EU plans to move its translation service to Luxembourg. Most people in Malta can get by in both English and Maltese. Only San Marino and Liechtenstein are somewhat linguistically isolated, at least as far as standard national languages are concerned. So most of the microstates have no difficulty in finding translators and interpreters who are, after all, essential to the tourist trade.

Dress

The microstates of Europe, though conservative, are just about as modern as their neighbors when it comes to clothing, so don't

The "Dancing Procession" takes place in Echternach on Whit-Tuesday.
LUXEMBOURG TOURIST BOARD.

Women in colorful Maltese costumes.
MALTA TOURIST OFFICE, NEW YORK.

expect to see natives dressed in their quaint costumes going about their daily routine. The exception, of course, is the Vatican. Practically every resident belongs to some religious order or another, so that many people are customarily dressed in their habits. The Swiss Guard, on the other hand, usually wear colorful Renaissance-style uniforms and helmets, said to have been designed by Michelangelo. In the other microstates, traditional costumes are worn on special occasions, such as the biannual investiture of the captains regent in San Marino. The Sammarinese also dress up for military parades and for archery demonstrations. At the daily changing of the guard in Monaco, the ceremonial troops are decked out in their finery. In Luxembourg, people dress in traditional garb for the so-called handkerchief procession dedicated to St. Willibrord, the world's only dancing religious procession. Traditional dress is also used in the microstates during performances of traditional music or dancing. For example, in Liechtenstein, brass bands wear traditional costume; in Andorra and Malta, people often break out their traditional costume to perform their national dances, respectively called the *sardana* and *il-maltija*.

Sports

The people of the microstates of Europe are quite sports-minded, and their preferences are probably influenced by their geography. Walking, hiking, and biking are popular in all of the microstates. Since their territories are small, these seem to be efficient ways of seeing the country as well as exercising. Three of the countries—Andorra, Liechtenstein, and Luxembourg—have cold winters and mountains amenable to skiing, a sport popular among tourists and natives alike. The people of the microstates are perhaps bigger car-lovers than they might have been had they better mass transit. And it may be this familiarity with cars that led Monaco, San Marino, and Luxembourg to hold annual Grand Prix races as part of the Formula One championship. Swimming and sailing are popular in Malta and Monaco, the two microstates with seacoasts. The only microstate without a sporting tradition is the Vatican. So it is not surprising that all but the Vatican participate in the Olympic games. The heir apparent of Monaco himself, Prince Albert, led a bobsled team in the Winter Olympics in 1988. Not deterred by their small chances for gold medals, the microstates have even set up their own Olympics, called the Games of the Small States. They were first held in San Marino in 1985, and have been held every other year since, rotationally, in one of the eight European states (six of the seven microstates, plus Cyprus and Iceland) with populations under 1 million.

Crime

The microstates leave much of their judicial systems to their big sisters. This is possible because the crime rate in the microstates is extremely low, thus there are few crimes to prosecute. And this is natural, since their people are so wealthy and busily employed. Still, though violent crime may be minimal, the microstates of Europe are not without higher-profile crimes. All but San Marino—including the Vatican—have been cited for money laundering. Also, for many years, Malta has had to deal with corrupt governments and a strident civil service sector. In the Vatican in 1998, a Swiss Guard killed his superior, the superior's wife, and then himself—and a greater scandal arose when it was discovered that the murdered man had been a spy for East Germany since 1979. Even the princely family of Monaco has been a kind of crime victim. Princess Stephanie divorced her first husband after she was shown incriminating photographs of him and another woman. Recently, the rejected husband won a civil court case against this woman for entrapment.

Micromanagement:
Government in the Microstates

For the governments of the microstates of Europe, once again smallness becomes both a challenge and an advantage. They need to run a whole country with a small number of people, yet their intimate groups allow for innovations not possible elsewhere. Economic policy, too, can be flexible, and the microstates vary from open-market capitalism to pure socialism. The governments range from absolute dictatorship to strong participatory democracy.

Democracy

If the trend of history is toward more democratic governments, the microstates are no exception. All but Monaco, the Vatican, and possibly Liechtenstein are true democracies. San Marino's democracy dates as far back as its legendary founding in the fourth century; it is the oldest republic in the world. The Arengo, an assembly of heads of families, was the earliest of San Marino's five branches of government, and is still around today, although in a different form. With an average voter participation rate of 80 percent, San Marino's democracy is so strong that they neither have nor need a constitution to protect it.

The election of the pope may be the only democratic element of modern Vatican City, but the papacy is probably the world's oldest elective office. Since the beginnings of Christianity, the bishop of Rome was given the automatic honor of heading the Catholic Church. Like other bishops, he was elected by the clergy and laypeople of the diocese, until the year 1079, when the voting was limited to cardinals. Since then, the cardinals have been shut up in a room to deliberate, beginning about two weeks following the death of a pontiff. If their debates lasted too long, the daily amount of food sent in was reduced to concentrate their attention. Because they were so isolated, they had to resort to a signaling system of smoke coming from the chimney of their fireplace after each session. Black smoke indicated deadlock, white smoke meant *habemus papam,* "we have a pope." Pope John Paul II has eliminated some of the secrecy and pressure tactics, but not the smoke signals, and this is the extent of democratic reform in the Vatican.

The other microstates experienced more recent democratizations, mostly in the nineteenth century. The most recent transition to democracy took place in Andorra, which was ruled jointly by the president of France and the bishop of the town of Urgell in Spain. Since 1419, heads of families in Andorra were allowed to meet and discuss local problems, but before the 1930s, you could vote only if you were a male and your father was no longer living. In the early 1970s, women got the right to vote, and plans were made to modernize the state. In 1973, the coprinces from Spain and France met for the first time since 1278, to discuss these plans. It wasn't until all the internal reforms were complete, in 1990, that the president of France allowed the people of Andorra to handle their own relations with other countries. Andorra, one of the world's oldest political divisions, transformed essentially from a medieval state to a modern one in less than twenty years.

Types of Government

Two of Europe's microstates are republics and five, monarchies. None of the latter has a king or queen, and only two of the monarchs are powerful rulers. Two of the monarchies, Liechtenstein and Monaco, have princes, Andorra has two "coprinces," and Luxembourg has a grand duke or grand duchess. Accordingly, Liechtenstein, Monaco, and Andorra are called "principalities," while Luxembourg is known as a "grand duchy." The Vatican has a prince of the church, but for political purposes the pope is known as the "sovereign" of the Vatican City State. Practically speaking, there is not much difference among these noble titles, except for Andorra's coprinces. Their title seems to be honorary, since neither the president of France nor the bishop of Urgell need be noblemen to hold their respective offices. Like Andorra, the Republic of San Marino has two heads of state, the captains regent. They are elected, but only for six-month terms, and they must wait for three years to run for this office again. They must agree on any action they perform, as did the coprinces of Andorra when they had real political power. Perhaps only in a microstate is this bifurcated kind of leadership possible. Only Malta has the familiar president as head of state, except that he or she is not elected by the people, but chosen by the Maltese parliament.

In most modern countries, a royal head of state does not hold much power these days. Microstates are somewhat exceptional, however, because their leaders have more duties and powers than, say, the queen of England or the emperor of Japan. Apart from their titled ruler, each of the microstates has a parliament or legislature, which enacts the laws. Only in Monaco and the Vatican does the head of state still have the power to veto any law; a new constitution, approved in 2003, has clarified that this power belongs to the prince of Liechtenstein as well.

A head of state is not necessarily a head of government. The "government" can be thought of as the executive branch of government, or the "administration," the branch that carries out the laws enacted by the legislative division. The other common branch of government is the judiciary, which normally determines whether laws have been broken, and by whom. The judiciary may also judge the constitutionality of laws that is, it will determine whether an enacted law itself does or does not break one of the

Captains Regent coming out of Government Building during ceremony.
STATE TOURIST BUREAU OF THE REPUBLIC OF SAN MARINO.

fundamental laws of the country. In the United States, all three branches are separate with "checks and balances" on each other, as set out in the Constitution. In the United Kingdom, no constitution spells out their separation, but by tradition Parliament, the royal cabinet, and the judicial system have quite a bit of independence from each other. This independence is often used as a measure of how democratic any government really is.

In four of the seven microstates of Europe, the branches of government are independent. In the other three—Monaco, Vatican City, and San Marino—they are somewhat or totally interdependent. In Monaco, the judiciary is independent; in fact, most of its judges must come from France. There, only the prince can propose a law and, as he can reject any law passed by the National Council, Monaco's legislature is not very powerful. According to the Vatican's fundamental law, "the supreme pontiff, sovereign of the Vatican City State, has full legislative, executive and judicial powers." If they are all responsible to one man, those branches of Vatican government cannot be considered independent. Recently, Pope John Paul II has introduced a strict separation at least between ecclesiastical and temporal courts. San Marino's judges are responsible to the legislature, so they are not strictly independent, either.

Vatican City and Monaco have "top-down" governments, and the other microstates of Europe have "bottom-up" government. The pope, and the prince of Monaco, have all or most of the political power, and the people must obey them and their surrogates. In the other microstates, the people ultimately rule, and the government serves the people, even if they all are simultaneously subjects of a largely symbolic monarch. Perhaps Liechtenstein can be considered an extreme version of bottom-up rule. Like its neighbor Switzerland, it frequently holds referendum and initiative elections on matters that would be handled by the legislatures of most other countries. The Vatican and Monaco are run more like corporations than modern governments, since their heads resemble chief executive officers, delegating power to lower-ranked officials. The government of the Vatican controls all economic activity;

in Monaco, the government often intervenes in the economy and it owns the richest corporation doing business there. The citizens of Monaco and the Vatican appear quite happy with this arrangement.

Legislatures

The legislatures of the microstates of Europe range in size from the seven-member pontifical commission of the Vatican to the sixty-five-member House of Representatives of Malta. On average, there are only a few thousand people per representative, though there are only 417 people for each member of San Marino's Great and General Council. Compared with the 630,000 Americans per U.S. representative, the people of the microstates, especially the Sammarinese, have unusually close contact with their national government. The ratio of 116 residents per cardinal in the pontifical commission is really meaningless, of course, since the pontifical commission is appointed, not elected. Andorra's legislature has 28 members, half elected at large, half selected in pairs from each of the seven parishes of the country. Members of Andorra's General Council or of Liechtenstein's Diet are elected to four-year terms, and the other microstate representatives hold five-year terms.

Because the microstate legislatures follow parliamentary traditions, they can be "dissolved" at any time, so the four- or five-year terms of office are not always completed. In most cases, the head of state ceremonially dismisses parliament, usually because of a parliamentary vote of no-confidence in the government. Then elections are held, and a new government is formed by the party winning the most votes or else by a coalition of parties. In the Vatican and Monaco, where there are no political parties, governments do not "fall" in this way. But the powerful head of state can dismiss the government or the parliament at any time. The pope can even dismiss individual members of his commission.

The parliaments of the microstates of Europe mostly have the same rights and duties as any other legislature. They must approve the national budget. They vote on laws, treaties, and other proposals, usually submitted by the administration. Some of the microstates allow the head of state or the people to propose laws through a referendum. But in Monaco, only the prince may propose a law. The grand duke of Luxembourg, too, proposes all laws to the chamber of deputies, but there the administration may suggest laws to the grand duke. In any case, all laws may be amended or divided by the legislature. Curiously, each law is normally voted on twice in Luxembourg's chamber of deputies, with an interval of three months between each vote. In each of the microstates, there is a head of the parliament, called "president" in four of them. These presidents have very few reserved powers, much like the speaker of the parliament in Britain. In fact, this position is called the speaker in Malta, because there the head of state is already called the president. Only in San Marino does anyone with any power preside over parliament—there it's the two captains regent, the coheads of state.

Most of the microstate legislatures also have the right to ask questions of the government, and even to investigate it. These powers are absent in Monaco and the Vatican. All the European microstates have unicameral legislatures; that is, there is only one house of parliament. At one time Luxembourg had an upper house of parliament called the council of state. Today, this body must give its opinion on all laws proposed or passed by the chamber of deputies, but it has no power to vote a law up or down. The twenty-one lifetime members are appointed by the grand duke.

Five of the seven microstates have governmental bodies whose only real purpose is to give advice or opinions on the functioning of the government. In Monaco, the prince may consult the Crown Council for help when he wants it, but he *must* consult them on certain issues, such as international treaties or granting of citizenship. However, their opinion is never binding. In San Marino, after the captains regents' six-month term is over, what they did or did not do in office is subject to citizens' complaints for three consecutive days before the two-person Syndicate of Regency. And in the Vatican, the pope is advised by the *consulta,* a body of twenty-four experts, including laymen, which he appoints himself. The idea of a governmental body with only advisory powers seems to be especially popular in the microstates, if not unique to them. Perhaps the smallness of the populations makes it less likely that an expert will hold an office where experience is needed, and consultation becomes more important than in other countries.

Another unusual feature of a microstate legislature is Malta's official leader of the opposition. Like the leader of the government, the leader of a party is chosen by the president, but in this case it's the second largest party, not the largest. During his term in office, the prime minister must consult this leader of the opposition when appointing a temporary president, or when appointing members of the electoral commission, the public service commission, the broadcasting authority, or other commissions where fairness is important.

In the microstates, after an election, when it is clear that one party or a coalition of parties has a majority of seats in the parliament, the head of state usually appoints the head of the biggest party as prime minister. Other members of the party in power are then chosen to head the various departments or ministries that carry out the everyday work of the government. But in Andorra, the representatives chosen as government ministers may no longer participate in the parliament, and in Liechtenstein, the prime minister is a civil servant, not chosen from among members of the Diet. Perhaps this is because only he and his deputy are employed full time by the government.

Administrations and Politics

The number of government ministers in the microstates generally varies from three to thirteen. Luxembourg, however, has a total of twenty-six ministries or departments. This is possible because in

Luxembourg—and also in Liechtenstein—several ministers typically head two or more ministries. The practice of giving a minister more than one portfolio is also common in non-European microstates, for example, in the island nations of Seychelles and Nauru. In Malta, it often happens that related persons are chosen as members of the government. Until recently, a pope would customarily hire his own nephews for various positions in the Vatican. All this coziness and multiple responsibility must be due at least partly to the small size of the microstates, and the small number of people available for the positions.

Another characteristic of microstate government seems to be cooperation—even between opposing political parties—and the prevalence of grand coalition governments. Liechtenstein's two major parties shared government power in a peaceful coalition that lasted from 1938 until 1997. In Luxembourg, the Christian Social People's Party typically forms a coalition government with one other party. There have been two major coalitions ruling San Marino continuously since World War II, one of them including the Communist Party. Today it's the Christian Democrats and the Socialist Party who govern this microstate. Only Andorra and Malta have true contention, where either of two parties wins a majority and governs on its own. On the other hand, Vatican City does not have political parties, and Monaco's National Democratic Union seems never to lose an election.

About the only thing that Malta's Labor and Nationalist parties could ever agree on was the need for the some kind of democracy in Malta. Before independence in 1964, Dom Mintoff, the head of Labor, worked out an agreement to actually integrate Malta into the United Kingdom, giving it seats in the British parliament. When the Nationalists won in 1962, they reversed course and obtained full independence for Malta with the queen of England as its head of state, as in Canada. When Mintoff and his labor party returned to power about ten years later, they broke with the monarchy and made Malta a republic, although it remained in the Commonwealth. Since then, the Maltese government has gone back and forth between Labor and the Nationalists several times.

Once, the elections were so close and forming a government so difficult, that Malta changed its constitution, guaranteeing a majority of seats in parliament to the party with the most votes. Generally, Labor advocates anticolonialism, a neutral foreign policy, friendly relations with the Third World (including Libya), and restriction of the powers of the Catholic Church. The Nationalists advocated membership in NATO and friendly relations with the Church, and today they champion membership in the European Union. In this respect, Malta's disunity and shifting government created confusion if not embarrassment in Europe. In the early 1990s the Nationalists applied for Malta's membership in the EU, but soon Labor took office and withdrew the application. Then in 1998, the Nationalists won and resubmitted the application. In May 2004, Malta joined the EU along with several Eastern European countries and Cyprus, but it has cut all its ties to NATO.

Until 1993, political parties were technically illegal in Andorra, but there were informal groupings in the General Council as early as the 1970s. And in 1982, after hundreds of years of direct rule from Spain and France, Oscar Ribas Reig, the leader of the National Democratic Grouping, became Andorra's first head of government. During his political career, Ribas Reig resigned several times, sometimes on principle, in his struggle to bring democracy to Andorra. For instance, in 1992 he resigned when conservatives blocked his effort to introduce a constitution guaranteeing civil rights. This tactic eventually succeeded, and it was the beginning of Andorra's new history as a modern state. Power has since shifted back and forth between the National Democratic Grouping and the conservative Liberal Union, which is in power today.

Judiciaries

A strict separation of the judiciary from other areas of government is essential for modern democracies. There must be some authority that can fairly dispense justice to all people accused by

Casa de les Valls, the seat of government in Andorra.

MINISTRY OF TOURISM OF THE GOVERNMENT OF ANDORRA.

the government and be sure that the government is adhering to all the rules it has agreed to follow. Generally this is the practice in the microstates of Europe. In most of them, there are lower courts, courts of appeal, and courts that can judge the constitutionality of laws passed by the government. There are criminal courts and civil courts. San Marino is exceptional, because it has no civil code of laws.

In most cases, the head of state appoints judges, usually on the advice of the government or a body of experts. San Marino again is different, because there judges are appointed by the legislature, the Grand and General Council. Andorra is another exception. Although the coprinces appoint judges to the higher courts, the Supreme Council of Justice appoints lower court judges in Andorra. A more interesting question is where the judges come from. Only in Andorra, Luxembourg, and Malta are judges always natives. In Liechtenstein, they often come from Austria and Switzerland, which is where most of the Liechtenstein's legal traditions come from as well. In Monaco, the majority of judges must be French. In the Vatican, judges must be male and Catholic, and can come from practically anywhere, as do most Vatican citizens anyway. But in San Marino, by law all judges must come from Italy.

The judiciaries of the European microstates are largely modeled on those of their big sisters. In Liechtenstein, criminal and civil law is based on the Austrian model, while corporate law is based on the Swiss. Andorran civil law is also based on two traditions, the Spanish and the French. Legal traditions in Luxembourg come mostly from Belgium, but also from Holland, France, and Germany. Monaco's civil code is similar to that of France. And both the San Marino and Vatican judiciary systems are influenced by Italy's. Although Malta has no big sister as a neighbor, it has adopted English common law and it uses Roman civil law.

Every European microstate, even the Vatican, has at least one prison, but some microstates traditionally send their prisoners abroad to serve their time there. If the sentence is greater than three months, then a prisoner in Andorra can choose between

France and Spain for captivity. After six months, a prisoner in Liechtenstein may be transferred to one of the Swiss cantons. There is a similar provision in San Marino, but it is rarely used. On the other hand, prisoners are only temporarily detained in Monaco, and must serve their time in France. The same is true in the Vatican, where prisoners are regularly sent to Italy immediately. Only Luxembourg and isolated Malta deal with all their prisoners internally.

Before serving time, a convicted prisoner may want to appeal. A judgment in a Liechtenstein court can still be appealed to a Swiss court of *cassation*. And until recently, final appeal in Andorra was either to the Supreme Court of Perpingnon, France, or to the ecclesiastical court in the Seu d'Urgell, Spain. Thus, the judiciary systems of the microstates are still somewhat dependent on their neighbors, partly because of tradition and partly because of their small size.

Constitutions

San Marino is the only European microstate without a written constitution. Some of the most democratic countries manage without one, the UK being one well-known example. If the democratic tradition is strong, then nobody needs to be reminded how to behave. But San Marino *does* have a bill of rights, passed in 1974, called the Fundamental Law. It can be changed only by a two-thirds majority in the Great and General Council. All the other microstates of Europe have written constitutions, and all but the Vatican's lay out their citizens' human rights. Some, like those of Andorra, Luxembourg, Malta, and Monaco prohibit the death penalty—none gives the right to bear arms. These constitutions all promise the basic individual rights, such as freedom of expression, of assembly, of religion, of equality before the law, of suffrage, of privacy, of free movement, and so on. Luxembourg's guarantees that its citizens will not be forced to take part in religious observances. Most of the constitutions also guarantee certain economic rights, such as the right to form labor unions, to strike, to own property, to set up businesses, or to participate in trade. Luxembourg and Monaco guarantee their citizens the right to an education and to health care, things on which the government has to spend money. Malta's constitution classifies these as "guiding principles," not rights, apparently concerned that budgets may not always allow them to be guaranteed every year. Several of the constitutions also guarantee the right to work, but it is not clear if this means that the government must offer a citizen a job if the private sector cannot.

Malta's constitution is the longest of the microstates'; almost thirty-three thousand words, it fills nearly one hundred pages. It spells out many things that most governments take for granted; for example, that parliament will set an official length for the workweek. It even states that all revenues collected must be consolidated into one fund and may not be spent without appropriation by parliament. Perhaps their founding fathers were afraid that democratic traditions were not so strong as to "go without saying." San Marino's fundamental law is the shortest, only 950 words. The constitutions of Andorra, Liechtenstein, and the Vatican are an order of magnitude larger, a bit less than ten thousand words, while Luxembourg's and Monaco's are about half that size. In addition to spelling out their citizens' rights, the constitutions of the microstates usually describe the general format the government is to take.

Human Rights

You can judge how well a state protects its citizens' rights not only by its constitution, but also by what treaties it signs. All the microstates of Europe except Monaco and the Vatican are members of the Council of Europe and have ratified the European Convention for the Protection of Human Rights and Fundamental Freedoms. They recognize the competence and jurisdiction of the European Commission and of the European Court of Human

Rights, concerning violations and interpretation of the Convention. Allowing outsiders to judge violations of human rights within one's own country is certainly a sign of confidence that one is in compliance.

The other two microstates have poor records on human rights. The ruling family of Monaco regularly censors the local press, removing anything detrimental to their image. And Monaco's form of government is not democratic enough to allow participation in this Convention. The same is true about the Vatican, but the pope also has reservations about some of the human rights language as well. The Vatican has recently described the new Charter of Fundamental Rights as "ungodly," because it sanctions homosexual unions and their adoption of children. Obviously, there is no freedom of religion in the Vatican.

On the other hand, all of the microstates of Europe have ratified the UN Convention on the Rights of the Child, including Monaco and the Vatican. Except for this treaty, Monaco and the Vatican do not participate in any of the human rights treaties mentioned below. As far as the other microstates are concerned, only San Marino has not ratified the UN Convention on the Elimination of All Forms of Discrimination against Women; but San Marino has ratified both the International Covenant on Economic, Social, and Cultural Rights and the International Covenant on Civil and Political Rights. Andorra and Liechtenstein have not, possibly a reflection of their laissez-faire economic positions. Luxembourg and Malta win the human rights prize, though, because they have ratified every one of the human rights conventions discussed here.

Because all the microstates except Malta have many foreigners living within their borders, they experience pressures relating to elections, since temporary or even permanent foreign-born residents do not have the same voting rights as the natives. Andorra has modified its laws to give the vote to all people born there who are more than twenty-eight years old, yet still only about one-seventh of the total population votes. Voting is compulsory in Luxembourg, and nonvoters are fined. As a member of the European Union, Luxembourg is required to allow noncitizen residents to vote at least in local elections. Their large numbers of disenfranchised residents may be one reason most of the microstates have not qualified to join the EU.

All but Monaco and Luxembourg are committed to a neutral foreign policy. Actually, the foreign policies of these two exceptions are rather neutral in practice and only technically aligned. Andorra, Liechtenstein, San Marino, and the Vatican try to use their respective position in the United Nations to vote for causes that they believe are beneficial for the whole world, except perhaps in matters where their own interests are at stake. (Being as they are microstates, such matters hardly ever arise.) Furthermore, the Vatican is known for its successful efforts as a mediator in negotiations between feuding Catholic countries.

A Worm's-Eye History of Europe

Microstate History

Most of the microstates are among the oldest lands of Europe. Their history is part of the history of Europe itself, but with a major difference: because of their minute size, these countries hardly ever *made* history, but were more often *affected* by history. From Caesar through Napoleon to Hitler, the microstates have been invaded, bombed, traipsed through, or simply forced to play diplomatic games to preserve their independence. Except for the Vatican and its predecessor, the Papal States, the seven have not had much influence on their neighbors nor on Europe as a whole. This very lack of influence may have convinced other countries that the microstates were not important enough to annex to their own territory.

Of course, each of the microstates has a distinct and unique history. But this chapter deals with some of the historical events and people shared by all the European microstates. Events unique to individual microstates are treated in Part II, which examines the countries one by one.

In some ways, the history of one microstate may be compared with that of another. For example, San Marino, founded in the second century AD, could be compared to Rome, the Papal States, and the Vatican with regard to total years of recorded history; their fates often intertwined. Monaco and Andorra were created early in the second millennium and have retained a shaky or semi-independence since then. Luxembourg and Liechtenstein were a by-product of the German Confederation in the late 1800s. Malta, unlike its miniature cousins, was ruled by imperial powers right up to the 1960s, and its independence may be considered part of the world decolonialization trend of that time.

Foundations

San Marino and the Vatican, surrounded by Italy, have their origins in ancient Rome. According to tradition, St. Marinus, the Christian stonecutter, wanted to escape the religious persecution of Roman emperor Diocletian, so he sailed across the Adriatic from Dalmatia to Mount Titano on the Italian peninsula, where he founded San Marino. Whether or not the legend is true, we know that by the middle of the fifth century a community was established there. A few centuries earlier, in the capital of the empire, Rome, St. Peter was crucified and buried at the end of the first century AD, near where the Vatican stands today. He is considered the first pope and predecessor of the all sovereigns of Vatican City. The first St. Peter's Basilica was built on this traditional spot in the fourth century. Modern popes live near the new St. Peter's, built there in the 1500s. It was not until 1929 that the Lateran Treaty with Italy officially established the microstate of Vatican City or the Holy See.

Andorra and Monaco were created in the early second millennium. In the eighth century, Charlemagne created Andorra as a "March," or buffer, state to protect France from Arab-occupied

Spain. The diocese of the Spanish border town Urgell was given control of the fiefdom of Andorra, and in AD 1000 the bishop asked the lord of Caboet to help him rule it. Later, a French nobleman, the count of Foix, inherited this responsibility through marriage. It wasn't until 1278 that squabbling for control of Andorra between Spain and France was settled in a treaty making them joint rulers of this coprincipality.

In southern France, the first fort at Monaco was built in 1215 by ruling families from Genoa. Disguised as a monk, François Grimaldi penetrated this fortress in 1297, took over, and began the Grimaldi dynasty. The Grimaldis briefly lost control of Monaco from 1301 to 1331, but from then on they have remained in charge of the principality.

Besides Andorra, Charlemagne also controlled the Vaduz region between Switzerland and Austria. After his death, it was divided into two independent states, Vaduz and Schellenberg. A thousand years later, a prince from Vienna purchased the two areas for himself and the Holy Roman Empire. It was renamed Liechtenstein, after the family of this prince, Johann-Adam. They still reign over the principality today. Luxembourg, too, achieved recognition as an entity within the Holy Roman Empire during the Middle Ages. This happened when Siegfried, count of Ardennes, exchanged his lands for a small Roman castle in the area of the present-day grand duchy. Neither Liechtenstein nor Luxembourg became independent until the nineteenth century.

Being an island in the Mediterranean, Malta, like its neighbor Sicily, is well documented in history from antiquity. And, like Sicily, it has been invaded many times and been influenced by many cultures. It is difficult to set a precise date for the foundation of Malta. As the Maltese language is closely related to Arabic, perhaps an appropriate year would be AD 870, when Arabs took the island and held it for two hundred years. Malta was given independence in 1964 from its last colonial ruler, Great Britain. It is still a member of the British Commonwealth of Nations.

Ancient Empires

The recorded history of the European microstates really begins with the Phoenicians, a Semitic people, who settled on Malta in about 1000 BC. In about 700 BC, they landed in Monoïkos. Monaco, like Malta, became an important trading center. The African Carthaginians also probably inhabited both Malta and Monaco. Their general, Hannibal, conquered the Andorrans as well. By 600 BC the city of Rome had been conquered by the Etruscans, and by 400 BC Etruscans occupied the area of San Marino. The ancient Greeks, too, probably had colonies in all of the microstates just mentioned, around the sixth century BC. In the seventh century BC, the Rhaetians, a people related to the Etruscans, inhabited the area of Liechtenstein.

Needless to say, the ancient Roman Empire occupied the city of Rome and the Vatican Hill since its inception. Emperor Nero held his circus and had gardens there. The Romans also held the ancient city of Ariminum, now Rimini, and the area of San Marino as early as 298 BC. Malta fell to the Romans as a result of the Punic wars in 218 BC, and Andorra was in their hands by 201 BC. Provence was settled by the Romans since 122 BC, and Julius Caesar is known to have set sail from Monaco to fight the Greeks. In 52 BC, Caesar conquered Gaul and the territory now called Luxembourg. The last of the microstate regions to fall was Liechtenstein, taken by Augustus's armies in 15 BC. The Roman Empire united the territories of the microstates for a few hundred years, and eventually brought Christianity to them. After the fall of Rome, territory containing all the microstates of Europe was never again held by a single ruler, with the sole exception of Napoleon.

Christianity

The next invader of Europe was Christianity, spreading through the territories previously conquered by Rome. In AD 60, St. Paul was shipwrecked at Malta on his way to Rome to appeal a charge of heresy. He established a foothold on the island, and Christianity probably took hold faster there than in the capital of the empire. The anti-Christian emperor Diocletian seems to have had an unintended effect on two of the microstates of Europe: he drove St. Marinus into founding the Christian community at San Marino. And, according to legend, St. Devota suffered martyrdom in Corsica under Diocletian and her relics were brought to Monaco where she is now patron saint. Christianity arrived in the region of Liechtenstein in the fourth century, with St. Lucius the first to be venerated there. It probably reached Andorra and Luxembourg in the sixth century. It is known that St. Justus, bishop of Urgell near Andorra, attended the second council of Toledo in the year 527. St. Willibrord played a large role in the conversion of Luxembourg in the next century, founding a Benedictine abbey in Echternach. Just as the Roman Empire spread from south to north in Western Europe, so did Christianity. Today, the seven microstates of Europe remain almost completely Roman Catholic, for the Christian Schism and the Protestant Reformation never reached them.

Holy Roman Empire

As the Roman Empire fell, Europe was overrun by Saracens, Slavs, Celts, Hungarians, Vikings, and Germanic "barbarians." The Germans were the most successful, and they reorganized their Holy Roman Empire into various subkingdoms until the nineteenth century, when it became the German Confederation. Italy, too, was disunited until 1870, and made up of various kingdoms, with the Papal States more or less in the middle. By tradition, the pope crowned the Holy Roman Emperors, so he had a strong influence on them.

The largely Germanic Holy Roman Empire had its strongest effects on the two Germanic microstates of Luxembourg and

Liechtenstein. In 1308, the ruler of a large fiefdom called Luxembourg became Henry VII, Holy Roman Emperor. He would be the first of four Holy Roman Emperors from the Luxembourg dynasty. Henry's grandson, Charles IV, made Luxembourg a duchy in 1354. The next emperor, Wenceslas, also of the Luxembourg dynasty, gave "imperial immediacy" to another fledgling microstate, Liechtenstein. This meant that it was now subject to the emperor alone, and that was a step toward independence.

By the middle of the fifteenth century, the Habsburg family had inherited the Holy Roman Empire. Luxembourg and Liechtenstein came with it. The Habsburgs would rule until the empire was dissolved centuries later. Rather than conquering territories, the Habsburgs tended to obtain lands through strategic marriages, and in 1520 Charles V inherited Malta. Ten years later, he gave the island to the Knights Hospitallers, or the Order of St. John, who ruled it for the next 250 years.

Guelfs and Ghibellines

The Guelfs and Ghibellines were opposing factions in medieval German and Italian politics, whose struggles affected four of the microstates of Europe. Both of their names derive from feuding German dynastic families. The Guelfs favored the papacy, while the Ghibellines favored the Holy Roman Emperor. The fortress that François Grimaldi besieged in Monaco had been built by the Ghibellines. The Grimaldis, being Guelfs, fought bloody battles with them until 1419.

The Guelfs and the Ghibellines eventually became synonymous with the idea of feuding families, and Shakespeare used them in *Romeo and Juliet*. Its setting is Verona, not far from San Marino, where Juliet Capulet's family are Guelfs and Romeo Montague's family are Ghibellines. San Marino itself took the side of a Ghibelline family named Montefeltro, against the Guelf Malatestas. The Italian poet Dante was a Guelf; despite his positioning

Ghibelline Guido da Montefeltro in the eighth circle of hell in his epic poem, *Inferno*, Dante favored the accession of Ghibelline Holy Roman Emperor Henry VII of Luxembourg as a means to reduce friction between the two factions. Henry VII had been a Guelf, until he had a tax dispute with the Guelf city of Milan, causing him to go over to the Ghibelline side. Needless to say the popes and their Papal States always took the Guelf side.

The Papacy

Popes controlled the Papal States, but originally they were not associated with the Vatican area of Rome. They lived in the Lateran castle in Rome until Pope Clement V fled to Avignon, France, in 1309. From then until 1377, the popes were under the control of the king of France, and the Papal States were in chaos. When Pope Gregory XI returned to Rome, the castle had been burned, so he moved to the Vatican. Almost immediately a schism occurred when Romans rioted, thinking Gregory might move back to Avignon. In actuality, it was an antipope who fled to Avignon. The canonical papacy has remained in the Vatican since then.

About a century later, a son of Pope Alexander VI, the Machiavellian politician Cesare Borgia, captured San Marino. His father and benefactor died a few months later, and San Marino was free. The other lands he had conquered went to the Papal States, and the papacy finally consolidated its control of these States. In 1631, Urban VIII officially recognized the independence of San Marino, which was surrounded by his Papal States. Later popes protected San Marino. In 1739 the rogue cardinal Giulio Alberoni, contrary to the orders of Clement XII, invaded San Marino in an attempt to annex it to the Papal States. Civil disobedience and clandestine messages to the pope helped liberate San Marino, which has remained intact ever since.

Pawns on a European Chessboard

San Marino, isolated in the Apennines, suffered only brief subjugation. Andorra and Liechtenstein, secluded in the mountains, also escaped many of the vicissitudes of European history. But Malta, Monaco, and Luxembourg were not so lucky.

Malta, in the middle of the Mediterranean, was in the middle of all the action. In AD 395, the east-west division of the Roman Empire was completed, and Malta became part of the Byzantine Empire under Constantinople, not Rome. In 870, Aghlobite Arabs invaded and held Malta until 1090, when Norman kings of Sicily took it. The French and then the Germans subsequently held Malta before it was taken by the Aragonese Spanish and eventually given to the Knights Hospitallers. In 1565, Malta was besieged by Arabs, but the Knights defeated them and held onto Malta. Then there was a period of stability for about two hundred years.

Monaco's coastal position, plus its powerful neighbor, France, made it a difficult prize for the Grimaldi family to retain. Before the Grimaldis arrived, Monaco was controlled first by the German Lombards and then by the French kingdom of Arles. The Saracens (Arabs) took over Monaco about the same time that Malta was taken. Afterwards, Genoa took Monaco and then it passed to the Grimaldi family in 1297. The Grimaldis looked first to France for protection, and in 1489 King Charles VIII recognized Monaco's independence. Then, in 1524, Prince Augustin I turned to Spain for the protection of Monaco. Spanish protection of the sixteenth century marked a difficult period for the principality, filled with revolts, violence, and palace intrigue. Finally, in 1641, the Grimaldis turned to French again for protection, which lasted another century. Monaco was under Sardinian-Corsican protection from 1815 through 1861.

Luxembourg has three neighbors to contend with, namely, France, Germany, and Belgium, and it has been taken over by each of them or their rulers throughout its history. About a hundred years after Luxembourg was made a duchy in the Holy Roman Empire, Philip the Good of Burgundy seized it in 1443. It went back to the empire under the Habsburgs. Then it was taken by France in 1684, but they had to restore it to Habsburg Spain in 1697. In 1714, the low countries were transferred from the Spanish to the Austrian Habsburgs, and Luxembourg went with them. The nineteenth century saw independence and freedom for Luxembourg, but in the twentieth it was occupied by Germany during each world war.

Napoleon

The microstates enjoyed stability during most of the eighteenth century, but this was disrupted by events emanating from France. The French Revolution of 1789 immediately created a crisis in Andorra when one of its coprinces, the king of France, was deposed, and the revolutionary government refused to rule Andorra. This was later resolved when Napoleon I was asked to rule Andorra and he accepted in 1806. The revolutionary French government behaved differently toward Monaco, which it annexed in 1793, and renamed "Fort Hercules." The prince and his family were arrested, and the palace was turned into a work-house. French troops also occupied Luxembourg in 1795, and Luxembourg was formally annexed to France as the "Department of Forests" by the treaty of Campo Formio in 1797. By then Napoleon had conquered half of Europe, including the Papal States. He had a plan to crush the British Empire by taking Egypt and, on his way there, he added Malta to his empire. However, in the process, he received a major setback from Admiral Nelson, who destroyed Napoleon's fleet. Britain ousted the French from Malta in 1800, and for most of the next century the island was

Napoleon at St. Bernard (1801).
JACQUES LOUIS DAVID (1748–1825).

ruled by a British military governor. War was ended by the treaty of Amiens in 1802, in which Britain agreed to return Malta to the Knights Hospitallers. However, they delayed doing so for a year, and hostilities broke out again in 1803.

Liechtenstein, on the other hand, was brought under Napoleon by its inclusion in the Rhine Confederation in 1806, not by war. In 1809, Napoleon formally annexed the Papal States and made Pope Pius VII a prisoner. The emperor created the Kingdom of Italy in the lands surrounding San Marino and made his stepson viceroy. He considered San Marino "an example of freedom," so he preserved its independence, and he even offered them some Italian territory. It is ironic that, today, a museum dedicated to Napoleon exists in Monaco, which he annexed, but there is no such tribute to him in San Marino.

The Congress of Vienna

After the defeat of Napoleon, the map of Europe was in tatters, and the Congress of Vienna attempted to repair it in 1814. All European states that had legally existed before Napoleon—including the microstates—were allowed to attend the Congress. Liechtenstein and Luxembourg, not yet officially independent, were added to the German Confederation, with Luxembourg getting much autonomy from the Netherlands, and being raised to the status of grand duchy. The British kept Malta, as they considered it a strategic base to help them keep the balance of power on the continent. So the "Knights of Malta" lost their home, and although they retain the name, their headquarters are now in Rome. Monaco and the Papal States were restored to their previous status, and placed under Sardinian and Austrian protection, respectively. The Papal States also moved back more or less to their original area, part of which surrounded San Marino. Andorra and San Marino, which had been on good terms with Napoleon, needed no protection, and simply went back to their original status.

The Risorgimento

Italian nationalists were disappointed that the Congress of Vienna returned the Papal States to the papacy, leaving thes Italian peninsula divided into ten different states. The struggle for a united Italy was called the Risorgimento, and the names "Guelf" and "Ghibelline" were revived to signify those who favored the pope as monarch of Italy versus those who favored a nonreligious leader. Both Malta and San Marino took in many refugees from the violence of the Risorgimento. One nationalist leader, Garibaldi, had to flee from Rome after French troops came to defend the Papal States against the republican uprising he led there in 1849. He trekked across Italy and took refuge in San Marino. The pope must have regretted his predecessors' protection of that microstate. Near the end of the Risorgimento, in 1862, San Marino signed a treaty of friendship and economic cooperation with the United Kingdom of Italy. The Papal States, last holdout of the divided Italy, were formally dissolved in an election in 1870. Pius IX, who had forbidden Catholic subjects of his former territory to vote or participate in Italian politics, then shut himself up in the Vatican, declaring himself a prisoner. Sixty years later, the "Roman question" was resolved when the Lateran Treaty created Vatican City.

The March of Democracy

All the microstates are now full democracies, except for Monaco and the Vatican. But democracy was the exception, not the rule, for most of their history. Only San Marino established democratic traditions before the nineteenth century. San Marino originally had an Arengo, a group of heads of families, to rule it. In 1243, the two captains regent began to be elected every six months as the executive branch of the government. With some changes, San Marino still uses this format to govern itself.

Luxembourg, the most liberal of the microstates, was given autonomy from Wilhelm I of the Netherlands in 1838. In 1848, it was granted a constitution. A new constitution of 1868 was one of the most liberal in Europe and is still in use today, in an amended form. Liechtenstein got its first constitution in 1862, four years before its official independence, and in 1921 this was replaced by a new and more democratic one. Monaco got its first constitution in 1911, ending the absolute rule of Prince Albert and his predecessors. Forty-two years later, under pressure from France, Prince Rainier promulgated a new constitution that ended the death penalty and gave the vote to women. However, only 15 percent of the residents of Monaco are citizens and have the right to vote, thus the country's incomplete status as a democracy.

Malta's road to democracy was anything but straight. In 1849, Malta got its first partly elected legislature and limited self-government as a British colony. Its first constitution was adopted in 1921. Because of squabbles about role of the Catholic Church, this constitution was revoked in 1936. Again in 1947, Malta was given increased self-government. And once again it was revoked, in 1959, this time because of civil disturbances. In 1956, Malta agreed to a kind of political integration with Britain, which even granted it three members of Britain's House of Commons. In 1964, Malta was given complete independence, with Queen Elizabeth II of Britain as its monarch. But in 1974, the Maltese parliament rejected the monarchy and made the country a republic. Finally, in 1979, the British military presence on the island was ended.

Andorra had only semi-independence before 1993. In 1933, youths stormed the General Council and forced it to grant suffrage to all male citizens over the age of twenty-five. Previously, only male heads of households had the vote. In 1970, the voting age was lowered, and it was lowered again in 1985 to eighteen. The year 1993 was an important one for Andorra: it adopted its first constitution, limiting the roles of the coprinces, and vesting power in an elected prime minister and parliament. In that one year, Andorra essentially went from a fiefdom to a modern democracy, and it was admitted into the UN.

In 1846, having just been elected pope, Pius IX gave the Papal States its first constitution, which created an elected legislature. But the unrest of the Risorgimento changed Pius's mind about democracy; he became extremely conservative and terminated the legislature. The 1929 Lateran Treaty, which gave the Vatican its independence, actually reduced the independence of Italy, because it gave the Catholic Church enormous privileges there. In 1985, these privileges were finally revoked in a revised treaty.

Neutrality

In 1866, the German Confederation was dissolved, and the Netherlands offered to sell Luxembourg to France, almost provoking a war between France and Prussia. The Conference of London of 1867 confirmed Luxembourg's independence and declared it neutral territory. The breakup of the German Confederation also caused Liechtenstein to declare its own neutrality and to disband its entire army in 1868.

Two other microstates actually have neutrality written into their constitutions: Malta and the Vatican. Malta is the only European microstate member of the so-called nonaligned movement. Vatican neutrality is guaranteed in the Lateran Treaty, and it may not even take part in attempts to settle international disputes unless specifically requested.

Andorra has always maintained its neutrality, but recently has experimented with "active neutrality," taking part in UN debates on the side of peace, justice, and human rights. Neutrality has not always been successful for all the microstates—see Luxembourg, below, for example—nor has it been completely adhered to in practice.

World Wars

The first round of twentieth-century warfare in Europe was not one of great territorial invasion, and so most of the microstates were relatively unaffected by World War I. However, in both world wars, San Marino sent volunteers to fight on the side of the Italians, and Luxembourg, located right on the front lines, was quickly occupied by Germany. The major effects of the Great War on the microstates came when it was over in 1918. It was the Treaty of Versailles, which brought peace to Europe, that also contained clauses specifying that the successors to the throne of Monaco must be approved by the French government and that, if there is no successor, Monaco reverts to an autonomous state under France. In exchange, France agreed to protect Monaco. World War I also convinced Liechtenstein to break its ties to the former Austria-Hungary, a loser in the war, and to link its customs and foreign affairs to Switzerland.

World War II was more disruptive and had a serious effect on most of the microstates. Once again, Luxembourg was overrun at the outset. The grand duchess fled to London, where she and her cabinet established a government in exile. After France fell, Monaco was occupied in 1941, and Prince Louis II was deposed. Monaco was bombed by both Italy and Germany during World War II. The same fate awaited Malta, situated in the strategic shipping lane between Italy and Africa, where Axis bombing began in 1940. The Maltese took shelter in their many underground passages, and their airfields provided bases for planes defending Allied ships. Rationing was particularly severe, as Allied supply ships were often bombed and did not always make it through. The bravery of the Maltese people in the face of relentless bombing won them the George Cross from Britain in 1942. Today this cross appears in the canton of Malta's national flag.

San Marino was bombed once, perhaps accidentally, by Britain in 1944—though it was officially neutral, fascists controlled the government at that time. Liechtenstein's decision to link itself to Switzerland paid off, and its neutrality was respected. Andorra's ties to Spain kept it out of World War II, just as its ties to France had kept it out of the Spanish Civil War. The Vatican was officially neutral, and when hostilities broke out, diplomats from Allied countries had to move out of Mussolini's Rome and into cramped quarters within the Vatican. Once Rome was liberated, they switched places with Axis diplomats. The end of the Second World War saw a return to the prewar status of all the microstates. But two German invasions convinced Luxembourg to drop its neutrality and join NATO.

Present and Future of the Microstates

In the eighteenth and nineteenth centuries, most of the microstates began to transform their economies from subsistence agriculture into more profitable ventures. Poverty had kept them safely beyond the notice of expanding megastates, but most recently activities such offshore banking, gaming, tax havens, and tourism have raised their standard of living to the highest levels in Europe. Sometimes their economic success has produced jealous reactions among their neighbors. Often it has drawn in guest workers from these neighbors, many of whom are permanent residents, but none of whom are citizens with the right to vote. This problem of inequality has been an obstacle to joining the European Union, in addition to the question of representation of tiny microstates in an organization where each country has equal veto power. Only Luxembourg was lucky enough to be a founding member of the EU.

Sometimes the reactions of the microstates' neighbors are not entirely due to jealousy. France and Germany have accused

Monaco and Liechtenstein of money laundering. Britain has accused American tobacco companies of smuggling cigarettes through Andorra. Luxembourg recently closed the bank accounts of Sani Abacha of Nigeria, said to contain billions of dollars embezzled and smuggled in from abroad. The Organization for Economic Cooperation and Development has even blacklisted a couple of the microstates for not doing enough to reduce money laundering. Hopefully in the future they will be able to clean up their acts and exploit their "niche sovereignties" in a more palatable manner.

There have been several attempts to officially organize cooperation among the microstates of Europe, the more recent ones being the most successful. In 1959, Baron Falz-Fein from Liechtenstein held a "summit" of the tourist bureaus of four of the European microstates. Although the *New York Times* wished the summit well in an editorial, Prince Franz Josef thought that it "ridiculed Liechtenstein in the eyes of the world," and no further summits were held. Today the governments of the European microstates use such international forum organizations as the UN to consult one another and to lobby for equal treatment for all nations, regardless of their size.

Big Fish in Little Ponds:
Monarchy and Religion in
the Microstates

Monarchy and religion are tied together in many ways; for example, most monarchies in some way maintain the belief that they exist by divine right, and sometimes a monarch is the head of the state religion. Depending on how one defines "monarchy," between three and five of the seven European microstates are ruled by monarchs, compared with ten of the forty-one countries in all of Europe. As it happens, all of the European microstates are Roman Catholic, and the Church plays a strong role among them.

Three small countries—Liechtenstein, Luxembourg, and Monaco—are ordinary monarchies, that is, with a sole noble ruler. Another, Andorra, may be called a diarchy, because it has two princes as joint heads of state. The Vatican is a monarchical-sacerdotal state. San Marino is one of the rare European republics (there are believed to be three) that were never monarchies. And Malta is the only microstate to follow the trend of three quarters of Europe's larger states: it's a former monarchy that dismissed its royal head of state—Queen Elizabeth II—to become a republic.

Three of the modern constitutional microstate monarchies are considered principalities, but none are kingdoms. A principality is simply a country ruled by a prince, not a king. What is the difference between a prince and a king? Unfortunately, the word "prince" has many meanings, ranging from "the son of a king" to "the head of any state." Some dictionaries define a prince as the head of a principality and define a principality as a country ruled by a prince! But for microstate purposes, let us assume a prince is a monarch of lower rank than a king. Correspondingly, a kingdom is usually bigger than a principality. Luxembourg is a grand duchy, ruled by a grand duke. A duke is defined as a nobleman of the highest ranking, but practically speaking, there is little difference between Luxembourg's monarchy and those of the principalities.

Technically, none of the microstate monarchs are royalty; since "royal" means "kingly," the princes are usually referred to as their "(most) *serene* highnesses," rather than "*royal* highnesses." Only because the current grand duke's grandmother, Charlotte, married into royal blood are the monarchs of Luxembourg called "royal highnesses." Although the people of these principalities may occasionally refer to the state as "the crown," none of the microstates' monarchs has a crown, and none celebrates a coronation. These monarchs do have a throne, usually involved in the accession ceremony, which is a kind of swearing in, but with a bit more pomp than a presidential inauguration. Until the reign of John Paul I, all popes were crowned with a tiara, soon after their election, but this practice has apparently been discontinued.

Now, what exactly is a monarch, anyway? A monarch usually inherits his or her position as ruler, is usually the only one in that position, and typically holds that position for a lifetime. Some people associate monarchies with dictatorial rule, but that has never been a valid assumption. Monarchs have always delegated their duties, and many did not interfere with the carrying out of those duties. Today most monarchs' activities are strictly limited by law, and they are largely ceremonial. A pope has two of the three qualifications of a monarch, but he is elected, not born to the position. Ironically, a pope *does* have the absolute power of a dictator.

There are many advantages, as well as disadvantages, of a monarchical form of government. The monarch is a cultural symbol of the whole nation and represents continuity; and his or her handling of state ceremonies leaves more time for the real power holders to devote to the business of running the country. Under an executive president, people may fear to criticize the government, because the symbol of the nation is at its head. On the other hand, the inheritance of the office and lifetime rule make it difficult to replace incompetent or otherwise embarrassing monarchs.

Although modern monarchs are no longer very powerful, they are usually highly revered by their people. This is true even in the microstates, where you are more likely to meet up with the head of state in the street. Luxembourg's constitution says that "the person of the grand duke is sacred and inviolable." Liechtenstein's constitution says of the prince that "his person is sacred and inviolable." Monaco's does not call him sacred, but "*la personne du prince est inviolable*." And the Lateran Treaty of 1929 between Italy and the Vatican stated that, "considering the person of the Supreme Pontiff to be sacred and inviolable, Italy declares any attempt against His person or any incitement to commit such attempt to be punishable by the same penalties as all similar attempts and incitements to commit the same against the person of the king." Today some legal scholars interpret the word "inviolable" to signify that the monarch may not be arrested or sued, but this wording certainly has its origin in a tradition where the monarch derived his or her powers directly from God.

Monarchs generally have many given names, and the rulers of the microstates are no exception. Hans Adam II of Liechtenstein is short for Hans Adam Ferdinand Alois Josef Maria Marko d'Aviano Pius. Grand Duke Henri of Luxembourg is really Henri Albert Gabriel Felix Marie Guillaume. And Prince Rainier III of Monaco was born Rainier Louis Henri Maxence Bertrand.

Monarchs usually have more than one title, as well. The prince of Liechtenstein is also the duke of Jägerndorf and Troppau, as well as the count of Rietberg. The grand duke of Luxembourg is also known as duke of Nassau; prince of Bourbon and Parma; count palatine of the Rhine; count of Dietz, Katzenelnbogen, Königstein, and Sayn; burgrave of Hammerstein; and lord of Eppstein, Idstein, Limburg, Mahlberg, Merenberg, and Wiesbaden. Prince Rainier of

Monaco has the following additional titles: duke of Estouteville, Mayenne, Mazarin, and Valentinois; marquis of Baux, Chilly, and Guiscard; lord of Isenheim and Saint-Rémy; sire of Matignon; count of Belfort, Carlades, Ferrette, Longjumeau, Rosemont, Thann, and Thorigny; baron of Altkirch, Buis, Hambye, la Luthumière, Massy, and Saint-Lô; and prince of Château-Porcien. And a pope simultaneously serves as bishop of Rome, successor of St. Peter, supreme pontiff of the Universal Church, patriarch of the West, primate of Italy, archbishop and metropolitan of the Province of Rome, and sovereign of the Vatican City State.

Hiring and Firing a Monarch

In monarchies without a crown, the heir to the throne is not called a crown prince or princess. In a principality, he or she is the *hereditary* prince or princess. And the next in line to Luxembourg's throne is known as the *hereditary* grand duke or duchess. There is usually a small induction ceremony, as a confirmation of who is next in line to the throne. Except for Monaco's "marquis des Baux," there is no special title for the hereditary monarch corresponding to "prince of Wales."

You may have noticed that until now, no mention has been made of females. That is because all the current monarchs are men, and it is difficult-to-impossible for a woman to inherit a throne in the microstates of Europe. Of course, there can be no female popes. Liechtenstein's laws provide no way for a woman to inherit the throne, either. Only if no male hereditary lines exist will Luxembourg will allow a female heir. Perhaps Luxembourg is reluctant to liberalize its law of succession, because it was this "Salic law" that gave the country its independence from Holland. Although Princess Wilhelmina was able to inherit the Kingdom of the Netherlands from her father, Wilhelm II, she could not inherit the Grand Duchy of Luxembourg from him, so in 1890 her distant relative, Adolf, the duke of Nassau, became grand duke of a newly separated Luxembourg.

Liechtenstein's Hereditary Prince Alois and Hereditary Princess Sophie, with their children Prince Joseph Wenzel, Princess Marie Caroline and Prince Georg.

LIECHTENSTEIN TOURISM.

On the other hand, Monaco could lose its independence if there is no heir to its throne. Under the terms of a treaty with Paris in 1918, France even has the right to approve of the princely successor—theoretically, each time a monarch of Monaco dies, France has the chance to reject all successors and make Monaco its protectorate. So far this has not happened, as the French had wanted this power only to be certain that a German would not become prince. Otherwise, Monaco's laws of succession are similar to the traditional British regulations. The children of the monarch inherit the throne in order of age, by gender: all the males come first, and the throne does not pass to even a male sibling unless the hereditary prince, living or dead, has had no eligible children. Under the law, a childless reigning prince may adopt anyone as his heir, as a way to keep the principality independent.

By law, the monarchs of Monaco and Liechtenstein must be Roman Catholic. In Luxembourg there is no such law, only the strong pressure of tradition. Furthermore, the parents of any inheriting monarch must have been legitimately married. In Monaco, this stipulation recently gave the pope some input on the succession there. Since Princess Caroline was divorced from her second husband when she remarried, the children of the third marriage could not be considered legitimate in the eyes of the Catholic Church. Her father, Prince Rainier, withheld his multi-million-dollar annual contribution to the Church for several years until an annulment to her second marriage was granted and the children of her third legitimized.

In modern monarchies, the reigning head of state must approve of any marriage, otherwise the marrying heir and any off-spring will not be eligible to inherit the throne. In the microstates, generally the laws of the princely family prescribe who will succeed the monarch. It is not clear from these nations' constitutions who is the final arbiter on whether the laws have been followed during any princely succession. In perhaps the most famous instance, in 1936 the British parliament had the final say as to whether King Edward VIII could marry American divorcée Wallis Simpson, and he had to abdicate in order to do so. In our times, no such conflict has yet arisen in a microstate monarchy.

While the French government must approve of Monaco's head of state, it is the French people who elect one of Andorra's coheads of state, namely, the president of France. The French coprince was originally the count of Foix, but when Count Henry of Foix was elevated to King Henry IV of France, the French head of state became the Andorran coprince. (See the full chapter on Andorra for information about how pretender Boris de Skossyreff disputed the right of the president to inherit this office from the deposed king of France.) The other coruler, the bishop of Urgell, is appointed by the pope. Now, a bishop would not be able to assent to something that is a crime under divine or canonical law, such as the right to use contraception, so it's fortunate that the coprinces do not have to sign many laws anymore. In fact, the coprinces have very few powers today. It is questionable as to whether they should even be considered princes, since neither of them has a lifetime position, and neither inherits it. Nevertheless, Andorra calls itself a principality.

Every monarch's term in office must come to an end, but in the microstates of Europe this is not always at the end of his or her life. There is a tradition among the Benelux countries for older monarchs to abdicate, and in the year 2000, Grand Duke Jean of Luxembourg did just that, leaving office in favor of his son, Henri. There is nothing disgraceful in abdication as a kind of retirement—it demonstrates self-confidence that one has groomed one's successor well enough for him to take over. In Liechtenstein, the procedure seems to be for the monarch to hand over all his duties to his son, while remaining prince in name only. This happened in 1938, when Prince Franz Josef took over from his father, and again in 1984, when he handed over rule of the country to the current reigning prince, Hans Adam II. As of this writing, Prince Rainier III of Monaco is increasingly in ill health, but thus far he has not indicated any desire to abdicate, although hereditary Prince Albert is taking on more and more of the running of the state. And there has been much speculation about the possible resignation of the aging John Paul II as pope, which would not be without precedent in history. One reason for the speculation was the pope's insistence that other members of the hierarchy retire when reaching a certain age—retirement would be mandatory for the bishop of Urgell, for example.

Power and Wealth

The microstates of Europe are conservative and resistant to change, and this is reflected not only in the number of monarchies but also in the amount of political power that their monarchies still wield. Andorra's coprinces appear to be the weakest of them, yet they have rather important roles in Andorran relations with Spain and France. Even the two captains regent of San Marino are quite a bit more powerful than the coprinces of Andorra. As mentioned above, the coprinces do not sign all the laws in Andorra, but all the laws of the other microstates must have the signature of the head of state affixed to them in order to be valid. Though the president of Malta is not a prince, his role is so ceremonial that he has no choice but to sign every bill that is handed to him. In practice, the grand duke of Luxembourg does the same, although he could theoretically exercise a veto. The grand duke also is head of the executive branch of the government, but normally his cabinet acts in his name. The prince of Liechtenstein may not participate in the discussions of his government, but he can and does exercise his veto power. The prince of Liechtenstein and the grand duke of Luxembourg also have the right to reject judicial nominations.

All the heads of state also have the power to pardon convicted people. The prince of Monaco possesses all of the other microstates' princely powers, and in addition he chooses the judges and members of his cabinet. The prince of Monaco proposes and approves of all the laws as well. He could be called an absolute dictator, if it weren't for the veto power that the National Council effectively retains. In most countries, the situation is reversed: the head of state retains a veto power over laws proposed and passed by the parliament. As mentioned before, the pope retains absolutely all temporal as well as spiritual powers in Vatican City. However, in practice, he tends to delegate the actual running of the state to the Curia, so he can concentrate on spiritual matters.

An unusual aspect of some of the microstates is the enormous wealth of most of their princes. Although the pope does not own all the wealth of the Catholic Church, theoretically he controls it, and ultimately he decides how much and how it will be spent in Vatican City. Prince Hans Adam of Liechtenstein is said to be the richest monarch in Europe, and Prince Rainier of Monaco may be

Princely golden coach.
LIECHTENSTEIN TOURISM.

the wealthiest man in his principality of jet-setters. But it's not their absolute wealth that is so impressive, it's the proportion of the wealth of the entire countries that makes these men so powerful. A serious economic upheaval could occur among the thirty thousand Liechtensteiners if their prince were to leave, as he has threatened to do in the past. He currently has no "civil list," that is, nobody in the princely family needs to be supported by a stipend from the state. In this respect, the only microstate monarchy resembling a more typical one would be the Grand Duchy of Luxembourg.

And what about the spouse of the monarch? Obviously, a princess or grand duchess must be cohost at state occasions or even host in the absence of the monarch. Grand Duchess Josephine Charlotte of Luxembourg, Princess Marie of Liechtenstein, and Princess Grace of Monaco have been the president of the Red Cross Organization in their respective countries. After the death of Princess Grace, the position was given to Princess Caroline.

Prince Hans Adam II and Princess Marie von und zu Liechtenstein.

The Princely Families

Does a monarch have last name? Well, yes, but it likely retains an older form that most non-noble families have dropped. For example, Hans Adam's full name is Hans Adam II von und zu Liechtenstein. *"Von und zu"* means "of and at," and these prepositions are the sign of a noble family. After the prepositions comes a place name, showing what area the noble family rules. So "Liechtenstein" is the prince's family name, and it is also the name of his dynasty, the princely house of Liechtenstein. The Liechtenstein name is unusual, because the country was named after the family, rather than the family adopting the name of the state.

The Liechtenstein family comes originally from Austria, just south of Vienna. They took the name from the castle built on a high chalk cliff known as the *lichte stein*, or "stone of light." The first person known to have the name was Hugo of Liechtenstein, mentioned in documents from 1136. The Liechtensteins were quite a successful family, and they acquired much property in Moravia and in Bohemia (now the Czech Republic) just outside Prague. Though the Liechtensteins bought their principality in 1712, they didn't reside in Liechtenstein until 1938. (See the full chapter on Liechtenstein for more about the family's history.)

The name "Luxembourg" comes from a castle built around the year 1000 and called Lucilinburhuc, meaning "little fortress." Not many years later, a man called Conrad took for himself the title, the count of Luxembourg. But today the grand ducal family of Luxembourg goes by the name "Nassau." This house of Nassau used to rule the duchy of Nassau (now in Germany), not far to the east of Luxembourg. Luxembourg was given to them and raised to the status of grand duchy by the Congress of Vienna. Adolf of Nassau, who inherited Luxembourg from his distant relative William II of Nassau, had recently lost his duchy of Nassau, which was absorbed into Prussia. So at that point, it might have been logical for the family to adopt the name "Luxembourg." But the name "Nassau" seems to have a lot of staying power, since the family again retained this name, even when Grand Duchess Charlotte married Prince Felix of Bourbon-Parma, whose name the family should have adopted.

Because the family laws of Luxembourg and Liechtenstein make it difficult for a woman to inherit the throne, the rulers of those countries don't often change their family names when they marry. But the Grimaldi family of Monaco employs another method to keep their dynastic name attached to their country— they require the new ruler and spouse to adopt the name "Grimaldi" as a condition for inheriting the principality. In 1133, a certain Otto Canella was a consul of Genoa. The descendents of his youngest son, Grimaldo, modified and adopted the son's given name as their dynastic name, Grimaldi. It wasn't until 1297 that Francois Grimaldi seized Monaco by disguising himself as a monk as a way to let himself and his cohorts into the fortress that the Genoese had built there. After losing the fortress a couple of times to its former owners, the Grimaldis finally established themselves as the ruling house of Monaco.

Currently there are ten ruling monarchies in Europe, but there are many more ex-monarchies. Their noble families typically live in exile in other European countries. Add to this number the nobility of former countries or territories—the duchy of Nassau is only one example—and you have hundreds of families and thousands of people who can claim to be the rightful ruler of somewhere or other. In the past, many of these people tried to marry others of similar or higher noble ranking in order to control more territory, and today many still marry for the prestige or for money. So all the noble houses of Europe are related to each other by blood, some more closely than others.

Because there are so many members of all the noble houses, each marrying people not too closely related to themselves, no house is "pure," and it is hard to generalize about them. But it appears that the monarchies of Luxembourg and Liechtenstein are fairly closely related to each other, while the princes of Monaco are relatively isolated from them and other European monarchies. In this respect, Luxembourg and Liechtenstein are both especially close to Belgium and Portugal, as well. Prince Hans Adam and Grand Duke Henri are third cousins, related through Michael, a nineteenth-century king of Portugal. Actually, they are a little more closely related than most third cousins, because two of Michael's daughters married Luxembourg nobility, and the result is that King Michael is Grand Duke Henri's great-great-grandfather in two ways. Grand Duke Henri and Prince Rainier of Monaco are fourth cousins once removed. And Prince Rainier is a fifth cousin of Prince Hans Adam of Liechtenstein.

Of the three microstate hereditary monarchs, Prince Rainier III of Monaco is the oldest. Born in 1923, he has lived through most of the twentieth century, including Nazi occupation of his country. Rainier's great-grandfather was Prince Albert I, a marine biologist by profession, who founded not only the Oceanographic Institute, but also the Anthropological Institute and the famous Exotic Gardens. Albert's son, Louis II, had no legitimate children, but adopted his natural daughter Charlotte, who was to be Rainier's mother. Rainier did much to take Monaco into the twentieth century, battling Aristotle Onassis for control of the casino, and fighting Charles de Gaulle to preserve Monaco as a tax haven. Perhaps Rainier's best business decision was marrying the beautiful American movie star Grace Kelly. She brought renewed interest in the principality plus tourists from all over the world, especially from America. It seemed that the spurning of Wallis Simpson would now be revenged and an American would finally marry "royalty." This marriage would be ended by a dreadful car accident many years later, but long after the birth of two daughters and hereditary Prince Albert. Unfortunately, the behavior of the children has not been exemplary. Prince Rainier has had to put up with several divorces and remarriages, and the one person for whom a successful marriage would be most important, Prince Albert, is still a bachelor. If Albert produces no heirs, probably he will adopt one of his sisters' children to ensure the future of the Grimaldi dynasty, and the very existence of Monaco.

The second oldest microstate monarch is Hans Adam II of Liechtenstein, born in 1945. The Liechtensteins seem to be the most snobbish and conservative of the three dynasties. For hundreds of years, they were absentee monarchs, preferring life in the court of the Habsburg emperors to living in the second-rate Vaduz castle. Hans Adam's father, Franz Josef II, was the first prince to occupy the castle. (In the chapter on Liechtenstein, you can read more about how circumstances leading to World War II convinced him to move to the principality.) Directly before him, Franz Josef's first cousin, twice removed, was Prince Johannes II. But Johannes produced no sons, and neither did his brother, the next prince, Franz I, and so the principality went to the grandson (Franz Josef) of their cousin (Alfred). Cousin Alfred also married the two brothers' sister, Henrietta. This unusual alliance gave

Franz Josef one great-grandfather, but no grandfather who had been a reigning prince. Like Rainier in Monaco, Franz Josef and Hans Adam II did much to modernize Liechtenstein, raising the standard of living there from poor to one of the highest in the world. Today, Hans Adam II has his own ideas on the future of Liechtenstein, which don't always agree with those of the Diet or his ministers. He wants to grant Liechtenstein citizenship to more of the principality's foreign residents, and he would like to revise the language of the constitution to reduce the official role of the Catholic Church. Like a good Liechtensteiner, Hans Adam II has produced several sons, and hereditary Prince Alois already has three sons of his own. In fact, Hans Adam II has thirteen male descendents, virtually assuring that his direct line will continue inheriting the throne, despite the Salic laws.

The youngest of the current microstate monarchs is Henri I of Luxembourg, born in 1955. Henri is the great-great-grandson of the first grand duke of independent Luxembourg, Adolf I, who began his reign in 1890. Adolf was succeeded by his son, Wilhelm IV. Wilhelm had no sons, but rather than seeking a male further afield, his daughter Marie Adelaide was allowed to succeed him. After World War I, many accused her of being too friendly to the invading Germans, so she abdicated in favor of her sister, Charlotte. Charlotte had no better luck with Germans, and she was forced to flee from them to Portugal during their second invasion of World War II, where her son Jean met his future wife, another refugee, Belgian Princess Josephine. Jean and Josephine recently abdicated in favor of their son Henri. The Nassaus of Luxembourg seem to be the most accommodating of the three hereditary microstate monarchs. Their constitution affords them many powers, but they choose not to exercise them, preferring not to veto anything, and selecting a cabinet that they know the parliament will approve of. Grand Duke Henri has been a board member of the Charles Darwin Foundation for many years, as a result of his interest in the environment. He also founded the Galapagos Darwin Trust, and visited them when an oil tanker spilled its fuel near those islands endangering the rare wildlife there. A colonel in the Luxembourg army, the grand duke has four sons and one daughter, including the hereditary grand duke, Guillaume, born in 1981.

Although Malta has no monarch, it does have a class of nobility. The Sicilian Normans introduced nobility to Malta, granting the titles of baron, count, and marquis to the locals in return for military service. These nobles usually made up the local government on Malta. They were unhappy to be displaced by the Knights Hospitallers, and they welcomed the British invasion two hundred years later.

Religion

The people of the seven microstates of Europe are almost all Roman Catholics. Christianity reached all the microstates of Europe, but Protestantism did not. While Andorra, San Marino, Monaco, and the Vatican lie deep within the Catholic area of Europe, the other microstates are near the periphery. Liechtenstein is a neighbor of Switzerland, which is half Protestant Calvinist. Its other neighbor, Austria, remained completely Catholic. Vaduz and Schellenberg were always owned by Catholic Austrian counts, and when they were combined into principality of Liechtenstein, it was under the Catholic princes who lived near Vienna. Luxembourg was ruled by the Protestant Dutch monarch just before its independence. It had been ruled by Catholics during and after the Reformation. When it wasn't under the Catholic Austrian Habsburgs, Luxembourg was under the Spanish Habsburgs or else Catholic France. By the time it became a grand duchy under the Protestant king of the Netherlands, monarchs were no longer so insistent on having the same religion as their subjects. Of course, the Reformation never approached Mediterranean Malta. Though Arabs from northern Africa gave their language to the Maltese, they did not leave their Islamic religion. When Europeans recovered Malta, they persecuted any Muslims left there and harried them off the island.

A procession of Maltese clergy.
MALTA TOURIST OFFICE, NEW YORK.

A "concordat" is the usual name for a treaty between the Vatican and another country, defining the relationship between the Church and the state, and guaranteeing the Church certain rights and privileges. There were no major concordats signed by the microstates, but many were signed by their big sisters. Concordats typically established Catholicism as the state religion, gave the ruler input on the selection of bishops, placed education in the control of the Church, and sometimes allowed the Church to censor the press. And if these Church powers were taken for granted in the neighboring states, they were well established in the microstates as well. As mentioned earlier, Prince Hans Adam II of Liechtenstein has advocated reducing the official role of the Catholic Church in his country, and he has ruled out signing a concordat with the Vatican.

Today, Roman Catholicism is the state religion of five European microstates, and its special relationship with the state is recognized in Andorra. Only Luxembourg's constitution makes no special mention of the Catholic Church. Interestingly, Luxembourg's government pays the salaries of all clergy, no matter what religion. Except for Vatican City, there is complete freedom of religion in every European microstate, but the Catholic Church still has considerable privileges. For example, Catholicism must be taught in all of Malta's schools, although a student may be excused from these studies. The Church still runs all the schools in Andorra, half being Spanish and the other half French, except for one Catalan school. And the bond between church and state is so strong in the Vatican that it will not recognize the credentials of any foreign ambassador who has been divorced.

So, Catholicism is very important in the microstates. But how important are the microstates to the Catholic Church? Perhaps one can get some idea by observing which microstates have been given their own dioceses. Andorra does not have its own diocese, but is administered ecclesiastically from Urgell, Spain. Until 1997 Liechtenstein was part of the Chur diocese of Switzerland. And San Marino is part of the San Marino–Montefeltro diocese.

Although Monaco is the second-smallest microstate, there has been a separate diocese of Monaco since 1868. Luxembourg, the largest microstate, is an archdiocese, meaning it has its own cardinal. The two largest islands of Malta, Malta and Gozo, each constitute a diocese. Presumably, Vatican City is covered by the diocese of Rome, since the pope is the bishop of Rome. But the seat of the diocese is all the way across town at St. John Lateran.

In many ways, both established state religion and monarchy are ideas of the past. This is because they do not treat all people equally, and they give privileges to some people because of their birth or their beliefs. To inherit a throne, a person usually must profess the right religion, must be legitimate, and in some cases must be male. Maintaining one's beliefs and customs can be difficult when one's government openly supports another religion. For these reasons, the governments of some of the microstates are modifying their constitutions to conform better to the norms of international treaties, such as the European Convention for the Protection of Human Rights and Fundamental Freedoms.

Small Talk:
Language and Education in
the Microstates

Being small creates big problems when it comes to language and education. A microstate may have no alternative to using the language and schools of its big sister. Trying to maintain a language or higher education system can be a complicated and expensive proposition. To keep a language alive, people need to be taught to respect it and use it in an official capacity. But a small country simply may not be able to afford to maintain a university for a limited number of students.

If you thought the definition of an independent state was fuzzy, you're likely to find yourself in a thicker haze when it comes to the definition of a language. The problem is with the border between languages, or really, the lack of boundaries between languages. As a speaker of English, you may be used to understanding almost everyone who speaks your language, and not understanding anyone who does not. The situation is rather different with most other languages. Most people grow up speaking to their neighbors in a way that would not be understood by most of their countrymen. When they go to school, they learn to speak the standard language. You may have already experienced this phenomenon if you have not been able to understand the English of someone from a remote corner of the British Isles.

But one thing that English-speakers never experience is being able to understand much of a foreign language that they never learned. This is because the origin of English, England, is part of an island, and it was isolated by water from other countries. In most other countries, the speech of people in the border area usually resembles that of people just over the border who officially speak another language.

In Europe, if you take the right route, you can probably still travel all the way from Portugal through Sicily without noticing any place where spoken language changes distinctly. Within that region, there is an unbroken chain of people who speak various mutually intelligible forms of the Romance languages. Of course, people who speak Portuguese cannot understand everything said by people who speak Sicilian Italian. So in a sense, there are either many Romance languages or only one. Some people like to say "a language is dialect with an army." That is, national languages are chosen by governments, which usually have the armies to enforce their decisions. Other people think that a language is a dialect with an alphabet. In this chapter, you will see that writing their "native" as opposed to official language is indeed a problem for people of some microstates.

Andorra, Monaco, San Marino, and Vatican City are in the Romance language area of Europe. Liechtenstein and Luxembourg are in the Germanic language area. Malta is all alone in speaking a Semitic language closely related to Arabic and more distantly related to Hebrew. According to the broader, rarely used definition of a language, there would be only three languages among the seven microstates of Europe. Actually, linguists believe that the Germanic languages and the Romance languages are distantly related as part of a bigger Indo-European family, and some believe that the Semitic languages are even more distantly related to Indo-European, "related" meaning that they had a common ancestor language sometime in the past. For example, Latin is the ancestor of the Romance languages: Spanish, French, Italian, and Portuguese (and also Romanian).

Official and Unofficial Languages

Several of the microstates are on border areas between bigger countries. In most cases, this means that their people speak a dialect intermediate between the official languages on either side. It is only a question of whether this dialect is any country's official language and is respected as such. Luckily for Andorra, Catalan (Català) is the language spoken in the area near the border of Spain and France, and it has been written down for centuries. Luckily for Catalan-speakers, the existence of Andorra allows them to say they speak some country's national language. Although Spanish and French are widely spoken there, only Catalan is official in Andorra. Luxembourgish (Letzebuergesch), on the other hand, would simply be called the West Franconian dialect of German, if Luxembourg weren't an independent country. And French and German are also official languages there. Although Luxembourg has been closely tied to Belgium and also to the Netherlands, Dutch is not one of its official languages. In English, Luxembourgish is also known as Luxembourgian.

As in Luxembourg, in Monaco the natives speak a language with a name similar to their country, that is, Monégasque (Monegù). But the only official language in Monaco is French. In Liechtenstein and San Marino, there isn't even a name for the language of the natives. Liechtenstein's official language is German, but Liechtensteiners learn the High Alemmanic German dialect at their mothers' knee. At least until recently, Sammarinese learned the Romagnolo dialect of Italian as children, but they must use only Italian in school and at work. Because there is no native population born in the Vatican, you can't say that Vatican citizens grow up learning the Roman dialect of Italian, although many of the people employed there have done so. The official language of the Vatican is Italian, but the official language of the Holy See is Latin, an otherwise dead language. Maltese (Maltì), of course, is one official national language of Malta—English is the other.

Nurturing a Language

Needless to say, French, Italian, and German have been spoken and written for hundreds of years. This is also true of Catalan, although it was prohibited in Spain and discouraged in France for many years. But Luxembourgish, Maltese, Monégasque, and to some extent, Latin, have not been counted among the languages of the world as a matter of course. They have had to be created or revived by the microstates themselves. Although Maltese has been spoken in Malta for centuries, it was only in 1934 that it became an official language there. Luxembourgish is about as old as Maltese, and it became an official language only in 1939. Unfortunately, Monégasque is still not an official language in Monaco, but the government is now making some efforts to promote it. Latin is now somewhat of an artificial language, and there is no universal agreement on how to translate such terms as "software" and "Internet," which did not exist when Latin was in its heyday. Little or nothing is being done in Liechtenstein or San Marino to promote the local dialect or even rename it to Liechtensteinisch or Sammarinese. More is being done outside these countries, among Romagnolo organizations in Italy and Alemmanic groups in Switzerland devoted to these dialects. Barcelona is the center for the promotion of Catalan, which is the official language of the autonomous region of Catalonia in Spain. As for Monaco, Nice is the center for Monégasque culture. The Acadèmia de Niça gives courses in "Nissard" and Monégasque.

Why should anyone care about their national language? Many people consider their language to be part of their culture and national heritage. Perhaps grammar is too abstract to associate with other aspects of culture, but consider the Catalan word *aplec*, for example—the word for their festival gathering. The particular kind of dancing and arrangement of the participants is native to the Catalonia area alone. It happens that this word is not to be found in Spanish or French. If the cultural festival ever disappears, so will the word disappear from the face of the earth. Language and culture are that tightly bound together.

How did the microstates create their languages? Well, they didn't really create them, but some countries ensured their survival by teaching them and creating a writing system for them. Perhaps because of Rome's relative proximity, all the microstates use the Roman alphabet to transcribe their languages. This is unusual in the case of Maltese, because all other Semitic languages are written in non-Roman alphabets, such as Hebrew or Arabic. The alphabetization used in Malta was settled on in 1921 and officially adopted in 1934. Before the standardization, various versions were in use since the late 1700s. Though Luxembourg was an independent country a century before Malta, it got a later start in standardizing its spelling. Luxembourgish seems to have been written first in 1806, but it was not until 1975 that the government finalized an orthography and printed a dictionary. In 1984, the parliament designated Luxembourgish as the official national language, but it still writes the laws in French. German and French are now known as "administrative" languages. Monégasque schoolchildren are now learning their local language in schools, but almost as a foreign language, since few if any grow up speaking it. It has been claimed that Monégasque is really a dead language—a prominent Monégasque linguist stated that there were only a few dozen speakers left in 1927. As noted above, Liechtenstein and San Marino have not even attempted to standardize their local languages. The Roman dialect does not differ drastically from standard Italian, so few people see any need to write it, and the Holy See is certainly not among them.

Malta, right in the middle of the Mediterranean Sea, has been subject to many invasions and foreign rulers. Each brought a new official language, but not all of them stuck. Phoenicians and Greeks were early colonists until about 200 BC, and the Arabs may have encountered both Phoenician and Greek spoken on Malta as well as on neighboring Sicily when they invaded in AD 870—this, despite Roman rule and official Latin for the intervening eleven centuries. Possibly because Phoenician is also a Semitic tongue, the Maltese took to Arabic, while the Sicilians may have retained more of their Greek. In any case, Arabic became the official language for the next two hundred years. Late in the eleventh century, Normans conquered both islands, and they again made Latin official, although they also brought the vernacular dialects from southern Italy. Perhaps it was because Malta was a bit of a backwater, and was somewhat ignored, that southern Italian did not totally supplant Arabic, as it did in Sicily. It seems odd that the Maltese people adopted and held on to their Christianity from the days of the Roman occupation, but that Latin and Italian never caught on. What the Maltese did adopt were hundreds and hundreds of Italian and Sicilian Italian words imported into their basically Arabic language.

During the Norman rule of Malta and also under the Knights of Malta, Sicilian and then standard Italian were used by the upper classes, and Italian replaced Latin in all official uses. During most of British rule, the Maltese people basically ignored English and respected Italian as official, while continuing to speak their Arabic tongue. This was probably due to the strong influence of Catholicism and the popes in neighboring Italy. In 1921 their English rulers actually made Italian official, along with English. In 1934 Maltese took the place of Italian. Slowly but surely Maltese became more respected and replaced Italian in one official capacity after another. For a number of years, evidence had been given in Maltese, but all other court proceedings were in Italian, including verdict and sentencing. At the same time, English was becoming a second language, especially in the area of education. Today many foreigners actually go to Malta to study English in a more affordable location than England or America. Most recently, more than one Maltese scholar has reported that the Maltese are beginning to mix their English and Maltese, and some fear that a pidgin language will soon emerge, incomprehensible to speakers of pure English or Maltese. Incidentally, young Maltese are using more and more Italian expressions these days, because of the strong influence of Italian television programs, which are received in Malta.

Like Maltese in Malta, Luxembourgish has for centuries been the vernacular language of everyday speech in Luxembourg. But following the Belgian model, French was the official language for all formal business, government or civil. Perhaps because it could be considered a dialect of German, Luxembourgish was largely ignored as the language of the streets. If someone didn't like French, he could fairly easily learn to read, write, and speak German. So Luxembourg got an even later start than Malta in writing down its local language.

There were several attempts to write Luxembourgish, and at least two different official orthographies. One early version was taught in schools, and later used by the Luxembourg Resistance of World War II for leaflets and an underground newspaper during the German occupation. It was both a code and a symbol of nationalism against Nazi pan-Germanism. But after the war, newspapers reverted to German, which had been the traditional language for the printed media. One problem with the proposed orthographies was that they were too good. That is, they reflected Luxembourgish pronunciation so well that people found them too foreign, too different from the German they were used to reading. (Imagine trying to adjust to all written materials being produced in English "phonics"!) Finally in 1984 a new compromise spelling was adopted.

Far from being an all-purpose language, Luxembourgish is still in an early state of half-implementation. Luxembourgers can't seem to decide which is more important to them, saving their own culture or participating in world culture. Trying to do both is something of a losing proposition. Luxembourgers sometimes complain that their language lacks the vocabulary and grammar to express many of nuances of today's global concepts. By switching to French or German they can express themselves more quickly and with more certainty in a country with so many foreigners. On the other hand, by avoiding Luxembourgish, they also avoid updating their language with the innovations that constant use creates. A similar dilemma affects any microstate in its attempt to join an international organization. By not pressing for any kind of official status for its lan-guage, Luxembourg may have assured its acceptance as a full member in the early stages of the European Union. By the same token, Luxembourgish missed an opportunity to raise its profile and encourage more people to use it.

In today's Luxembourg, road signs are still in French and so are all legislation and official announcements. Newspapers are generally in German. As was the custom in Malta, testimony is done in the local language while lawyers speak to the judges in another language, French. But the grand duke—a national symbol himself—addresses the nation in Luxembourgish. There are radio and television programs in all three languages. Remarkably, most of these language assignments are customs and traditions, and are not dictated by law. For years, French was always the language of the educated, and German the language of the semieducated. Of course today everyone is educated, and German is also generally used in commerce. To some degree, it is still the case that French is the most prestigious. French is used almost exclusively in secondary education, while German and Luxembourgish have a bigger place in primary education. Most Luxembourgers are trilingual by adulthood, and have a natural advantage in a multilingual Europe. There are also disadvantages to this, besides the expense—some Luxembourgers fear they will never excel in any language.

Latin is another language managed by a microstate. In this case, it's the Holy See's use of Church Latin, which differs somewhat from the classical Latin of Cicero and other ancient Romans. For one thing, Church Latin is pronounced more like Italian than the older Classical Latin. The letters *c* and *g* are pronounced like English *ch* and *j* when they occur before *I* and *E*. They were always "hard" in Classical Latin. Also some vocabulary items took on new meanings, for example, *salus*, "health," also meant "salvation" among the Christians. Now, the earliest liturgical language of Christians was New Testament Greek. But by the fourth century, so many Western Christians used Latin as their official language, that the early Church came under pressure to use it. Dropping Greek was also a good way to underline the differ-ence between the Roman and the Orthodox Churches. St. Jerome translated the Bible, and the Mass was translated into a pious-sounding Latin as well.

Over the centuries, Latin developed different styles among lay and clerical users. Eventually, lay people abandoned it in favor of vernacular languages closer to everyday speech. But the Church only started saying mass in the vernacular in the twentieth century. Today, official communications and documents, such as encyclicals, often come out originally in Latin and are translated to other languages. The Esperanto of the Second Vatican Council was Latin, of course, which is still used whenever the cardinals from all over the linguistic world need to communicate.

Speaking of Esperanto, this international auxiliary language is regularly used in some of the Vatican's shortwave radio broadcasts. There are national Esperanto organizations in Luxembourg, Malta, and San Marino, and the Akademio Internacia de la Sciencoj holds a study conference biannually in San Marino. Perhaps microstates show an above-average support for a neutral international language in reaction to the dominance of the languages of their big sisters.

A Little Linguistic Geography

Except for isolated Malta, the microstates speak related Romance or Germanic languages. Actually, three of the four in the Romance area are considered dialects of Italian, and even Arabic Maltese has close connections with Italian. The Roman dialect is Central Italian, though it is just on the regional linguistic border with Southern Italian, from which Maltese borrowed so many words. Romagnolo and Monégasque are in the Gallo-Italian region, meaning that these dialects somewhat resemble southern French. They are also known as Emilian and Ligurian, respectively, after their Italian regions. But San Marino is just on the border with Central Italian, and Monaco is very close to French Provençal, so Romagnolo and Monégasque are about as far apart as any two Gallo-Italian dialects can be. Provençal has often been associated with its neighbor, Catalan, the language of Andorra. Technically, Catalan is considered to be a Western Romance

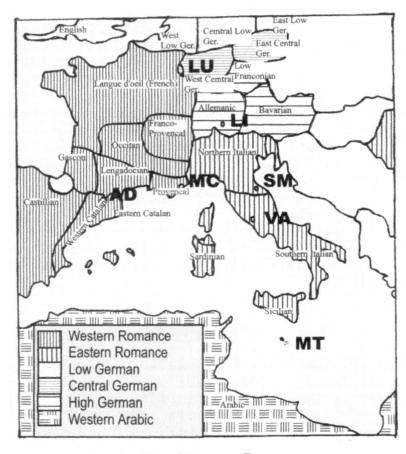

Language and Dialect Map of Microstate Europe.

THOMAS M. ECCARDT.

language, whereas the others are Eastern Romance, though the importance of this distinction may be overdone. Catalan itself has two principal types, Eastern and Western. Although Andorra is technically in the Eastern zone, it's just about on the linguistic border between the two. Of course Latin, specifically Vulgar Latin, was the ancestor of all the Romance languages.

Among the Western Germanic languages, a major division separates the Low German languages such as English and Dutch from the High German ones, such as Standard German and Alemmanic. Actually, the dividing line runs right across Germany, and "high" simply refers to the German spoken in southern mountainous areas while "low" refers to the lowlands of the north. Like Monégasque and Romagnolo, Luxembourgish and the High Alemmanic of Liechtenstein belong to the same region—High German—but are located on opposite ends of it. Liechtenstein's dialect is close to Swiss High German in the Alps, while Luxembourgish, next to Belgium, has a few elements of Low German. Maltese is considered to be a dialect of Western Arabic, because it seems closest to Tunisian Arabic. But it also has a few features of Eastern Arabic, and in fact not much of it is understood by speakers of Arabic in general.

The local microstate languages in Europe are not only considered dialects, but some of them have dialect subdivisions themselves. None of these internal dialects presents any difficulties of communication, however. In Malta, dwellers in the capital city of Valletta tend to speak an upper-class dialect that differs from the rural dialect around it. There are also differences in the speech on the other main island, Gozo. Liechtenstein apparently underwent an ancient migration of the Walser people from across Switzerland to the Triesenberg region so, despite its tiny size, Liechtenstein actually contains two varieties of High Alemmanic. Luxembourgish has two main dialects: a northern one with some similarities to Dutch and a southern one with similarities to Alemmanic.

Each of the microstate local languages except Maltese and Latin are part of a greater local language area, and crossing the national border does not imply crossing a communications boundary. Essentially, their languages are spoken in the neighboring lands and several of the languages are also spoken in emigrant communities as well.

A Multilingual Prayer

The following chart compares a sample of the local language of each microstate with that of the others, and with English as well. The text is the Lord's Prayer, familiar to just about every European microstate inhabitant, as there are few non-Christians. To eliminate distractions, all punctuation and capitalization have been removed. In some cases, the order of the phrases has been slightly changed to align each language into ten similar rows. The more similar languages have been placed next to each other, except of course for English and Maltese. Also note that Latin and Romagnolo are really not comparable, since one is ancient and the other modern. Finally, notice that sometimes the traditional translation varies a little; for example, in line 1 of Romagnolo, the words for "our father" literally mean "father of all."

In English, we say "this book" or "these books," but not "this books." This matching of the senses of words is called agreement. It is found much more frequently in the languages of Europe than in English. For example, notice that in Catalan line 7, *nostres ofenses* (our sins), versus line 6, *nostre pa* (our bread), –*s* is added not only to *ofense,* but to *nostre* as well. Agreement happens in a few other areas besides singular / plural. In most European languages, including all the microstate languages, everything has a gender, masculine or feminine (and sometimes neuter), whether or not it's a living thing with a natural sex. In lines 2–4 of Catalan, Monégasque, Romagnolo, and Latin, "name" and "kingdom" have the same gender, but "will" has another. The tipoff is the few words preceding (or, in Latin, following) them: Every one of these languages has a separate word for "your" to match the gender of the word for "name" or "kingdom," different from the

Line	English	Liechtenstein—Alemmanic	Luxembourg—Luxembourgish	Andorra—Catalan	Monaco—Monégasque	San Marino—Romagnolo	Vatican City—Latin	Malta—Maltese
1	our father who art in heaven	fader unser du in himile bist	eise papp am himmel	pare nostre del cel	paire nostru che si' ünt'u celu	babb ed tòtt che tsi in zil	pater noster qui es in coelis	missierna li inti fis-smewwiet
2	hallowed be thy name	din name vuerde geheiliget	däin numm sief gehellegt	sigui santificat el teu nom	sice santificau u to' nume	che seia santifichè e tu nom	sanctificetur nomen tuum	jitqaddes ismek
3	thy kingdom come	din riche chome	däi räich soll kommen	vingui el teu regne	che u to' regnu arrive scìu de nui	che vègna e tu regn	adveniat regnum tuum	tigi saltnatek
4	thy will be done	din wille gesckche	däi wëll soll geschéien	faci's la teva voluntat	che sec fà a to vuruntà	da seia fata la tu voluntè	fiat voluntas tua	ikun li trid int
5	as in heaven on earth as well	in erdo also in himele	wéi am himmel sou op der äerd	com al cel així també a la terra	ün celu cume ün terra	tant in zil acsé in tèra	sicut in coelo et in terra	kif fis-sema hekkda fl-art
6	give us this day our daily bread	unser tagoliche brot kib uns hiuto	gëf äis haut eist deeglecht brout	dóna'ns avui el nostre pa de cada dia	dane anchoei cuma tüti i giurni u nostru pan	das e nostar pan d'totti i dé	panem nostrum quotidianum da nobis hodie	hobżna ta' kuljum aghtina llum
7	and forgive us our wrongs	unde unsere schulde belass uns	verzei äis eis schold	i perdona'ns les nostres ofenses	perduna i nostri pecài	scanzela i nostar debit	et dimitte nobis debita nostra	ahfrilna dnubietna
8	as we forgive those who wrong us	also auch wir belazend unsern schludigen	wéi mir och dene verzeien déi an eiser schold sin	com també nos-altres hem perdonat els qui ens ofenen	cuma perdunamu ün acheli che n'an fau de mà	cume nò a fasè cun i nostar debitùr	sicut et nos dim-itimus debitoribus nostris	bhalma nahfru lil min hu hati ghalina
9	and lead us not into temptation	und in chorunga mit leitest du unsich	féier äis nët an d'versuchung	i no deixis que caiguem en la temptació	num ne lascià piyà d'a tentaçiun	no fès caschè in tentazión	et ne nos inducas in tentationem	u la ddaħħalniex fit-tiġrib
10	but deliver us from evil	nu belose unsich fom uble	mä maach äis fräi vum bëisen	ans deslliura'ns del maligne	e libèrane d'u mà	e tés luntan da tott i mel	sed libera nos a malo	iżda eħlisna mid-deni

version of "your" used to match the word for "will." For example, in Catalan it's *el teu* (your, masculine) before *nom* (name) and *regne* (kingdom) but *la teva* (feminine) before *voluntat* (will). Actually, in Latin, *nomen* and *regnum* are in the neuter gender, which disappeared in the modern Romance languages. Additionally, there is a gender difference in lines 1 and 6 of Luxembourgish as well: *eise* (our) is masculine for *papp* (father), but *eist* (our) is neuter for *brout* (bread). At one time English maintained a similar distinction, but this has been lost. Allemanic has three genders as well, but it is not obvious from this particular text.

Another feature common to Latin, Alemmanic, and Luxembourgish is grammatical case. Sometimes a word's case is determined by a preposition, such as "from." So in line 10 of Latin, the word *malo* (evil) is in the ablative case because of *a* (from). If it hadn't been for the preposition, "evil" might have been *malum*. In Alemmanic and Luxembourgish, examples of the dative case can be found in the words *fom* and *vum*, which are actually abbreviations for the phrase "of the." The letter *m* at the end of each represents "the" in the dative case. Case is no longer used in the Romance languages.

In the Lord's Prayer text, Luxembourgish and Alemmanic bear a resemblance to German. Romagnolo and Monégasque show similarities to Italian, while Catalan is similar to Spanish and French. There are also similarities between Alemmanic, Luxembourgish, and English; for example, the words *wille, wëll,* and *will* in line 4. These same words match up nicely among the translations in Catalan, Monégasque, Romagnolo, and Latin: *voluntat, vuruntà, vuluntè,* and *voluntas*. Notice that *trid,* in Maltese, resembles none of them. All this shows the differences and resemblances between Germanic, Romance, and Semitic languages. In fact *vol,* the first syllable of *voluntas,* is distantly related to English *will*. This is an example of the similarity of the Germanic and Romance divisions of the Indo-European family, as opposed to the alien-sounding Semitic family.

A difference between High German and Low German can be found in the consonants at the beginnings of words. Even though

Luxembourgish is still considered to be in the High German area, occasionally it resembles the Low Germanic languages, such as English. For example, in line 6, *tagoliche* (daily) begins with *t* in Alemmanic, yet *deeglecht* begins with *d* in Luxembourgish, as it does in English. The difference between the Western Romance languages, (such as Catalan) versus the Eastern Romance languages (such as Monégasque and Romagnolo) can be seen in the way they form the plural. Western Romance languages tend to use the letter *s* as in Catalan line 7, *les nostres ofenses* (our wrongs), while Eastern Romance uses vowels, such as *i*, as in *i nostri pecài* (Monégasque) and *i nostar debit* (Romagnolo).

Maltese is in a league of its own. It tends to connect words much more than Indo-European languages do. For example, "thy" is represented in lines 2–3 by the letters *–ek* at the end of *ismek* (thy name) and *saltnatek* (thy kingdom). Look for examples of the ending *–na* meaning "our." The same ending is used to mean "us" in *aħfrilna* (forgive us). Maltese sometimes even connects what would be three English words, as in line 10, *mid-deni* (from the evil). Finally, you may remember that Maltese is supposed to have imported a lot of Italian words. Only one shows up in the Lord's Prayer, namely, in the words "our father," *misserna*. *Missier* is from the Sicilian word *messere*, meaning "gentleman," and is related to the French word *monsieur*.

Education in the Microstates

Nowadays, elementary through upper school education is mandatory and free in all the microstates. But things were not always so simple. For many years, parents in Liechtenstein had to pay tuition for elementary schools, although the neediest could get financial aid from the government. In Malta and Andorra, the Catholic Church has traditionally been in charge of much of education. In 1983, resentment of the dominance of the Church in Maltese life caused the government to confiscate more than 75 percent of Church property—most of it devoted to schools—and

Junior high school.
STATE TOURIST BUREAU OF THE
REPUBLIC OF SAN MARINO.

prohibit charging of fees by private schools. Catholic officials then closed all of their schools in protest, leaving half of Malta's children without classes. A negotiated settlement reopened the schools, with the government insisting on free education but promising noninterference in teaching. In Andorra, the Catholic Church runs the entire system—really two systems: one in Spanish, the other in French. The curriculum resembles the one used in Spain, but the French government subsidizes the schools that teach in French. Recently, the Church has opened a school for students who want to study in Catalan.

Most of public education in the microstates mirrors the systems of their big sisters, and in fact the local language often suffers because of it. Even though Catalan is the only official language of Andorra, education was given mostly in French and Spanish, as it was in the Catholic schools of France and Spain. The Romagnolo and Monégasque dialects were regularly ignored in the schools of San Marino and Monaco, because the Italian and French school systems were emulated in those microstates. Monaco has introduced its local language as an academic subject, but most classes are still taught in French. Liechtenstein's schools follow the systems of several German-speaking countries, namely, Germany, Austria, and Switzerland. There, too, no attention is paid to the local Allemanic. The Vatican has no need for a public education system, since the small number of children of the Swiss Guards can go to elementary school in Rome.

Only Malta and Luxembourg seriously promote their native languages through their public school systems. Luxembourgish is used exclusively in preschools, and foreign children are encouraged to learn to speak it. In primary schools, German is introduced, and it gradually becomes the language of instruction. French is the language of instruction in the upper grades and university. By the time they finish their education, most students have mastered speaking, reading, and writing in all three languages. On Malta, Maltese is generally the language of instruction. But due to the influence of 150 years of English rule, English is taught extensively and the English educational system is used.

The result of the public education systems in the microstates of Europe is a very high literacy rate. Literacy is 100 percent in all but San Marino (99.1 percent) and Malta (92.1 percent). Perhaps the lower rate in Malta can be explained by the fact that the use of Maltese, the first language of most of the population, was discouraged for so many years in favor of Italian and English. The microstates maintain a low student to teacher ratio, generally ranging from one teacher for every seventeen students to one per fourteen. Interestingly, San Marino has one teacher for every six students.

Though Malta may have had the most problems with its public education system, it was the first by far to have its own university, founded by Jesuits in 1592. The University of Malta was established as a state institution in 1769, and today it offers courses in all the important fields. And although the Vatican offers no public education for children, it has several private universities, generally for theological studies. These are scattered throughout Rome, and are not housed within the walls of the Vatican. Only toward the end of the twentieth century did most of the other microstates found universities. Before then, most students went abroad to get higher education. Some microstates had specialized schools, such as Liechtenstein's academy of music, or the University of Southern Europe in Monaco, which offers Masters of Business Administration and the like. Luxembourg has had an International University of Comparative Science for a good many years. But recently, sometimes with the help of the Internet, the microstates have been setting up their own universities. San Marino has a University of Study on the Republic of San Marino with an Institute for Computer Science. And Liechtenstein now has an International Academy for Philosophy.

There is a new University of Andorra, as well, and much of it is devoted to computer science. However, it now has a multidisciplinary doctoral program in the study of the future of the microstates. The students make use of campuses outside Andorra as they attempt to anticipate future developments through the use of generalized systems theory. The University of Malta has also created an Islands and Small States Institute. It organizes seminars and conferences all over the world on the problems of small states and islands and runs programs leading to advanced degrees in small states studies. At least in Andorra and Malta, the subject of micropatrology is taken quite seriously.

PART II

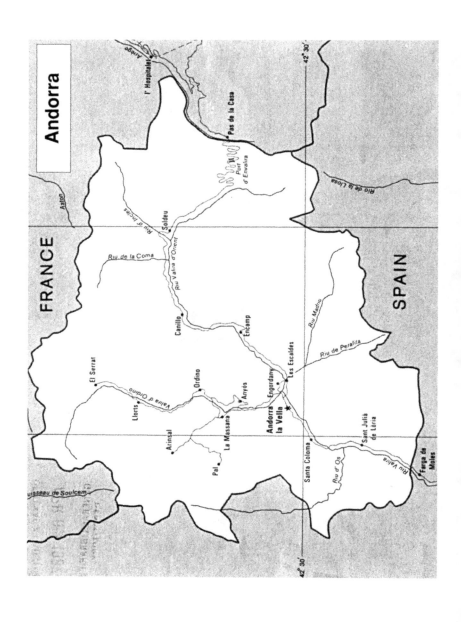

Andorra:
The Pyrenean Microstate

You will never see a landscape photograph of Andorra without mountains. That is because Andorra is *all* mountains. They are everywhere—whether snow-covered at their peaks or full of summer wildflowers in their valleys. Unlike some of its European microstate cousins, Andorra is not merely at the foot of mountains, or near a big river valley—it is right in the middle of the Pyrenees Mountains. And it would be difficult to pick a more mountainous or isolated spot within the Pyrenees for a tiny country.

Andorra would resemble any other isolated area of the Pyrenees, except for the seventy thousand residents who pack the valleys, jam traffic, and welcome almost 11 million visitors per year. With six ski resorts in an area of 174 square miles, this country must hold the world's record for ski resort density. As most of the visitors come for the duty-free shopping, Andorra probably also holds the record for portion of population engaged in the retail trades.

Andorra is so mountainous that there are only three main roads, or four if you count the continuations separately. The advantage of this is that everything is either on or near one of them. The main roads follow riverbeds in valleys. Road number one comes up from the town of Seu d'Urgell in Catalonia, Spain, and continues to Andorra la Vella, the capital. A little further on, it divides into roads two and three. Road two is the longest, and it meanders northeast, eventually reaching the town of Pas de la Casa on the French border. Roads one and two are the heaviest traveled, and also the oldest, providing access to Andorra la Vella from Spain and France. Roads three and four go northwest from the capital, road four exiting into Spain at a new crossing called Pas de Cabus, and road three being a dead end. If you are interested in seeing the old Andorra, note that roads three and four are the least developed and most unspoiled. There are a few other minor roads, as well, and there are also several beautiful hiking trails.

Andorra may be unique among tourist destinations in another way: most visitors come to Andorra for a reason. Either they come for the shopping; or for skiing, hiking, or camping; or else for a convention. Hardly anyone comes "to see Andorra." After reading this chapter, perhaps you will be convinced that Andorra is a truly unique nation, with a people and culture worth experiencing.

When you visit Andorra, you may notice that there is a lot of modern architecture, and some very old Romanesque architecture, but very little in between. This may leave you with the impression that history does not flow in this isolated country, but comes in sporadic floods, only to recede for long periods of time. That impression would not be mistaken. Andorrans seem to prefer being left alone, and to change only when change is completely unavoidable. This chapter covers only some major incidents in Andorran history, but you need not feel that you missed anything.

A History of Fits and Starts

Andorrans are proud that their recorded history goes back to Charlemagne. They are also proud of their historical documents, although some of these documents may not be authentic. For example, the Carta de la Fundació d'Andorra is a document supposedly written by Charlemagne to his son, Louis the Pious, establishing the independence of Andorra. More likely it was

Skier on Andorran slope.

MINISTRY OF TOURISM OF THE GOVERNMENT OF ANDORRA.

Andorran six-petal daffodils, said to represent the six traditional parishes.
MINISTRY OF TOURISM OF THE GOVERNMENT OF ANDORRA.

written by Andorrans many years later to fend off claimants to their territory. Nevertheless, the Carta is kept in a locked cupboard in the government headquarters, the Casa de la Vall in the capital. The cupboard has six locks, each of whose key is held by one of the representatives of Andorra's six traditional parishes, now seven modern political divisions.

These six parishes are mentioned in Andorra's oldest authentic historical document, from AD 839, the Act of Consecration of the Cathedral of Seu d'Urgell, indicating that the parishes belong to its diocese. Soon after, the fiefdom of Andorra was actually given to the bishop of Urgell as a present from the count of Urgell, Ermengol IV. From then on, the bishop and his successors would be rulers or corulers of Andorra. At that time, it was normal for Catholic clergy to have temporal powers, but it has never been easy for them to maintain political and religious control simultaneously and, about two hundred years later, they assigned the defense of Andorra to the Caboet family. As the Caboets gained more and more control of Andorra, they married into the noble Foix family from France. At this time France was still not a unified country.

The bishop of Urgell eventually began disputing the right of the counts of Foix to control Andorra, especially since the Foix family had inherited it only through marriage. Spain was not a unified country, either, when the king of Aragón, Peter III, sided with the bishop. His brother, James II, controlled some of the territory on the French side, so Peter used his influence to force a peaceable settlement. That settlement, the *paréage* of 1278, essentially froze Andorra in political time for the next 715 years. The *paréage* required the Andorrans to pay a biannual tribute to each of the corulers, the counts of Foix and the bishop of Urgell. And in addition to about eight dollars, the bishops got six hams, six cheeses, and twelve hens every other year until 1993. When later one of the counts of Foix was elevated to king of France, his corulership was elevated permanently to that position. If Spain were now to try to absorb Andorra into its territory, as it did with surrounding Catalonia, it would have to answer to the king of France. Similarly, if

Monument to the signing of the paréages.

France wanted to absorb Andorra, as it did with the province of Roussillon (also known as Catalonia North), it would have to answer to the bishop of Urgell, and ultimately to the pope. Incidentally, it seems to have been pure Andorran luck that the count of Foix became the king of France just when he did, because the territory that included Foix was drawing closer and closer to Spain, and had practically become a dependency of Aragón.

What would happen if a small border territory were ruled jointly by high-ranking officials of two countries that only became countries long after the agreement for joint control? If the two sides never gave up their rights to the territory, but neither found it worth going to war over, the result might be a country like Andorra, which for about seven hundred years existed in a state of limbo, neither a part of France nor Spain nor a totally independent country.

This standoff between France and Spain, established by the *paréage* document, was quite effective, and the borders fixed by it have remained unchanged longer than those of any other European country. Some of Andorra's current political institutions were formed by the *paréage* as well; for example, the *batlles* (BAHL-lyuhs) or magistrates, some of whom are still appointed by the coprinces. Each of the coprinces would also appoint a *veguer* (buh-GAY), or lieutenant, to handle day-to-day affairs of the principality. Nowadays things are a little more indirect. The *veguers* live in Andorra, but each represents either the perfect of the French department of Pyrenees-Orientales or the vicar general of the Urgell diocese. The perfect and the vicar general reside in Perpignan, France, and Seu d'Urgell, Spain, respectively. And they, in turn, represent the president of France and the bishop of Urgell.

Soon after the *paréage* was signed, the count of Foix began building a castle above Santa Coloma. It was then thought necessary to sign a new *paréage*, in 1288. The new *paréage* bans all such building, and today you will find no castles in Andorra. Another result of the *paréage*s and corule is that many services in Andorra are run by the Spanish or the French government or by both. There are two postal systems and three primary education systems, and Andorrans can choose among them.

The other important document from the history of Andorra is the Manual Digest. In 1748, a doctor of the law, Antoni Fiter i Rossell, collected and copied out all the important Andorran documents he knew of, starting from the Carta de la Fundació. The Manual Digest also spells out Andorra's policy of neutrality in conflicts between France and Spain. One copy of the Manual Digest is in its author's hometown in the Casa d'Ordino, another in the Casa de les Valls d'Andorra, and a third in the Seu d'Urgell cathedral.

Between 1288 and 1933, very few changes took place in Andorra's form of government. In 1419, an emissary of the more important Andorran families received permission from the coprinces to set up the Council of the Land, a kind of parliament where important issues could be discussed. Only the heads of the important families were allowed to participate, and the Council had no real power, but could only advise the coprinces. More than four hundred years later, in 1866, the Council of the Land was reformed and renamed the General Council of the Valleys. Now heads of all families were allowed to participate, and it was given jurisdiction over some things like hunting and fishing, road maintenance, and local taxes. But still it had very few powers.

Toward the end of the nineteenth century and the beginning of the twentieth, Andorra was becoming more and more modern, as regarded its economy. The country was electrified and the modern roads to Spain and France were opened. Cars were replacing mules as the major form of transport. However, politically, Andorra was still a feudal country. Only the eldest male of a household was allowed to vote; a father had to be deceased before his son became eligible. With Andorra's long life spans, this meant that even middle-aged men usually couldn't vote. When the General Council started granting such franchises as the right to open a gambling house, those authorizations were repeatedly cancelled by the coprinces. By the 1930s, anarchism was a popular movement in neighboring Catalonia, which was now officially autonomous from Spain. Spain had overthrown its monarch, and had become a republic. The General Council began

Andorran shield in stone.

to think of itself as in charge of the internal affairs of Andorra, and they started printing "Republic of Andorra" on the passports. When the government of Spain asked the bishop of Urgell to give them his rights over Andorra, he refused, and the president of France supported the bishop's decision.

Eventually feelings for democracy boiled over and, in early April 1933, a group of young Andorran men stormed the Casa de les Valls and forced the General Council to agree to universal male suffrage. They had driven around the country in their cars yelling, "We want the vote," gathering supporters as they headed for the parliament building. Despite this early victory, the General Council members soon changed their minds and planned not to submit the agreement to the coprinces. Luckily for the rebels, there was an organization of Andorran expatriates in Barcelona, which sprang into action and threatened to kidnap the General Council if they reneged on the agreement. By the third week of April, they had joined with the youths and once again stormed a General Council meeting, forcing it to be opened to the public. On that day, for the first time in Andorran history, a young man who was not the head of a family had the chance to address the General Council, a body of old men. A few days later, the revolution had gained so much self-confidence, that its leader, Andrés Massó, was demanding that the French and Spanish coprinces renounce their claims on Andorra. "Nothing short of independence will do" was his position.

This did not impress the head of the General Council, the Syndic. By June he had dismissed the parliament and exiled Mr. Massó. But the General Council refused to recognize the dismissal, despite the demands of the French president that they desist. Now began a protracted struggle between France and the Andorran people, with the French sometimes sending in their gendarmes, and Andorrans practicing civil disobedience by using their donkeys to block the parliament building, and refusing to vote to elect a new General Council. Spain generally backed the Andorrans, but they had little influence, since it was the bishop of Urgell, not the Spanish government, who coruled Andorra.

Several times a date was set for the election of a new General Council, and then it was postponed because the Andorrans were insisting that young men have the right to vote in it. The revolutionaries were just about to bring their case before the League of Nations, when they put everything on hold because the tobacco crop needed harvesting. Finally in early September 1933, young Andorrans voted for the first time. After a few more squabbles, France and Spain settled their differences, and by the end of the year, all was peaceful in Andorra once again. But years later, in 1941, the Vichy French military government took universal male suffrage away again and it was not restored until 1947.

A King of Andorra?

1934 was to be no quieter than the previous revolutionary year. By then, news of the unrest in Andorra had spread all over the world. Rich foreigners were now offering large amounts of cash to Andorra in exchange for a title of nobility. The General Council rejected a $100,000 offer from a Chicagoan for a kingship, saying that Andorra was a principality, not a kingdom. This answer was somewhat disingenuous, because the future king of Andorra had already arrived from Palma de Mallorca. He was accompanied by his American benefactor, Mrs. Florence Marmon, the divorced wife of an Indiana automobile magnate. He may have been out of money, but he certainly looked the part, with his monocle and his command of many European languages. Baron Boris de Skossyreff, count of Orange, spent a few months in Andorra, studying its history and comparing his genealogy to that of the long-deposed kings of France. Then in the spring of 1934 he announced that, as count of Orange, he would act as "regent for the absent king of France" and become King Boris I of Andorra.

De Skossyreff's application for Andorran citizenship had already been approved by the General Council, and apparently his proposal now pleased them enough to accept him as their first king. Boris I's program included complete freedom of speech and of the press, and free public education for all. Boris's subjects would be encouraged to participate in sports. Some of King Boris's plans were amazingly prophetic, such as his idea to appoint a director of tourist travel and propaganda, and his desire to get Andorra admitted into the League of Nations. Boris then chose his biggest supporter, Syndic Pere Torres Ribas, to be prime minister. Ribas convinced all but one of his fellow General Council members to go along with the plan, which was essentially a risky declaration of independence from Spain and France.

Perhaps ashamed of their actions to keep Andorra nondemocratic in 1933, this time the French stayed out of the affair. But the one General Council member who dissented from the plan for a constitutional monarchy ran off to tell the bishop of Urgell, who was not in the least amused. By then, rightists were in charge of the shaky Spanish Republic, and the bishop had no difficulty getting Spanish civil guards to protect his ownership in the Andorran cofiefdom. In early July, they arrested de Skossyreff and brought him to Barcelona. Mrs. Marmon, who had been acting as his personal secretary, was allowed to stay at Seu d'Urgell. Boris I was indignant. From exile, he declared war on the bishop of Urgell and dissolved the General Council. These declarations were printed and pasted up all over Andorra.

Despite their apparent love for their new king, there was little the people of Andorra could do. Boris had been deposed by the bishop of Urgell, and now faced removal to Madrid in a third-class train compartment with two Spanish detectives. His explanations that he was only trying to protect Spanish interests in Andorra from French hegemony were unconvincing. Insult was added to injury when the difference between a first-class ticket and his third-class fare was not forthcoming from Mrs. Marmon, and Boris was shipped off to Madrid for further investigation. These investigations revealed that de Skossyreff was actually born in Lithuania, and was not the Dutch count he had claimed to be. Apparently nobody in the American colony at Palma de Mallorca had taken him very seriously, either, as he claimed to be a wealthy yachtsman, but never seemed have the cash to pay the check at a restaurant. On the other hand, de Skossyreff was already in violation of an old order of expulsion from Spain, and was persona non grata in England and France as well.

After a few months in a Madrid prison, Boris de Skossyreff was expelled from Spain to Portugal, as he had requested. He was immediately arrested in Portugal, as his papers were not in order. Mrs. Marmon returned to her brother in the United States. Not much was heard during the next decade from the former king of Andorra, who had been born in Vilnius, but considered himself a German. But toward the end of the Second World War, Boris de Skossyreff was apparently sent by Hitler on a circuitous route through Europe to Yalta in the Crimea, in order to try to influence the outcome of the famous peace conference held there.

Not much happened in Andorra for another forty years, except that it served as an important refuge for Spaniards fleeing their civil war and then for French people fleeing German occupation. During the postwar period, there were various power conflicts between the coprinces, who by tradition never consulted each other. Andorra had so little self-rule that it was hardly considered a country by international organizations. Andorra was not even allowed to join the International Postal Union or the World Tourism Organization. In 1973, the coprinces met for the first time, to begin plans to democratize Andorra. By 1993, this process resulted in the complete modernization of the Andorran government, following which the microstate joined the United Nations. The coprinces are now largely figureheads, but they must still approve treaties with Spain and France and other matters concerning boundaries, defense, and internal security.

A Catalan Culture

Andorra is now an independent country, and because of its intermediate position it has never been considered part of Spain or France. On the other hand, it is located in the middle of Catalonia, called Catalunya in the Catalan language. Andorra is the only

Plaza in Andorra la Vella.
THOMAS M. ECCARDT.

country in the world to make Catalan its official tongue, but language is not the only thing it shares with its surrounding area, which approximately covers northeast Spain and a sliver of southwest France. In particular, Andorra is in the mountainous Pyrenean region of Catalonia, which distinguishes it somewhat from the Mediterranean cultural area of Barcelona, the capital of Catalonia. It follows that many elements of Andorran culture relate to Catalan culture, not that of broader Spain or France.

Food in Andorra is generally Catalan in style. A favorite ingredient or condiment is *allioli* (ahl-yee-OH-lee), literally "garlic and oil." *Allioli* is actually a kind of eggless mayonnaise, made by crushing garlic and mixing it with olive oil. Catalan cooking is often done in the Catalan version of the casserole, a *cassola,* which is an earthenware pot glazed on the inside. An *escudella* is made in a *cassola* by simmering meats and vegetables together, and serving

Andorran cuisine.

the juice separately as soup and the solid ingredients as a main course. Other aspects of Andorran cooking differ from general Catalan cooking, because of the country's location in the mountainous Pyrenees. Andorra has no seacoast, so you will not find the wide varieties of seafood familiar in Valencian paellas; instead, Andorrans enjoy deliciously prepared freshwater trout. Because the microstate is located in a relatively isolated, largely rural area, hunting is popular, and rabbit, mountain pig, and goat are freely available for cooking. Of course, a full range of Spanish, French, and other international foods also are served in Andorra, catering to the tastes of its many visitors.

In Catalonia, folk dancing is very popular, and it is traditionally done in an *aplec* (uh-PLECK), a kind of festival gathering. Rather than walk in a procession, the townspeople form a ring and, holding their neighbors' hands in the air, dance the *sardana*. The *aplec* and the *sardana* are symbols of Catalan unity, whether it be officially in French or Spanish territory. They were a kind of cultural act of defiance against the Franco dictatorship for many years. As the only independent area of Catalonia, Andorra has always held a special place in the hearts of many Catalans. Nowadays, the General Council of Andorra and the Generalitat of the autonomous Spanish region of Catalonia sometimes sponsor cultural events in each other's countries. As for Andorran dances, each major town holds its own *aplec* on its patron saint's day, and some of them have distinctive dances. For example, the town Sant Julià de Lòria celebrates the festival of Santa Anna by dancing the best-known Andorran dance, the *marratxa*. It is a good idea, especially in summer, to check with the tourist office to see if an *aplec* will be held any time during your stay in Andorra.

Visiting Andorra

Most people arrive in Andorra through the town of Seu d'Urgell in Spain. There is a major road to it from Barcelona. Others arrive through France from the towns of L'Hospitalet or La Tour de Carol.

Hot springs of Caldea at Les Escaldes.
MINISTRY OF TOURISM OF THE GOVERNMENT OF ANDORRA.

If you come through France, don't miss the *petit train jaune*—the little yellow train—which wends its way through the beautiful French Pyrenees. In any case, if you're not going by car, the last leg of your trip into Andorra must be by bus, since no railroad goes there. As a matter of fact, buses are a convenient mode of transportation within Andorra, since parking may be difficult to find.

If you're not in Andorra for the best and cheapest skiing in the Pyrenees, there are several other sports in which you can participate. Camping and horseback riding are enjoyable in the mountainous scenery—you might even spot a herd of wild horses. Hiking is particularly popular in Andorra, and it's fun to imagine smugglers on donkeys following the same routes across the borders with Spain and France. Andorra has a unique system of twenty-six

Stanta Coloma round romanesque tower.

"refuges," formerly used mostly by shepherds, which are now freely available to hikers for overnight stays in summer. You can obtain a complete list and a map of the trails and refuges, from the tourist office. Finally, there is the great spa complex of thermally heated waters at Les Escaldes in the shape of a huge glass pyramid.

You need to allocate at least one day to see the cultural sites of Andorra. In one day, you could see Andorra la Vella, the capital, with its Casa de les Valls and Santa Coloma Romanesque church. With a little more time, you should at least visit Ordino in order to see the more traditional Andorra. Because it's off the beaten tourist path, Ordino has more traditional architecture, and conveniently it has several unusual museums. Museums in Andorra are not the typical galleries hung with paintings; in fact,

Restored 17ᵗʰ century kitchen, Rull House in Sispony.
MINISTRY OF TOURISM OF THE GOVERNMENT OF ANDORRA.

most of the frescos that decorated the walls of Romanesque churches have been removed to museums in Barcelona. In Ordino, there is a postage museum and also a museum of miniature pictures, so small that they have to be viewed through microscopes. Very appropriate for a microstate. Ordino was the center of the old iron industry, still preserved in its ironwork decorations. There are other museums in Ordino, including one displaying Slavic Orthodox religious icons of the seventeenth to nineteenth centuries. Elsewhere, there is an automobile museum, a modern sculpture museum, and there are original and re-created houses so you can see what life was like in past Andorran centuries.

Andorra's pride and joy are its stone Romanesque churches and bridges. The tourist office will give you a list of them; just about every major town has one. Santa Coloma in Andorra la Vella might even be considered the nation's trademark, with its unique rounded tower. The other famous symbol of Andorra is the six-armed but so-called seven-armed cross, on the old road from Meritxell to Canillo. Legend has it that it was erected with seven arms, but one miraculously disappeared when one of a group of seven boys was inadvertently shot to death in a prank. Others say the arms represent the traditional parishes of Andorra, as do the six petals of the national flower, the *grandalla*, a kind of daffodil.

Basic Data

Official Name	Principality of Andorra
Official Native Name	Principat d'Andorra
Nickname	The Pyrenean microstate
Origin of Name	The name of a valley, thought to be of Basque derivation
Capital	Andorra la Vella
Origin/Meaning of Name	Andorra City
Official Language(s)	Catalan
Motto	*Virtus unita fortior*
Motto in English	A united action is much stronger
Nationality	Andorran
Area in Square Miles	174
Latitude	42.3° north
Longitude	1.3° east
Time Zone	GMT+1
Big Sister	Spain, France
Big Sister Guidebooks to Use	Spain, Catalonia, Pyrenees
Convenient Cities	Barcelona, Toulouse, Seu d'Urgell

Seven-pointed cross.

New Meritxell Sanctuary. Our Lady of Meritxell is Andorra's patron saint.

Daffodil-filled Valley d'Incles.

MINISTRY OF TOURISM OF THE GOVERNMENT OF ANDORRA.

GDP	$1.3 billion (2000 estimate)
GDP per capita	$19,000 (2000 estimate)
Major Exports	Tobacco products, furniture
Present Currency	Euro
Currency before Euro	French franc and Spanish peseta
Exchange Rate / Dollar	1.19
Population	69,150 (July 2003 estimate)
Annual Population Growth	1.06% (2003 estimate)
Type of Government	Parliamentary democracy
Head of State	French president Jacques Chirac / Monsignor Joan Marti y Alanis
Head of Government	Head of Government, Marc Forné Molné
Name of Parliament	General Council
Date of Constitution	1993
National Holiday	Mare de Deu de Meritxell
National Holiday Date	September 8
Year of Foundation	1278
Year of Independence	1278
Womens' Suffrage	1970
UN Membership	1993
Diocese	Urgell (Spain)
Patron Saint	Our Lady of Meritxell
Telephone Code	376
Internet Suffix	.ad
Radio Stations	15
Television Channels	1
Official Web Site	http://www.turisme.ad/ angles/index.htm

Flag   Three equal vertical bands of
                    blue (hoist side), yellow,
                    and red with the national
                    coat of arms centered in the
                    yellow band

SOURCES: U.S. Central Intelligence Agency: *The World Factbook, 2003*; *Worldmark Encyclopedia of Nations*; *Europa World Yearbook*; *Political Handbook of the World*.

National Holidays

New Year's Day	January 1
Epiphany	January 6
Constitution Day	March 14
Good Friday	Friday before Easter
Easter Monday	Monday after Easter
Monday after Pentecost	Monday after Pentecost
May Day (labor)	May 1
Our Lady of Meritxell	September 8
All Saints' Day	November 1
Immaculate Conception	December 8
Christmas Day	December 25
St. Stephen's Day	December 26

Major Dates in Andorra's History

201 BC   Andorra becomes part of Roman Empire as result of
          Punic wars

AD 527   St. Justus, bishop of Urgell, attends second council
          of Toledo

770	Charlemagne founds Andorra as a march state, a buffer against Moorish Spain
850	Ermengol IV makes bishop of Urgell overlord of Andorra
1000	Urgell bishop asks Spanish nobleman for help; later, French count of Foix inherits
1278	Joint suzerainty of Spain (bishop) and France (count)
1607	Henri IV issues edict establishing French head-of-state as coprince
1789	Revolutionary France refuses to rule Andorra
1806	Andorrans ask Napoleon I to rule them
1850	Andorrans raise and smuggle tobacco
1933	Youths storm General Council to demand suffrage
1970	Women get the vote; voting age lowered to 21
1993	Andorra has new constitution, coprinces' power is limited, parliament rules
1993	Andorra joins UN

Foods

Food Name	Type	English Name	Ingredients
Allioli	General	Mayonnaise	Mayonnaise made from garlic and oil
Formatge de tupi	General	Goat cheese	Goat cheese with garlic and brandy
Pa amb tomaquet	General	Catalan pizza	Bread rubbed with tomato plus oil

Xicoira	General	Dandelion	Type of dandelion used in salads
Rostes amb mel	Entrée	Ham	Ham slices, honey, vinegar
Xai	Entrée	Lamb	Lamb
Conill amb all i oli	Entrée	Grilled rabbit	Rabbit with Catalan mayonnaise
Trinxat	Entrée	Hash	Boiled potatoes and cabbage with bacon slices
Escudella	Entrée	Stew	Meat and vegetable stew
Fideuà	Entrée	Noodle paella	Paella made with vermicelli instead of rice
Llebre	Entrée	Hare stew	Hare simmered in its own blood
Coques	Dessert	Flat cakes	Flat cakes with brandy

Places to Visit

Name and Description	City	Road #
Casa de la Vall parliament building in old quarter	Andorra	1
Plaça del Poble—beautiful main square of capital plus tourist office	Andorra	1

Santa Coloma Romanesque church with rounded tower	Andorra	1
Bridge of La Margineda	Andorra and St. Julia de Loria	1
Santuari de Meritxell with replica of old statue of patron saint of Andorra	Canillo	2
Casa Christo Museum— re-creation of traditional Andorran house	Encamp	2
National Car Museum	Encamp	2
Portella Blanca—where smugglers could step into Spain or France	Encamp	2
Andorra Model Museum—scale models of buildings in Andorra.	Engordany	2
Thermal baths of Caldea—huge spa complex with saunas, pools, etc.	Escaldes-Engordany	2
Viladomat Museum—250 works of Catalan sculptor	Escaldes-Engordany	2
Bridge of Sant Antoni de la Grella	Escaldes-Engordany and La Massana	3
Museum and house of Areny-Plandolit iron magnate family	Ordino	3
Museum of Miniatures—tiny microscopic images viewed with microscopes	Ordino	3
St. George Icon Museum—Slavic Orthodox religious icons from the seventeenth to nineteenth centuries	Ordino	3
Ordino-Arcalis Ski Resort—most pleasant, with north views	Ordino	3
Andorran Postage Museum in Borda del Raser barn	Ordino	3

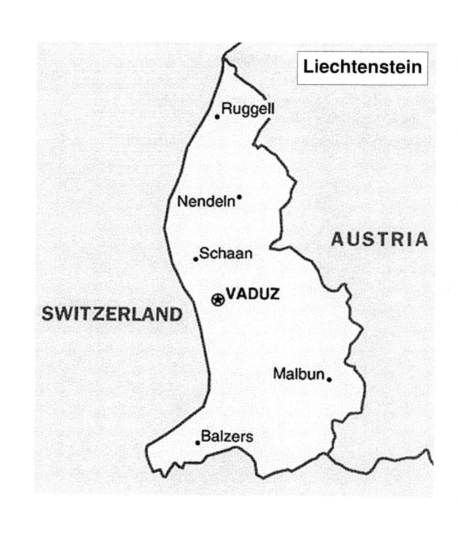

Liechtenstein:
The Business Microstate

There are many reasons to call Liechtenstein the business microstate. For one thing, Liechtenstein is the most industrialized country in Europe. For another, business taxes are low, and corporate laws are written to attract businesses. But Liechtenstein could not be called the business-as-usual microstate. Its industries produce very little pollution, without even marring the landscape. And about eighty thousand of the businesses with headquarters in Liechtenstein really do no business there.

You will not see any ugly factory buildings with huge smokestacks in Liechtenstein. What you will see are the idyllic Alps and Rhine river valley. Amid this scenery you will find chalet-type houses and a couple of castles besides. The Alps are on the eastern side of the country, and they continue into Austria. The Rhine River runs along the western border, and its valley continues a little ways into Switzerland before the Alps resume. Since Liechtenstein is much longer in the north-south direction than going east and west, it's convenient to divide it into north, middle, and south sections, though this is historically inaccurate. Liechtenstein was created out of the lordship of Schellenberg in the north and the county of Vaduz in the south. In keeping with Liechtenstein's business reputation, those parcels were a purchase of a rich prince who wouldn't live there.

Remote-control Rule

With their fabulously wealthy princely family plus billions of dollars of assets in their banking system, Liechtensteiners may now be the richest citizens of any country in the world. But it wasn't always that way. Originally the area wasn't even called "Liechtenstein," but nowadays it is the only country in Europe named after its rulers, the princes "von und zu" Liechtenstein. Although they have always called themselves the princes "of and at" Liechtenstein, their family purchased the territory around the year 1700 and continued to live near Vienna, Austria, for another two hundred years. They only earned the right to truthfully say "at Liechtenstein" when Prince Franz Josef II moved there in 1938.

Before the purchase by the Liechtenstein family, most of the area was called Vaduz, since Schellenberg makes up only a small part in the north. For many years, the two were politically unrelated areas under Charlemagne and then under the counts of Bregenz. It wasn't until the year 1300 that their borders were finally fixed as they are today. Often under the same ruler, they were legally separate, and were bought and sold individually. Vaduz was always the more important area, so you might say that Vaduz was Liechtenstein's former name.

"Vaduz" may be a combination of the words "valley" and "Teuton," so coined because Vaduz was in the Rhine valley, where the Germans lived. About the time that it formally became a county, the count of Vaduz built a castle just above its biggest city to protect it. The castle and the town were destroyed in the Sabian war a couple of centuries later but then rebuilt. Today you can see the rebuilt castle from the outside, but it's the private residence of the princely family, so it's closed to the public.

Princely palace in Vaduz.
LIECHTENSTEIN TOURISM.

In 1396 Vaduz was raised to the status of "imperial imme-diacy," which meant that it was subject to the Holy Roman Emperor alone. Because it is still a monarchy, today people say that Liechtenstein is the last remnant of the Holy Roman Empire. Thirty-eight years later, Schellenberg was joined with Vaduz in this status. Another landmark you can visit was built at about this time, called the Rotes Haus. This red house has a *torkel*, a kind of wine press, and it houses the prince's favorite restaurant.

The Middle Ages were not a happy time for Vaduz and Schel-lenberg. The area was wracked by wars, the plague, and even ram-pant witch hunting. Vaduzers were impoverished peasants, ruled from the castle by counts or their representatives. Their rulers appar-ently were not much better off financially: Vaduz and Schellenberg were sold off to new owners at least three times in order to pay the debts of their former owners. The territory of the business microstate was a sort of commodity in the dealings of the nobility in the Holy Roman Empire.

After so many years of bad luck, when Schellenberg went on the block in 1699, it would be for the last time. The owners, the counts of Hohenems, were so irresponsible and debt-ridden that the emperor appointed someone else to handle to job of finding a buyer and clearing up the debts. The buyer he found was Prince Johannes Adam I of Liechtenstein, also known as "Hans the Rich." Hans Adam and his father, Karl Eusebius, had done much to enrich the Liechtenstein family, and also began its art collection. They had two palaces in Austria and extensive land holdings there and in what is now the Czech Republic. One thing this prince had lacked, however, was sovereign territory. When he went on to purchase Vaduz in 1712, Hans Adam also obtained another thing he wanted, a seat in the Assembly of Imperial Princes, made possible because Vaduz had the imperial immediacy.

In the same year, Hans Adam died, and his cousin Anton Flo-rian became head of the house of Liechtenstein. Anton was already an important figure in the emperor's court, but in 1719, Vaduz and Schellenberg were together raised to the status of imperial principality. And so Anton Florian I became the first prince of the newly rechristened Liechtenstein. Although it now had a new name, Liechtenstein was not an independent country, nor was the Liechtenstein family interested in obtaining independence for their principality. The Liechtensteins were loyal servants of the Habsburgs, the Holy Roman Emperors. Anton Florian served as their ambassador to the Papal Court in Rome, as prime minister, and as educator of the emperor's son Archduke Karl; and Florian's nephew Prince Josef Wenzel served as imperial ambassador to the sumptuous royal court of Louis XV in Paris. In fact, no head of the house of Liechtenstein set foot into his principality until 1842. Instead, a governor or administrator appointed by the prince governed Liechtenstein from Vaduz Castle.

Prince Johannes I of Liechtenstein was another loyal servant of the Habsburgs—so loyal, in fact, that he fought the man who gave Liechtenstein its independence from them. That man was Napoleon, who in 1805 allowed Johannes's son Karl to become prince of the independent Principality of Liechtenstein within the Confederation of the Rhine. After Johannes helped defeat Napoleon, the Congress of Vienna rescinded Liechtenstein's independence, and it reverted to a principality under the German Confederation. And Johannes took back his position as ruler from his son.

During the nineteenth century, life in Liechtenstein finally began to improve, both economically and politically. Poor little Vaduz's ship had finally come in, in the form of a wealthy foreign prince. Prince Alois II visited his territory in midcentury, and was appalled at his subjects' poverty. Among other benevolent actions, he financed the building of a wall to reduce Rhine river flooding. In the 1860s Liechtenstein got its first constitution, became independent, disarmed, and declared itself permanently neutral in foreign affairs. Independence had come somewhat unexpectedly,

Panoramic view of Liechtenstein.
LIECHTENSTEIN TOURISM.

when the German Confederation was broken up. And the prince still could see no reason to leave his beloved Vienna.

But the first half of the twentieth century was like a glass of cold water thrown in Liechtenstein's face. Although it was able to maintain its neutrality during the World War I, the country's economic links to one of the losers, Austria, proved costly. The market for its exports almost evaporated. Then, at the end of the war, the Liechtenstein family's royal patrons, the Habsburgs, were forced to abdicate in Austria. So Liechtenstein shifted its orientation toward Switzerland, and established an economic union with its western neighbor. Perhaps this was a more suitable union, since Switzerland also had a neutral foreign policy.

For a while, Liechtenstein's fortunes seemed to be on the upswing. A new, more democratic constitution was adopted in 1921. In 1928, the new prime minister, Dr. Franz Josef Hoop, established a new economic policy, still partly in effect today.

Liechtenstein lowered its taxes and invited foreign investments on the easiest terms. For a while it was actually selling Liechtenstein citizenship to anyone who would pay $5,500. The princely family did not draw revenue from the people, but was really contributing to the economy as a kind of local benefactor.

This liberal welcoming of foreigners for a fee would have consequences in the next decade. While the government was prospering, many Liechtensteiners had lost their jobs in the worldwide Depression of the 1930s. Some found jobs in neighboring Austria, and there they were exposed to the new National Socialist or Nazi movement, popular even outside Germany. Now, among those who had purchased Liechtenstein citizenship was a number of Jews. Finding life very difficult in Austria and Germany, some had moved to Liechtenstein, including two brothers by the name of Rotter. They had run a theater in Berlin, which went bankrupt—under false pretenses, according to some Nazi paramilitarists. With the help of a few Nazi sympathizers within Liechtenstein, they kidnapped the Rotters in 1933, intending to bring them back to Germany. The brothers tried to escape and, in the struggle, one of the kidnappers' cars overturned, killing one brother and his wife. The other brother succeeded in escaping, and returned to Liechtenstein. A Liechtenstein hotel owner spent two years in jail for abetting the plot. Oddly, he was allowed to bring his piano into his jail cell.

With Nazi propaganda streaming in from across the border with Austria, and nationalistic calls for the unification of all the Germanic peoples into one nation, it is a wonder that the Nazi movement in Liechtenstein remained as small as it did. Microstate though it was, Liechtenstein was an attractive target for incorporation into the Reich. While Liechtenstein would have been difficult for the Swiss to defend, it could serve as a convenient launching pad for any attack on Switzerland across the Rhine. Capturing Liechtenstein would have also meant sweet revenge on the small number of refugees who had fled there to escape Nazi persecution.

Although the Liechtenstein family had renovated Vaduz Castle, they were still living in Austria. They didn't seem to be paying much attention to world political events, until they were overtaken by them. On March 12, 1938, Germany annexed Austria, in the so-called "Anschluss." Within a few days, the mayor of the Austrian border town of Feldkirch was already welcoming the German army and renaming the town square after Hitler. On March 15, Prime Minister Hoop spoke to a special session of the Diet, painting a grim picture of the new danger to Liechtenstein's independence. Then, a week after the Anschluss took place, Prince Franz's nephew, Franz Josef, mysteriously left Austria and moved into Vaduz Castle for a "lengthy sojourn." Next, the Diet passed a resolution proclaiming their loyalty to the prince, expressing their wish for closer relations with Switzerland, and establishing a coalition government. This coalition would last into the 1970s.

With no army, and given its tiny size, Liechtenstein's desire to keep its independence indeed seemed precarious. Dr. Hoop embarked on a mission to Bern and then to Berlin to solve this problem through diplomacy. In Bern, he tried to get assurances from the Swiss either to defend Liechtenstein in case of German attack or else to allow it to join Switzerland as a canton. In Berlin, he wanted assurances from Hitler that he would respect Liechtenstein's neutrality as he had promised to do for Switzerland. While no promises were forthcoming, Dr. Hoop's diplomatic skills may have saved Liechtenstein. No one can tell what actually convinced Hitler that Anschluss with Liechtenstein was "impracticable." Typically of this kind of diplomatic mission, discussions were kept secret, and the ostensible reason for Hoop's visit to Berlin was to discuss some issues with its new neighbor, greater Germany, arising from the fact that Liechtenstein's judicial system still had been tied in some ways to Austria's.

A Resident Ruler

At the end of March, Prince Franz of Liechtenstein relinquished his absentee rule from Austria in favor of his nephew Franz Josef, now living in Vaduz. At the stroke of a pen, Liechtenstein went from a kind of fiefdom to a normal constitutional monarchy. The very next year, a prince of Liechtenstein opened parliament for the first time in history. There was much speculation on the reasons that the prince finally moved to the land he was ruling, including the fact that the elderly Franz's wife was of Jewish extraction. In any case, Franz died in the summer, and Franz Josef was ceremonially sworn in during the late spring of 1939.

However, a couple of months before this accession ceremony, there was an attempted Nazi coup d'état in Vaduz. On March 28, 1939, about eighty Liechtenstein Nazis occupied the bridge over the Rhine at the town of Schaan, and were heading for Vaduz to take over government buildings there. But the plotters were routed by the tiny police force plus another group of Liechtensteiners, led by the Diet president, and armed with pitchforks, scythes, and fence slats. Many believed that the directive for this putsch came from Feldkirch, Austria, but it seems like a half-hearted attempt, to say the least. In any case, a few days later, about 95 percent of Liechtensteiners signed a petition similar to the Diet's previous declaration, pledging loyalty to the prince and favoring independence, but preferring the economic union with Switzerland over Germany.

Some Liechtensteiners later volunteered and fought in the German SS, and they were put in jail after the war. But the danger of involvement in the Second World War was over before the war started. Liechtenstein's neutrality was respected and it suffered no damage, despite the allied bombing of Feldkirch. The war was no fun, however, as rationing was imposed, and a flood of refugees spilled over Liechtenstein's border at war's end.

After World War II, Liechtenstein began taking on its modern shape, as a highly industrialized microstate with a well-developed banking sector. Franz Josef II, the first prince to live in the country, and his prime minister, Dr. Hoop, guided the country through this transition. In 1984, Franz Josef handed over the reigns of the state to his son, Hans Adam II. As a trained economist, Hans Adam II handled big capital projects, while the day-to-day affairs were handled by the Diet.

In 1989 Hans Adam II became prince in his own right, and in the next year it happened that Liechtenstein's long-standing application for membership in the United Nations was approved. In 1995 Liechtenstein was admitted into the European Economic Area and also the World Trade Organization. These memberships had been strongly advocated by the prince, and in that same year, a Liechtenstein judge suggested that such actions of the prince be subject to judicial review. The prince responded by threatening to dismiss the judge. The judge replied that he might in turn bring the matter before the European Court of Human Rights.

This was the beginning of a kind of power struggle between the prince and other parts of the government—especially the Diet. Apparently several issues had been bubbling beneath the surface between the monarch and his parliament and have now boiled over. The main dispute has been over the prince's proposed amended constitution, which "clarifies" certain sections in favor of the prince. An example is the prince's desire to nominate judges and to have the Diet approve them, rather than the other way around, which was the tradition. Another dispute is the prince's wish to build a proper museum to display his extensive art collection, on which the two parties can't seem to come to an agreement. At present, you can see a part of the collection housed in the new Kunstmuseum, a modern building in black stone and glass.

In the debate, the prince suggested that he and his family might move away from Liechtenstein if the people could not accept the monarchy on his terms. He referred to the wealth that might go with him if he were to leave. Would the country would be allowed keep the name Liechtenstein in such an event, or would he take away his family's name, too? Poor little Vaduz, whose ship came in when Hans Adam the Rich bought the country so many years ago, could see that ship sail away with Hans Adam II at the helm, as it says good-bye to its last two centuries of good fortune.

In March 2003, a referendum approved the new constitution, presumably convincing the Liechtenstein family to stay. But in order to keep their prince and his billions, Liechtensteiners may have made more concessions than they realize. Among the prince's new powers are the right to dismiss individual members of the government, the right to dismiss the entire government, and immunity from the country's constitutional court. The prince inserted a clause allowing for the possible abolition of the monarchy as a kind of counterbalance to all the new powers he was taking. But this was not enough to satisfy the Council of Europe, which considers the new constitution a step backward. Liechtenstein now risks being ejected from the Council and may have made itself insufficiently democratic to join the European Union if it ever desires to do so.

Visiting Liechtenstein

For now, Liechtenstein is still a prosperous country, probably the only one in the world that can afford guest workers from Switzerland. Visiting Liechtenstein may not be an inexpensive proposition, but there are several ways to make your money go further. Since this microstate is small, you can stay in a cheaper, less central location outside Vaduz without much inconvenience. Liechtenstein has a youth hostel, and there are several guesthouses where you can stay with a family in their private home. The other alternative is to stay in nearby Austria or Switzerland and take a quick bus ride to Liechtenstein. Of course there are plenty of comfortable full-priced hotels. Because Liechtenstein is not entirely mountainous, it is possible to rent a bike and make that your mode of transportation. There are specially marked routes to make biking more enjoyable. Because Liechtenstein is so small, you may even consider getting around by foot.

Cars and buses are the best motorized way to get to and around Liechtenstein. There is a train to Schaan, but Schaan is a local stop only. So it can be best to get a train ticket to Buchs, Switzerland or Feldkirch, Austria, and then take a bus to Vaduz. There is no airport in Liechtenstein, and the nearest big international airport is in Zurich, Switzerland. If you have a day to spend in Liechtenstein, you could see everything in Vaduz. Be sure to visit a tourist office when you arrive, because some attractions are open only by appointment. With more time, you could visit the attractions outside Vaduz. If you have a few days, you might want to spend some time in Triesenberg, with its distinctive Walser regional dialect and culture.

Some people visit Liechtenstein for its sporting facilities. There are the popular downhill and cross-country ski slopes of Malbun and Steg. There are also several hiking trails, some devoted to nature, others historic. Liechtensteiners are sports-minded, too, so there are plenty of bowling alleys and indoor and outdoor swimming pools. You can obtain more information about all of these at a tourist office.

Although Liechtenstein is situated in the Alps, it does not have a cold climate. The Föhn is a warm, dry wind blowing up from the Mediterranean to the Rhine river valley. It makes grape growing possible, and Liechtenstein produces about twenty-three thousand gallons of its own wine per year. Nearly the entire grape harvest is used for winemaking only. The Vaduzer is a fairly dry reddish-amber wine of the Pinot Noir type, the other popular Liechtenstein variety being Riesling. Groups can make an appointment for a wine tasting in a couple of wineries.

Liechtenstein cuisine is a mixture of Swiss and Austrian influences, as are other areas of culture. Meats such as sausage, wursts and schnitzel feature prominently in traditional eating. There are four interesting starch dishes: *rösti*, *hafaläb*, *käsknöpfle*, and *kratzete*. *Rösti* is a potato dish in the shape of a pancake, and *kratzete* are flour pancakes. *Hafaläb* and *käsknöpfle* are types of dumplings. Liechtenstein has no seacoast, but trout and other freshwater fish dishes are popular. Of course, everyday international items, such as pizza and Asian foods, are popular as well.

One way to start your visit to Liechtenstein might be to have a look at the relief model of the principality on display in the Landesmuseum in Vaduz. That would give you an idea of the layout of the land. There is also a miniature train tour of Vaduz. Some of the clean and attractive industries, such as the dental and false teeth center in Schaan, will give you a tour of their factories, usu-ally by appointment only.

The princely art collection is not the only place you will find artistry in Liechtenstein. Crafts such as pottery, sculpture, and carvings produced by Liechtensteiners are among the best in the Alps. There is a ceramics works in Nendeln in the north, where you can see pottery being made or purchase a souvenir.

Nor is the Liechtensteiner polka the only piece of music to come out of this microstate. The world-famous Romantic com-poser, Josef Gabriel Rheinberger, was the son of the prince's trea-surer. The house in Vaduz where he was born now contains the Liechtenstein School of Music, and you can pay your respects to the monument to him just outside. Perhaps due to the Austrian influence, Liechtensteiners are rather good musicians. They have two operetta companies, and numerous choirs and marching bands.

Liechtensteiners are good musicians, and they comprise numerous choirs and marching bands.

LIECHTENSTEIN TOURISM.

Some of those bands can be heard each year on the National Day celebrations on August 15. This day, the feast of the Assumption, is also known as Prince's Day, as it falls the day before the late Prince Franz Josef II's birthday. Every year the prince invites everyone in the country—including visitors—to the grounds of Vaduz Castle for a party. Many people dress up in traditional costumes, and there are reenactments of the legends of folklore on the princely grounds. At night, there are fireworks. This would be an ideal day on which to the visit the principality.

And now you can do more than visit Liechtenstein—you can rent it! The state tourism agency has set up a program where a business can replace the signs on many buildings with its own corporate logo, making it appear that they have "taken over" the entire country for their business meeting. For about $500 per person in groups of up to twelve hundred people, a company can have exclusive access to the country's hotels, restaurants, sports facilities and meeting places. Upon the announcement of the program, Liechtenstein became the butt of some joking in the media, which called it "rent-a-count," even though the princely family does not officially participate in the program. "Rent-a-state" and the row over the constitution are a far cry from the staid days of the 1960s, when the prince's father considered a conference of microstates set up by his tourism minister to be an embarrassment to the nation.

Basic Data

Official Name	Principality of Liechtenstein
Official Native Name	Fürstentum Liechtenstein
Nickname	The Business Microstate
Origin of Name	Anton Florian of Liechtenstein
Capital	Vaduz
Origin/Meaning of Name	Valley of the Germans (Teutons)

Official Language(s)	German
Motto	*Klar und fest*
Motto in English	Clear and firm (Prince)
Nationality	Liechtensteiner
Area in Square Miles	62
Latitude	47.8° north
Longitude	9.31° east
Time Zone	GMT+1
Big Sister	Switzerland, Austria
Big Sister Guidebooks to Use	Switzerland
Convenient Cities	Zurich, Innsbruck
GDP	$825 million (1999 estimate)
GDP per capita	$25,000 (1999 estimate)
Major Exports	Small specialty machinery, dental products, stamps, hardware, pottery
Present Currency	Swiss franc
Exchange Rate / Dollar	1.6303
Population	33,145 (July 2003 estimate)
Annual Population Growth	0.9% (2003 estimate)
Type of Government	Hereditary constitutional monarchy
Head of State	Prince Hans Adam II von und zu Liechtenstein
Head of Government	Prime minister, Otmar Hasler
Name of Parliament	Diet (Landtag)
Date of Constitution	1921
National Holiday	Assumption Day
National Holiday Date	August 15
Year of Foundation	1699

Year of Independence	1719
Womens' Suffrage	1984
UN Membership	1990
Diocese	Since 1997 Vaduz, formerly Chur (Switzerland)
Patron Saint	St. Lucius
Telephone Code	423
Internet Suffix	.li
Radio Stations	4
Television Channels	0
Official Web Site	http://www.liechtentein.li
Wine	Vaduzer, red burgundy type
Flag	Two equal horizontal bands of blue (top) and red with a gold crown on the hoist side of the blue band

SOURCES: U.S. Central Intelligence Agency: *The World Factbook, 2003*; *Worldmark Encyclopedia of Nations*; *Europa World Yearbook*; *Political Handbook of the World*.

National Holidays

New Year's Day	January 1
St. Berchtold's Day	January 2
Epiphany	January 6
Candlemas	February 2
Shrove Tuesday	Early February
St. Joseph's Day	March 19
Good Friday	Friday before Easter
Easter Monday	Monday after Easter
Labor Day	May 1

Ascension	40 days after Easter
Whit Monday	Monday after Pentecost
Corpus Christi	Late May / early June
Assumption—Prince's Day— National Day	August 15
Nativity of Our Lady	September 8
All Saints' Day	November 1
Immaculate Conception	December 8
Christmas Eve	December 24
Christmas Day	December 25
St. Stephen's Day	December 26
New Year's Eve	December 31

Major Dates in Liechtenstein's History

800 BC	Liechtenstein colonized by Etruscan-related Rhaetians
15 BC	Liechtenstein conquered by Romans
350	St. Luzius (St. Lucius) brings Christianity to Liechtenstein
1396	Ex-county Vaduz gets Imperial Immediacy (*Reichsunmittlebarkeit*, subject to Emperor alone)
1719	Austrian family Liechtenstein creates Liechtenstein from the county Vaduz plus the barony Schellenburg, under the Holy Roman Empire
1806	Liechtenstein is brought into the Rhine Confederation by Napoleon
1815	Liechtenstein enters the German Confederation
1862	Liechtenstein gets its first constitution
1866	Liechtenstein becomes independent
1868	Liechtenstein declares permanent neutrality

1918	Liechtenstein breaks ties with Austria-Hungary; customs, foreign affiliations are linked to Switzerland
1921	Liechtenstein gets new and democratic constitution
1939	Liechtenstein escapes World War II
1990	Liechtenstein joins UN

Foods

Food Name	Type	English Name	Ingredients
Käsknöpfle	General	Cheese dumplings	Dumplings or noodles baked in a casserole with cheese, sautéed onions, and butter
Hafaläb	General	Fried bagels	Dough boiled then dried, fried in butter
Schwingerhörnli	General	Noodles	Filling pasta dish available in winter
Rösti / Alplerrösti	General	Shredded potatoes	Potato pancake with bacon fried in butter
Kratzete mit Apfelmus	General	Pancake	Pancake with applesauce
Bauernwurst	General	Farmer wurst	Coarse sausage with mustard seeds and marjoram

Schwartenmagen	General	Black stomach	Type of head cheese with diced pork and natural spices in a gelatin base
Törkarebl / Ribel	General	Polenta	Porridge/ dumpling mix of corn flour, milk, water, fried in butter
Rauchteller	Entrée	Smoked plate	Cold plate of smoked meats
Geschnetzelte Schweinsleber mit Rösti	Entrée	Sliced liver with *rösti*	Sliced pork liver with *rösti*
Geschnetzeltes Schweinefleisch	Entrée	Sliced pork	Thinly sliced pork with onions
Buretopf	Dessert	Fruit compote	Apricots, pears or plums in Kirsch

Places to Visit

Name and Description	Town	Region	Year
Church Hillock—where Liechtenstein was born in 1699	Bendern	North	1280
Ceramics Works—production and sales	Nendeln	North	
Excavated ruins of a Roman villa	Nendeln	North	
Ruggeller Riet—nature reserve of rare animals and plants	Ruggell	North	

Ruins of upper and lower burg of Schellenberg plus Russian war monument	Schellenberg	North	
Museum of Rural Homes	Schellenberg	North	
Theater am Kirchplatz— plays, concerts, ballet, pantomime, etc.	Schaan	Mid	
St. Laurentius Church plus Railroad Station—patron saint of Liechtenstein	Schaan	Mid	
Museum of Calculators	Schaan	Mid	
Schloss Vaduz (prince's castle)	Vaduz	Mid	1150
Rathausplatz with town hall	Vaduz	Mid	
Landesmuseum with relief model of principality	Vaduz	Mid	
Skiing museum—100 years of skiing history	Vaduz	Mid	
Old Walser settlement—oldest Walser church (14th century)	Vaduz	Mid	
Ruins of Wildschloss	Vaduz	Mid	
Postal Museum—Engländerbau	Vaduz	Mid	
Rotes Haus (Red House) with wine press	Vaduz	Mid	1400
House of and monument to composer J. G. Rheinberger	Vaduz	Mid	
National Art Museum— Kunstmuseum Liechtenstein	Vaduz	Mid	
Citytrain—miniature train for tour of Vaduz	Vaduz	Mid	
Wine cellars of the prince of Liechtenstein (reservation necessary)	Vaduz	Mid	

Löwen Inn—oldest guesthouse in Liechtenstein	Vaduz	Mid	1380
Government Building—one building for all of Liechtenstein's government	Vaduz	Mid	1903
Castle Gutenberg	Balzers	South	1250
Ski resorts of Malbun and Steg	Malbun	South	
Chairlift from Malbun to Sareis	Malbun	South	
Walser Heimatmuseum— history of Walser people	Triesenberg	South	
Walser Settlement—old Walser homes, view of Switzerland	Triesenberg	South	1250

Luxembourg

BELGIUM

GERMANY

•Troisvierges

Diekirch•

Mertert•
Grevenmacher•

LUXEMBOURG✪

•Differdange
•Esch
•Dudelange

FRANCE

Luxembourg
The Giant Microstate

The world's only grand duchy is also the grandest of the microstates of Europe. Although a bit smaller than Rhode Island, the smallest American state, Luxembourg is large enough to have two climate zones and multiple railway lines. It has many of the things only normally associated with bigger countries, not with microstates. Luxembourg is the only microstate whose vernacular distinguished itself from similar neighboring dialects and became respected as a national language. And no other microstate besides Malta has its own airline and airport. (Malta's language and air transportation really stem from its isolation, not from its size.)

As a matter of fact, Luxembourg would not have been a microstate at all, if it hadn't lost so much territory over the years before its independence. Originally, Luxembourg was about four times bigger than it is today—in total, about half the size of the next biggest European country, Slovenia. But because of three different partitions, which removed three-quarters of its original territory, today Luxembourg is a microstate, not just a ministate. Luxembourg was the only microstate to be a founding member of the United Nations and the European Union. Perhaps its previous size—comparable to its neighbors, Belgium and Holland—convinced people to take it more seriously than they did the other microstates.

Inside Vianden Castle.
LUXEMBOURG TOURIST BOARD.

Vianden Castle.
LUXEMBOURG TOURIST BOARD.

The Good Old Days

Luxembourg is named for a Roman fortress, Lucilinburhuc, meaning "little fortress." The fortress was built on a rocky out- cropping above the Alzette River called the Bock. It was pur- chased by Count Siegfried of the Ardennes in the year 963, when for the first time this part of the early Holy Roman Empire became a political entity, a county. Siegfried also built a new castle on the Bock, which he called Letzelburg. From this, Lux- embourg-Ville developed. Siegfried's successors, the counts of Luxembourg, ruled for two hundred years until the male line ran out and the emperor awarded the land to Henri IV of Namur.

The Middle Ages were, in a sense, the glory days of Luxem- bourg, for during this period Luxembourg grew to its maximum size, and four Holy Roman Emperors were selected from the Luxembourg family. Henri of Namur's daughter Ermesinde, unlike her father, would become one of Luxembourg's greatest rulers. As it happened, Ermesinde was not even supposed to have been born. Her father had been childless, and separated from her mother for years. He had already designated his nephew Baldwin as his heir. But in 1186 some Guelf (papal) supporters convinced Henri to disinherit Ghibelline (secularist) supporter Baldwin by reconciling with his wife and having a child. Henri promised Ermesinde's hand to the count of Champagne, hoping to ensure his family's right to Namur. But the emperor unfailingly sup- ported Baldwin, so the count of Champagne gave up the game and went off to Jerusalem, marrying someone else. It was up to Henri to recover his child Ermesinde, who at age four was already in the hands of the count's men in Champagne.

Ermesinde's father died when she was only ten years old, but not before arranging for her to marry Theobald, count of Bar. Arranged marriages of course were the custom of the time, and later Ermesinde herself would not be above choosing a husband for mainly political reasons. Theobald was quite a good choice, as he helped Ermesinde maintain her claim to Luxembourg, despite the Salic laws against women inheriting titles. Luxembourg

Luxembourg-Ville, view of the twin spires of the Cathedral of Our Lady of Luxembourg.

LUXEMBOURG TOURIST BOARD.

should have reverted to the Holy Roman Empire, but Theobald cleverly maneuvered between the Guelfs and the Ghibellines and actually recovered some possessions that Ermesinde's father had lost. Before Theobald died in 1213, he and Ermesinde had four children, all of whom died before 1215, except a daughter, Elizabeth.

As a widow, Ermesinde would have lost Luxembourg to Theobald's son from his previous marriage, but she preserved her control over Luxembourg by marrying Waleran, the Lord of Montjoie, only three months after Theobald's death. Ermesinde's daughter from the first marriage profited from her mother's remarriage, too, marrying Waleran's son. Ermesinde and Waleran ruled Luxembourg jointly for eleven years. They had three children, and they managed to arrange the right combination of marriages and alliances to keep the inheritance of Luxembourg intact for their eldest son Henri. Henri was not yet of age when his father died and, with a lot more personal experience behind her, Ermesinde was able to take the reins of government for herself.

Ermesinde's regime was unlike those of her father or her stepson. Instead of going to war, she used peaceful tactics to her own advantage. She made deals with her subjects, offering them civil liberties and limited self-rule in exchange for territories, cash payments, and the use of castles during wartime. Her benign rule gained her the loyalty of her subjects, in the face of competing monarchs who were less well loved. She granted charters of freedom to the people of various towns, and a frieze depicting her handing over one such charter to the people of Luxembourg-Ville can be seen at the Cercle Municipal, which houses the tourist offices. Ermesinde thought that certain families had become too powerful, so she created new political institutions that replaced hereditary positions with non-nobles. Some of these reforms outlasted her reign for centuries. Another legacy of Ermesinde was a tripling of the area of Luxembourg.

Ermesinde should have given up her reign when her son Henri came of age, but she ruled until she died in 1247, aged sixty-one. Henri apparently didn't mind, for after his mother's death he helped create a kind of cult around her. He endowed the monastery at Clairfontaine—now in Belgium—where she is buried. And he encouraged the belief that Ermesinde was the second founder of Luxembourg after Siegfried. This belief is still popular today. In 1308 Ermesinde's great-grandson, Henry VII, was the first Luxembourger to become Holy Roman Emperor. His son and successor, John the Blind, had the motto *Ich dien,* "I serve." Having lost his sight, John nevertheless took part in the battle of Crécy, where he died. John's motto was adopted by the victor in this battle, Edward III of England, and he passed it on to all successive Princes of Wales, who still retain it on their shields. John's son Charles IV was the second of the Luxembourg Holy Roman Emperors. He raised the status of Luxembourg to a duchy. Two more dukes of Luxembourg became emperors, but this was the end of the glory days of Luxembourg.

The Bad Old Days

Soon Luxembourg fell on hard times. The duchy was sold several times to pay off debts, until it was taken over by the French under Philip the Good. It passed between Spain and France a couple of times as well. The Thirty Years' War and the plague both devastated Luxembourg. In the Peace of the Pyrenees, between France and Spain, Luxembourg lost about one-tenth of its southernmost territory to France.

By 1713, Luxembourg went back to the Holy Roman Empire under the Habsburgs of Austria, joined to Belgium and the Netherlands. Peace lasted until the French Revolution and Napoleon I, when Luxembourg briefly became a French department, that is, part of France. The Congress of Vienna liberated Luxembourg, raised it to the status of grand duchy, and put it under the protection of the German Confederation. Unfortunately, it also partitioned Luxembourg for a second time, giving about one-third of its eastern territory to Prussia.

Independence

It is difficult to pinpoint the exact date when Luxembourg became an independent state. Because it happened in gradual steps, perhaps it's best to say that Luxembourg was born sometime in the nineteenth century. First, the Congress of Vienna freed Luxembourg of Spanish, French, and Austrian domination in 1815, putting it under the Kingdom of the Netherlands, which included Belgium. Though Luxembourg was considered a personal possession of the Dutch king, it was also part of the German Confederation, and Prussian troops were stationed in Luxembourg-Ville.

Then in 1830 Belgium revolted and separated itself from the Netherlands. A settlement was reached in 1839 awarding most of the microstate to Belgium as the new internal province of Luxembourg, and bringing about Luxembourg's third partition. Most of this western part spoke French, so now Luxembourg was an entirely Luxembourgish-speaking country. Furthermore, it had been granted autonomy from the Netherlands.

When the German Confederation broke up in 1866, the Dutch king decided to sell Luxembourg to France. The German kaiser was irked about this, and threatened war, so the Dutch king retracted the offer. The next year the fate of Luxembourg was settled by the Treaty of London, making Luxembourg an independent nation, with its neutrality guaranteed by each of the Great Powers. The Prussian troops were withdrawn from Luxembourg-Ville, but Luxembourg itself was nominally still under the king of the Netherlands. Luxembourg was also granted a foundation charter. In 1890, the Salic law prevented the newly crowned Queen Wilhelmina of Holland from inheriting the Grand Duchy of Luxembourg from her father, so a separate line of the Nassau family began to rule it, cutting the last ties to the Netherlands. Finally, Luxembourg was a completely independent nation.

World Wars

If you get the feeling that the Salic law was invoked more as an opportunity to create a separate Luxembourg dynasty than anything else, you may not be far from the truth. The very next grand duke died without male heirs, but in 1912 his daughter, Marie-Adelaide, was allowed to succeed him as Luxembourg's first grand duchess. It may have not been the wisest of choices. Marie-Adelaide was a bit of an interventionist into Luxembourg politics, which by then were understood to be separate from the ceremonial affairs of a monarch. World War I would only cause more resentment, and Marie-Adelaide was accused of collaboration with the Germans, who occupied her country from its outbreak.

Incidentally, the very first military action in that war occurred in the northern Luxembourg city of Troisvierges.

It may be that much of Marie-Adelaide's alleged collaboration was fabricated, such as the telegraph she supposedly sent the kaiser "praying God for the success of the German cause." But under the pressure of occupation, she did receive the kaiser during his visit to Luxembourg. Luxembourgers suffered from food shortages during the war and, by the war's end, they had had enough of their monarch. There had already been a couple of ominous votes in parliament showing a great loss of confidence in her among her government, when in 1919 noisy demonstrations were held by people advocating the abolition of the monarchy and the establishment of a Republic of Luxembourg. These demonstrations were easily ended by General Pershing and his victorious American army, but other issues were looming. Luxembourg was still a young country, and Belgium was pressing the allies to allow it to annex the rest of Luxembourg. Meanwhile, France and others were resentful of Luxembourg's apparent collaboration. So Marie-Adelaide abdicated in favor of her sister Charlotte. Then a referendum was held asking whether Luxembourgers favored their new grand duchess, the former one, a republic, or unification with France or Belgium. Seventy-seven percent voted for Charlotte, and this result was accepted by the allied peace conference.

Charlotte was to be much more successful than her sister, who went into exile in an Italian convent and died at age twenty-nine. Although Luxembourg maintained its neutral policy again before World War II, it was ready to deal with another German invasion. When news came of German troops approaching the border, Grand Duchess Charlotte and her government fled to France before dawn on May 10, 1940. This time, Paris was not able to provide refuge from the invasion, so they went on to London through France, Spain, and Portugal. Although the grand duchess did not share in her subjects' suffering, at least she did not appear to be collaborating, making frequent broadcasts to her people from across the English Channel. Her husband and son joined the British armed services and fought to retake their country.

Luxembourg suffered the same hardships under the Nazis as the French, such as forced labor and deportation of Jews and others to death camps. But because they were a Germanic people, Luxembourgers were expected to become Germans as well. They were conscripted into the German army. The Luxembourgish language was banned. Even personal given names had to be changed to standard German ones, and if a family name had been changed to a French version, it had to revert to its German one. Confident that pan-Germanism would catch on in Luxembourg, the occupying Germans held a couple of surveys that didn't go their way and had to be abandoned. One asked Luxembourgers to list their nationality as either French or German. True to their national motto, "We want to remain what we are," 97 percent of them responded by writing in "Luxembourgish." The Nazis also circulated a petition for the "reunion" of Luxembourg into the Reich. Those civil servants who did not sign were removed from office, deprived of their pensions, or even shipped off to concentration camps. Nevertheless, the results must not have been satisfactory, because they were not published. Regardless of the patriotism of its natives, Luxembourg was annexed into Germany in the summer of 1942. The resulting protests and general strikes were punished with arrests and deportations.

One of the biggest and most important battles of World War II took place in northern Luxembourg, after the country had already been liberated. Germany's last gasp took place in the Ardennes mountains in what the Americans called the Battle of the Bulge. The German army attacked a poorly defended section of the front line, creating a bulge and almost breaking through, with heavy loss of American soldiers. Many castles and other treasures of Luxembourg's heritage were damaged there and had to be rebuilt after the war. Several war memorials and museums commemorate such battles, as well as the cemetery for American soldiers donated by the people of Luxembourg, where General Patton is buried. Luxembourgers were enduringly grateful for their liberation, and have since maintained what have probably been the most

Esch-sur-Sûre, an idyllic market-town in the Luxembourg Ardennes.
LUXEMBOURG TOURIST BOARD.

friendly relations with the United States of all the microstates of Europe.

A few years after the war was over, an American diplomatic appointment to Luxembourg created a stir, and, curiously, another such appointment caused another stir almost exactly fifty years later. The first appointment was of socialite Perle Mesta to be head minister at the U.S. mission in Luxembourg-Ville. Mesta was a strong supporter and fundraiser for the Democratic Party and a fabulous party hostess on the Washington scene. She was only the third American woman appointed to such a high diplomatic position, and her story inspired Irving Berlin to write the musical, *Call Me Madam*. Incidentally, the name of the musical's fictional microstate, "Lichtenburg," was inspired by the two real microstates, Liechtenstein and Luxembourg. Although her nomination sailed through the Foreign Relations Committee, one U.S. senator—a political enemy of President Truman—tried unsuccessfully to filibuster the appointment, saying, "I have no objection to a woman holding high office, if she is qualified, but merely being a woman does not qualify her." The second appointment was of James C. Hormel, a philanthropist and advocate of civil rights, to the post of U.S. ambassador to Luxembourg. This time, several senators stopped the nomination from even reaching a vote in 1999, because Hormel is openly gay. The sexual orientation of Hormel did not insult or scandalize Luxembourgers, as feared; the senators were really playing up to the neoconservative sentiments of some of their own constituents. Perle Mesta's appointment had been less welcome in Luxembourg than James Hormel's, because she was a political appointee without diplomatic experience. Finally, President Clinton had to resort to a "recess appointment" to get Hormel through while the senate was not in session.

Visiting Luxembourg

Touristically as well, Luxembourg is the most comparable of the microstates to larger states. Three of the five regions of Luxembourg are often compared to other areas of Europe. The northern mountainous zone of Luxembourg, the Oesling, is also known as "Little Switzerland." The eastern, wine-tasting area on the banks of the Moselle is also known for its water sports, and it's sometimes called the "Little Riviera." And because of the rocky fortification on the Bock, Luxembourg-Ville has the nickname "Gibraltar of the North." The other two regions are the industrial southwest, now reviving itself with museums and pedestrian malls, and the central Mullerthal section, where you will find the town of Echternacht, the religious foundation of the country.

Cathedral to the Blessed Virgin (1613) in Luxembourg-Ville.
THOMAS M. ECCARDT.

Luxembourg-Ville, view over the Grund suburb.
LUXEMBOURG TOURIST BOARD.

If you like good food, you will love Luxembourg, which benefits from the cuisine of its neighbors. It is often said that Luxembourg food has French quality and comes in German portions. Most recently its cooking has been influenced by the large numbers of Portuguese immigrants. Per capita and per square mile as well, Luxembourg has more Michelin star-rated restaurants than any other country in the world. Its culinary trademarks are *judd mat gaarde-bounen* (smoked collar of pork with broad beans) and Ardennes ham. These are washed down with beer or the famous Moselle-district wines.

Luxembourg-Ville, Petrusse Valley.
THOMAS M. ECCARDT.

When you go to Luxembourg, your first stop will probably be the capital, Luxembourg-Ville. You can fly into Findel International Airport, northeast of the city, and get a bus to the train station. The station is in the newer section of the town, where you may find somewhat cheaper accommodations. By train, Luxembourg-Ville is quickly accessible from Brussels, Liege, Frankfurt, or Strasbourg. Luxembourg has recently signed an agreement with France to extend the high-speed TGV train, which will connect Luxembourg-Ville and Paris. Northwards and a good walk from the station is the old city, where most of the attractions are found. You will often find yourself crossing one of Luxembourg-Ville's 110 bridges that span the beautiful valleys of the Alzette or

Petrusse Rivers, which converge at the city. Pause a moment to take in the views of the city from the bridges and numerous other promontories.

Luxembourg's fortifications are the raison d'être of the entire city. Built up and dismantled several times over the years, they had their origin in founder Siegfried's castle. There are other remnants as well, plus the cavernous Bock casemates, a huge system of tunnels, now a highlight of most visits. According to legend, Siegfried married Melusina after agreeing to her mysterious request that he leave her alone for a full day each month. On that day she would disappear into her rooms in the casemates and would not reemerge until the next day. On one occasion, Siegfried gave into temptation and peeped through a keyhole. He saw his wife in the bathtub, with a large fishtail hanging out of the side. Of course, a mermaid like Melusina would certainly sense she was being observed, and she jumped out the window, returning forever to the river Alzette. If you stare into river long enough, you may see a beautiful girl's head or a fishtail pop out of the calm waters of the Alzette.

If you are not driving, you can easily get around Luxembourg by bus, by train, or even by boat. Should you have only a day to spend in Luxembourg, you will have to restrict yourself to the capital city. With a little more time, you could see the capital and then take a trip to another region. It would probably take you a week to thoroughly explore Luxembourg. Although it's possible to make day trips from Luxembourg-Ville, it's also enjoyable to stay in one of the smaller towns. You might enjoy a relaxing boat ride down the Moselle River in the wine district.

If you're interested in the European Union, you can visit the government complex on the Kirchberg Plateau just outside Luxembourg-Ville. Several departments of the European Commission are located there plus the European Investment Bank, Eurostat, and the European Court of Auditors. An increasingly more important arm of the EU, the European Court of Justice, is open to visitors. The other parts of the EU government are located in nearby Strasbourg and Brussels.

Luxembourg and the World

As an EU administrative center, Luxembourg's influence may seem out of proportion to its size. Luxembourgers have twice held the post of European Commission President—not even the giants Germany or Britain have done that. No wonder Luxembourg is the EU's most enthusiastic member. But this influence didn't start with the EU and doesn't end there. Luxembourgers created three major global corporations, and these are not "letter-box" companies headquartered there for tax purposes. The first was ARBED, now Arcelor, the steel corporation. The second was RTL, a broadcasting system, recently bought by Bertelsmann. RTL started out as the Luxembourg Radio Broadcasting Company, a privately owned corporation founded in 1931. Because its internal market was limited to half a million people, the company began transmitting radio and TV programs to other countries, with much success. Luxembourg's multilingual population undoubtedly proved an asset, and the fact that RTL's competition was government-controlled stations in other countries also helped make RTL a household name in much of Europe. RTL grew big enough to employ its own orchestra, another world-class organization. The third big corporation is the SES communications company, whose geostationary satellite serves Western Europe. Its control center is located in Betzdorf, Luxembourg, birthplace of Grand Duke Henri.

Luxembourg is also a significant player in the European Union, defending the interests of smaller countries. In addition to hosting the European Investment Bank, Luxembourg has major banking and securities industries of its own, and the major European banks have branches in Luxembourg-Ville. With its relatively small parliament a consensus can often be reached faster, and Luxembourg is often the first to conform its laws to new EU regulations, giving Luxembourg industries a head start in taking advantage of changes.

Betzdorf satelite dishes.
Luxembourg Tourist Board.

Having lost most of its historical territory to its neighbors, Luxembourg is now getting a kind of revenge. The grand duchy has become the hub of La Grande Region, a booming economic zone taking in neighboring parts of Belgium, France, and Germany. More than ninety thousand workers commute to Luxembourg daily in a mutually beneficial relationship: Luxembourg gets people to ease its tight labor market, and the surrounding region's unemployment rates are reduced. The regional authorities and Luxembourg even send joint trade delegations abroad to attract business to the entire area.

Basic Data

Official Name	Grand Duchy of Luxembourg
Official Native Name	Grousherzogdem Lëtzebuerg
Nickname	Giant Microstate
Origin of Name	The name of a castle, Lucilinburhuc, "little fortress"
Capital	Luxembourg-Ville
Origin/Meaning of Name	Luxembourg-Ville
Official Language(s)	Letzebuergisch
Motto	*Mir wëlle bleiwe wat mir sin / Ich dien* (motto of counts of Lux and prince of Wales)
Motto in English	We want to remain what we are / I serve
Nationality	Luxembourger
Area in Square Miles	998
Latitude	50° north
Longitude	6° east
Time Zone	GMT+1
Big Sister	Belgium
Big Sister Guidebooks to Use	Belgium and Luxembourg, Benelux
Convenient Cities	Liege, Brussels, Strassbourg
GDP	$21.94 billion (2002 estimate)
GDP per capita	$48,900 (2002 estimate)
Major Exports	Machinery and equipment, steel products, chemicals, rubber products, glass
Present Currency	Euro

Currency before Euro	Luxembourg franc (LuxF) tied to Belgian franc
Exchange Rate / Dollar	1.19
Population	454,157 (July 2003 estimate)
Annual Population Growth	1.23% (2003 estimate)
Type of Government	Constitutional monarchy
Head of State	Grand Duke Henri
Head of Government	Prime Minister Jean-Claude Juncker
Name of Parliament	Chamber of Deputies
Date of Constitution	1868
National Holiday	Former grand duke's birthday
National Holiday Date	June 23
Year of Foundation	963
Year of Independence	1867
Womens' Suffrage	1919
UN Membership	1945
Diocese	Luxembourg (archdiocese)
Patron Saint	St. Willibrord
Telephone Code	352
Internet Suffix	.lu
Radio Stations	13
Television Channels	5
Official Web Site	http://www.visitluxembourg.com/
Wine	Moselle wines: Ebling, Rivaner, Riesling
Flag	Three equal horizontal bands of red (top), white, and light blue

Sources: U.S. Central Intelligence Agency: *The World Factbook, 2003*; *Worldmark Encyclopedia of Nations*; *Europa World Yearbook*; *Political Handbook of the World*.

National Holidays

New Year's Day	January 1
Carnival	Just before Lent
Good Friday	Friday before Easter
Easter Monday	Monday after Easter
May Day (labor)	May 1
Ascension	40 days after Easter
Whit Monday	Monday after Pentecost
Corpus Christi	Late May / early June
National Day—	
Grand Duke's Birthday	June 23
Assumption Day	August 15
Luxembourg-Ville Kermesse	September 1
All Saints' Day	November 1
Christmas Day	December 25
St. Stephen's Day	December 26

Major Dates in Luxembourg's History

52 BC	Luxembourg becomes Roman territory
AD 600s	St. Willibrord helped bring Christianity to Luxembourg
963	Siegfried, count of Ardennes, establishes castle and founds Luxembourg as independent state
1308	Ruler of large fiefdom of Luxembourg becomes Henry VII, Holy Roman Emperor
1354	Henry's grandson, Charles IV, creates Duchy of Luxembourg

1443	Philip the Good of Burgundy seizes Luxembourg
1482	Luxembourg passes to house of Habsburg
1684	France controls Luxembourg
1697	Spain controls Luxembourg
1714	Austria controls Luxembourg
1795	Luxembourg becomes part of France
1797	Luxembourg ceded to Revolutionary France in Treaty of Campo Formio
1814	Congress of Vienna makes Luxembourg a grand duchy, part of German Confederation under the Netherlands (but largely self-governed)
1835	Official year of independence
1838	William I of the Netherlands gives Luxembourg autonomy
1839	Major part (Belgian province of Luxembourg) goes to Belgium
1848	Luxembourg gets constitution
1867	Luxembourg declared neutral territory by European powers in Treaty of London
1890	Luxembourg breaks from the Netherlands, because a queen (Wilhelmina) may not rule
1914	Luxembourg occupied by Germany
1921	Customs union with Belgium
1940	Luxembourg occupied by Germany
1945	Luxembourg joins UN
1948	Luxembourg joins Benelux
1949	Luxembourg joins NATO
1956	Luxembourg signs treaty of Rome, founds / joins EEC
1993	Luxembourg founds / joins European Union

Foods

Food Name	Type	English Name	Ingredients
Thuringer	General	Sausage	Spicy version of German bratwurst
Luxembourg ham	General	Ham	Smoke-cured uncooked ham resembling Italian prosciutto
Gromper Keeschelche	General	Potato pancakes	Deep-fried potato pancakes
Kach Keis	General	Luxembourg cooked cheese	Soft cheese spread (like Camembert)
Jambon d'Ardennes	General	Ardennes ham	Cold smoked ham with pickled onions
Fierkelsjhelli	Appetizer	Suckling pig in aspic	Pig bones, feet, and rind in a vegetable and herb jelly
Hong am Rèisleck	Entrée	Chicken in white wine	Chicken flambéed in cognac, in Riesling and cream sauce
Kuddelfleck	Entrée	Tripe	Tripe in a sauce of shallot, gherkins, and capers
Huesenziwwi	Entrée	Jugged hare	Hare marinated in a thick flambé sauce with cognac and mushrooms

Judd mat Gaardebou'nen	Entrée	Pork with broad beans	Smoked collar of pork with broad beans (Luxembourg national dish)
Hiecht mat Kraïderzooss	Entrée	Pike in green sauce	Boiled pike in a sauce of sorrel and chervil
Liewekniddelen mat Sauerkraut	Entrée	Liver meatballs with sauerkraut	Chopped liver balls, sauerkraut
Quetscheflued	Dessert	Plum tart	Plum tart
Verwurrelt Gedanken	Dessert	Random Thoughts	Shrove Tuesday cake
Kèiskuch	Dessert	Cheesecake	A cake topped with a cheese filling

Places to Visit

Name and Description	Neighborhood	Region
Bock casemates	Bock	Luxembourg-Ville
Place d'Armes and Place Guillaume II—two main city squares	Center of Luxembourg-Ville	Luxembourg-Ville
Chemin de la Corniche—Pedestrian Promenade	Chemin de la Corniche	Luxembourg-Ville
American military cemetary with statue of General George Patton	Hamm	Luxembourg-Ville

European Union Headquarters	Kirchberg Plateau	Luxembourg-Ville
National Museum of Art and History	Marche-aux-Poissons	Luxembourg-Ville
Casements of Luxembourg-Ville	Montée de Clausen	Luxembourg-Ville
Maquette de la Fortress (model of old city, 1804)	Place d'Armes	Luxembourg-Ville
Cathédrale Notre-Dame	Place de la Constitution	Luxembourg-Ville
View of Petrusse Valley and Luxembourg-Ville Bridges	Place de la Constitution	Luxembourg-Ville
Plateau du St. Esprit— panoramas of the city	Plateau du St. Esprit	Luxembourg-Ville
Museum of the History of Luxembourg-Ville	Rue du St. Esprit 14	Luxembourg-Ville
Casino Luxembourg (not a casino, but a venue for contemporary art exhibitions)	Rue Notre Dame 41	Luxembourg-Ville
Boat ride on the Moselle—provides view of vineyards, castles	Moselle River	Moselle
Route du Vin—connects wine villages along the Moselle	Moselle River Valley	Moselle
St. Willibrord's Benedictine Abbey	Echternach	Muellerthal

Chateau de Bourscheid—a thousand-year-old castle with a great view	Bourscheid	Oesling
Castle —with "Family of Man" photographs by Edward Steichen	Clervaux	Oesling
National Military Museum	Diekirch	Oesling
Municipal Museum— Roman mosaics	Diekirch	Oesling
Esch-sur-Sûre— ruined castle, picturesque village	Esch-sur-Sûre	Oesling
Victor Hugo Museum	Vianden	Oesling
Museum of Toys and Rustic Arts	Vianden	Oesling
Vianden Castle	Vianden	Oesling
Castle	Wiltz	Oesling
Museum of Arts and Ancient Crafts	Wiltz	Oesling
National Resistance Museum (WWII occupation)	Esch-sur-Alzette	Southwest

Gozo
• Rabat

Mediterranean
Sea

Comino

Malta

Rabat•

VALLETTA ✪

Marsaxlokk
•
Birżebbuġa•

Mediterranean
Sea

° Filfla

Malta:
Microstate in the Middle

Malta must be the most distinctive of the European micro-states. Like most of the world's non-European microstates, it is an island. It also happens that Malta is located in the exact center of the Mediterranean, from both a north-south and an east-west perspective. Unlike its fellow mainland European micro-states, Malta has no big sister—it does not use the language of a big neighbor. Unable to take advantage of transshipment of goods and the tax systems of adjacent countries, Malta is also the least wealthy of the European microstates. But Malta's beauty more than makes up for its economic position: a million tourists per year come for its sunny climate and its artistic and cultural trea-sures, not just for shopping or stamps.

The Republic of Malta actually consists of five islands: Malta, Gozo, and Comino, plus the tiny rocks of Filfla and Cominotto, which are uninhabited. Unlike the other European microstates, for most of its history Malta was occupied or colonized by foreign powers, and it became independent only in the 1960s.

If Malta had to be compared to any other place, that place would be Sicily, its closest neighbor. Both are relatively treeless, semitropical Mediterranean islands, less developed than main-land countries. Both have been strongly influenced by Arabian

Aerial view of Valetta's bays.
MALTA TOURIST OFFICE, NEW YORK.

Ship at Valetta.
MALTA TOURIST OFFICE, NEW YORK.

invaders, Italy, and the conservative Catholic Church. And both suffered the destruction of much of their medieval architecture in the earthquake of 1693. Situated at the crossroads of Europe, they clearly benefited from the cultures of many nations, reflected in the remains of their ancient buildings. They were in the middle of everything.

Malta's scenery is flat, without mountains—it is either barren pinkish limestone or else clayish soil with a few green shrubs or olive trees. Since most buildings in Malta were constructed of the native limestone, the built-up areas have the same pinkish color as the limestone plateaus. The Victoria lines are the main geological rift running east and west across the island. Because Malta lacks freshwater rivers and lakes, the Maltese must get their water from the sea, via an expensive desalinization process.

The island of Malta is about three times bigger than Gozo, but it has about ten times the population. As is usual in microstates, most of this population is concentrated around the urban center of Valletta, the capital. Situated on the northeastern coast, this conglomeration of cities also includes the more modern Sliema and the three cities of Senglea, Cospicua, and Vittoriosa, all centered around Valetta's harbors, plus the inland cities of Floriana, Paola, and Hamrun. Most people arrive through Malta's only airport, further inland, but arriving by ship provides you with a magnificent view of the harbors. As Malta is located midway between Europe and Africa, there is boat service from Sicily, Italy, and sometimes from Libya or Tunisia. If you visit quieter Gozo, you must go by ferry or helicopter.

Since there are no railways, you must travel around Malta and Gozo by car or bus. The bus service is good but, like cars, buses are subject to traffic jams, especially during the summer tourist season. Biking or motorbiking could be useful alternatives. Roads on Malta go in all directions, and also along most of the coast, but the roads of Gozo all radiate from its biggest city, Victoria (or Rabat). If you have only one day in Malta, you can spend all your time in the metropolis that includes Valletta. Boat tours of the harbors of Valletta provide an interesting overview. Another overview could be "The Malta Experience," a forty-minute sound and slide show playing daily in the former Hospital of the Order of St. John. If you have two days, visit the old inland capital of Mdina and also Rabat. In a few days to a week, you could enjoy all that Malta and Gozo have to offer. That means beaches, ancient and prehistoric temples and ruins, fishing villages, and, during a summer weekend, one of the many *festas*. Longer-term residents can do what the natives do—take a holiday in Sicily.

Malta's biggest industry is tourism, so there are hotels and restaurants galore. Fortunately, Malta is not a mere resort, but a nation, and there is a full range of prices available. This includes guesthouses with restaurants providing full and half board. Maltese food is similar to Italian, and the natives begin their meals with pasta or a minestra.

The beaches on Malta are located in the northeast, although the best one is considered to be Ghajn Tuffieha on the northwest coast. All are accessible by car or bus, but it can be rewarding to scramble down cliff sides to the less crowded ones. The best-preserved fishing village is Marsaxlokk, where Maltese fisherman still set out to find the lampuka fish, to be grilled, poached, or baked into pies.

The second Maltese island, Gozo, was never as fortified as Malta, and as a result, historically it suffered pillaging and much of its population was taken away to slavery. What Gozo lacks in architecture, it makes up for in agriculture. Most of the grapes made into Maltese wine are produced there. Life is slower in Gozo, but there is still much to see. You can get an overview in the multimedia show, "Gozo 360°." The Ggantija ("Giant") Neolithic Temples, the best preserved of Malta's ancient structures, are said to be the oldest in the world.

You can get a complete list of things to see from the tourist information offices in Valletta and Victoria on Gozo, or on the Internet. And there are several guidebooks and histories devoted exclusively to Malta (see bibliography).

Braġjoli (beef olives). This dish consists of a thin slice of beef wrapped around a stuffing of breadcrumbs, chopped bacon, hard-boiled eggs, and herbs, braised in red wine.

The Sovereign Military and Hospitaller Order of St. John of Jerusalem, Rhodes, and Malta

During the first half of the second millennium, Malta found itself in the middle of a struggle between Islam and Christianity. In 1090, after the Normans had driven the Saracens out of Malta, the Crusades began. In Jerusalem, the Order of St. John was formed to take care of sick pilgrims. Eventually they called themselves "knights" and took on the military role of protecting Christianity in the Holy Land. By 1291, they were defeated by Muslims and took refuge on the island of Rhodes, where they practiced piracy on passing Ottoman ships. By 1522 the Turks had had enough piracy, and the son of Süleyman the Magnificent drove the Knights off Rhodes. Fortunately for the Knights, he let them leave with honor, bringing all their records and some of their treasures with them. After a few years of wandering and petitioning various European rulers for a homeland, they were given the island of Malta by the Holy Roman Emperor, Charles V of Spain. As a symbolic payment, the emperor of Spain and the viceroy of Sicily were each to receive one falcon per year. These birds inspired the statuette in the famous book and movie, *The Maltese Falcon*. They're also reminiscent of the *quèstia* of chickens, cheeses, and hams given to the bishop of Urgell and the king of France biannually by the principality of Andorra.

From their arrival in 1530 to 1565, the Knights did little to protect Malta, always dreaming of returning to Rhodes. Meanwhile, the notorious pirate, Dragut Rais, harassed them in their new home. Finally Süleyman the Magnificent sent a force of thirty thousand to capture the islands with the help of Dragut as well. The Knights and the locals, numbering only about nine thousand, defended themselves valiantly in this Great Siege, until help came from Sicily. Süleyman was defeated and fled home to Turkey. Today this battle is reenacted in the *parata* sword dance performed during Malta's carnival each year in February.

Fort St. Angelo in Vittoriosa (with the Senglea vedette in the foreground).
MALTA TOURIST OFFICE, NEW YORK.

All Christian Europe celebrated this victory over the Ottomans, and money for the fortification of the island poured in, because the Knights still adhered to their noble mission. To become a Knight, you had to belong to a noble family of Europe, you had to pay a large initiation fee, and you had to leave four-fifths of your fortune to the order. The head of the order was called the "grand master," and the title exists even today.

The grand master who defeated the Turks was Jean de la Vallette, and immediately after the victory he began a building program to create a new capital. Unlike landlocked Mdina, Valletta was on the coast, and was to have a new fort, St. Elmo, from which Malta could be defended from sea attack. Today you can visit this fort, the other bastions surrounding the city, the auberges, and the other magnificent constructions in Valletta built during the 260-year reign of the Knights. As the Knights came from noble families throughout Europe, each speaking a different language, every Knight belonged to one of eight divisions, called *langues.* In the main part of Valletta, there is one auberge to serve as headquarters for each division. They now serve more modern functions, as government buildings, a museum, and even as the offices of the Malta Tourism Authority. Incidentally, the Maltese Cross has eight points representing the *langues* of the early Knights. It is properly called the Cross of St. John, the patron of the Hospitallers. The Knights also built themselves a cathedral in Valletta named after St. John. When you enter it, you see several bays on your right and left, eight of which are dedicated to one of the *langues* of the Knights. In another building, the National Library, you can see documents from the Knights' archives, such as its charter (AD 1113) and the Act of Donation (1530), giving them the island. It must have been the constructions built by the Knights that convinced the UN to name Valletta a world heritage site.

But the story of the Knights Hospitallers is not always an honorable one. Their treatment of their competition, the Knights Templars, was less than exemplary. The Templars were an order with a similar mission and history as the Knights of St. John. Their patron, St. Bernard of Clairivaux, was called by some "the second pope," because of his powerful spokesmanship in favor of Christianity. The Templars made their home for a while in or near Seborga, a small town near Monaco, which still claims to be a microstate principality independent from Italy. Unfortunately, the king of France, Philip the Fair, felt threatened by the Templars, so he accused them of heresy, among other sins. The Knights Hospitallers were only too happy to help in the demise of the Templars, and they inherited most of the Templars' assets. Perhaps under some pressure from King Philip, Pope Clement V "suppressed" the Templars, and their last grand master, Jacques de Molay, was burned at the stake in 1314. This ill treatment may have been what convinced the Masons to revive the Templars in the early 1700s as part of their "York Rite of Freemasonry." Of course, the

St. John's Co-Cathedral.

MALTA TOURIST OFFICE, NEW YORK.

Masons and the Catholics have been feuding for hundreds of years. Because the Hospitallers have been defenders of Catholicism, the Templars make a perfect foil to them as competition and enemies of the Church. Today both the Knights Templars and the Knights Hospitallers ostensibly have honorable missions of charity and faith in the Almighty; however, they are largely old-boy networks of the wealthy.

The Knights of St. John continued to build on Malta. In the early 1600s, the French grand master, Alof de Wignacourt, built an aqueduct to supply scarce water to Valletta. He also had a defensive tower, designed by Gafà, built in northern Malta on St. Paul's Bay. Around the year 1658, the Spanish grand master, Martin de Redin, had thirteen defense towers constructed all along the Maltese coast. And in the early 1700s the great builder, Portuguese grand master António Manoel de Vilhena, commissioned the beautiful Manoel Theater, which today includes a bust of its patron. He also built Fort Manoel, and the building that now houses the Museum of Natural History in Mdina. All these constructions are still standing today and help to make Malta a real gem in the Mediterranean.

Ironically, when the Knights Hospitallers finally got around to fortifying Malta, there was less reason to protect it. Islam had already peaked in its power and territory, and so the Knights' mission as defenders of Christianity diminished yearly. At the same time, the Knights were becoming corrupt, leading rather hedonistic lives. Their treatment of the native Maltese, including Maltese women, was less than exemplary. So it is not surprising that even the priests staged an uprising, which was brutally suppressed in 1775. The Knights had become an occupying power comprised of elite gentlemen from many foreign nations, especially France.

Once again, Malta found itself in the middle, between the Knights, France, and then Britain. When the French Revolution took place, Napoleon began his conquest of Europe. When he reached Malta, he found a population unhappy with its rulers, and an opportunity to confiscate the riches of the Knights and to appear as a great liberator of the oppressed. But once the French took over, their continued pillaging made them just as unpopular as the Knights. The Maltese people appealed to the British, and Lord Nelson soon defeated the French. Alexander Ball became the first British governor of Malta in 1799. Some fifteen years later, the Congress of Vienna officially restored Malta to the Knights, but the Maltese people protested, and as Malta was becoming more strategically interesting for the British, they stayed on Malta until 1964.

Meanwhile, some of the Knights had fled to Russia and others to Catania, Sicily. From Sicily they went to Ferrara, and then on to Rome and the protection of the pope. After their rout in Malta, the Knights practically disappeared, and they were largely reinvented in 1879, when the pope finally appointed a new grand master. Although they were re-created as a charitable organization, their origins in the nobility and their exclusion of anyone who was neither noble nor wealthy tended to ally them to right-wing interests. They have been accused of smuggling Nazis out of Europe after World War II, of secretly injecting foreign money into Italian politics, and even of supporting attempted right-wing coups d'état. Although the Knights have no territory, they have diplomatic relations with many countries, and they are an observer member of the United Nations. For good or for bad, the Knights Hospitallers have had a profound effect on the Maltese and it can be seen everywhere on their islands.

Art and Architecture

Among the arts of Malta, architecture has always been the most important. During their years under the Knights, the Maltese built great fortifications, churches, and other constructions. The Maltese people have also excelled in painting and sculpture. But literature, theater, and other language arts did not fare so well, mostly because the spoken language was traditionally not the

Boat in harbor, against the Dome of Carmelite Church and spire of St. Paul's Anglican Cathedral in Valetta skyline.

MALTA TOURIST OFFICE, NEW YORK.

same as the official language. Whatever the art, Malta has always looked abroad for inspiration, most often to Italy.

From Italy came Francesco Laparelli de Carotona to design the city of Valletta, the new capital of Malta under the Knights Hospitallers. Laparelli had worked with Michelangelo on the dome of St. Peter's in Rome. Pope Pius V sent both him and financial aid to create this new bulwark of Christendom. Laparelli designed the infrastructure, including the drainage system. To avoid another Great Siege, the city was to be fortified with ramparts surrounding it and a fort at the tip of the peninsula, opposite Mount Sceberras. Fort St. Elmo itself was designed by a Spaniard, Pedro Pardo. Laparelli also designed the grid pattern of streets that allows sea breezes to keep the city cooler in summer.

But it was a native Maltese who was to design the most important buildings inside the walled city. Gerolamo Cassar, a military architect, was a student of Laparelli's. When Laparelli left the island in 1570, Cassar began his enormous building program, which included the grand master's palace, the seven auberges, and St. John's Co-Cathedral, all in Valletta. But Cassar's buildings can be found everywhere on Malta, including the Verdala Castle in Rabat. Cassar's son, Vittorio, was not as prolific as Gerolamo, but among other things, he designed the city walls of Victoria on Gozo.

In 1693, a violent earthquake struck Malta, destroying much of its medieval architecture, including the original cathedral in the old capital of Mdina. A new cathedral was designed by Lorenzo Gafà, an architect of the baroque period. This is Gafà's masterpiece, and it includes a magnificent dome. Mattia Preti's mural, *The Shipwreck of St. Paul*, still survives the earthquake. Gafà also designed many of the churches in Malta, including Gozo's cathedral in Victoria and St. Paul's Church in Rabat, a redesigned Cassar original. Gafà's brother, Melchiore, was a talented sculptor, and he did the marble statue of St. Paul that can be found in the church's crypt.

Mixtures of architectural periods and styles are common in Malta, due to the rebuilding after the earthquake. St. John's Co-Cathedral in Valletta is no exception. Designed by Cassar in 1572, it was completed by 1578. Caravaggio, the great chiaroscuro painter, was commissioned by the Knights to do *St. Jerome* and what was to be his masterpiece, *The Beheading of St. John.* These still hang in the cathedral. When he received this commission, Caravaggio was in a kind of exile from Italy, due to his violent temper. A Sicilian called Mattia Preti had studied under him in Rome. From 1662 to 1667 Preti decorated the ceiling of St. John's, including the painting of eighteen episodes from the life of St. John the Baptist. Preti's works can be found all over Malta, including the *Shipwreck of St. Paul* in Mdina, and several paintings in the Hospital of the Order of St. John in Valletta. Preti is buried in a modest crypt in the Co-Cathedral.

An Archaeologist's Dreamland

Malta is one of the oldest known inhabited areas in the world, and you can get some idea of life in ancient civilizations through the ruins conquerors left behind. The ancient Roman occupiers of Malta left us a Roman villa in the city of Rabat. The Museum of Roman Antiquities is located there, too, as well as the early Christian catacombs of St. Agatha and St. Paul. In the same area, at Clapham Junction, you will find samples of the so-called "cart ruts" that crisscross various flat areas of the Maltese Islands. They appear to be tracks cut into the limestone, but nobody is certain exactly what they are. Finally, in the northwest, near Għajn Tuffieħa, there are the remains of Roman baths.

Before the Romans came to Malta, Phoenicians had settled there. Near the picturesque fishing village of Marsaxlokk are the ruins of the Tas Silġ sanctuary, dedicated to the Phoenician goddess, Astarte.

Interior of Mdina Cathedral, the first of Malta's two co-cathedrals.
MALTA TOURIST OFFICE, NEW YORK.

A corridor at the Mediterranean Conference Centre in Valletta, also called Sacra Infermeria (Hospital of the Knights).

Malta Tourist Office, New York.

Tarxien temples.
MALTA TOURIST OFFICE, NEW YORK.

But Malta's archaeological pride and joy are the temples built during the Copper Age, 4000–2000 BC. Whether it's the Tarxien temples, Ħaġar Qim, the underground Hypogeum, or the Ġgantija ("Gigantic") Temples on Gozo, you will be amazed by the huge, expertly cut limestone blocks that fit together without mortar. They are the oldest standing structures in the world. Nobody knows much about the culture that built them, since it is prehistoric. But certain details emerge from the items found in the temples, such as the ubiquitous "fat-woman" figurines. These apparent fertility goddesses can now be seen in museums, notably the National Museum of Archaeology in Valletta. A must for anyone remotely interested in archaeology, this museum contains

The Neolithic Goddess of fertility.
THOMAS M. ECCARDT.

most of the items removed from excavations and temples, and gives a wonderful overview of the prehistory of Malta. It is housed in the beautiful Auberge de Provence designed by Gerolamo Cassar.

Life on Malta

Life on Malta is a curious mixture of contrasts, or what outsiders might even call contradictions. The Maltese work a long business day, yet prize their leisure time. Like their other southern

European cousins, the Maltese interrupt their workday with a siesta, when some people take a nap, at least in summer. This also means that businesses close for a long lunch. But after that, they stay open until seven o'clock in the evening. Coming home from work, many Maltese then go out again for an early evening stroll called the *passeggiata*. They also like to relax in cafés any time of day and watch the world go by.

As you can see from the long table of holidays, the Maltese are great celebrants. Each year, there are no less than six political or historical holidays and seven religious holidays, plus New Year's Day. In addition, there are the local festivals, commemorating the patron saint of each town. The Maltese have always been exuberant about their *festas*—so exuberant, in fact, that the government found it necessary to move all the local feast days to the weekend, to ensure that no extra workdays would be missed by people traveling to other towns to join in the fun. A town celebrating its *festa* will be decorated by electric lights and papier-mâché figures of saints. A heavy statue of the town's patron saint is carried in a slow religious procession through the streets near the main church. Usually the local brass band will play and march in the procession, which ends where it started, at the church. There the saintly image will be restored to its glass case until next year. Then there is partying with fireworks in the evening.

Of course, the *festas* commemorate saints of the Roman Catholic Church. Traditionally, Malta has been staunchly Catholic, even to the point of unofficially giving up some of its sovereignty to Rome. Eighty-seven percent of the population are regular churchgoers, a very high figure for a European country. Despite their faithfulness to the Church, the Maltese people maintain other less canonical beliefs and legends. There is a legend about the shipwreck of St. Paul and a bonfire lit to warm him and St. Luke. As Paul was gathering wood for this fire, a poisonous snake sprang out and bit his hand. Miraculously, Paul was able to carry the snake to the bonfire, unaffected by the bite. From then on, goes the story, the snakes and scorpions of Malta became non-venomous. There are plenty of other legends, many explaining

The fishermen of Malta paint an eye of Osiris on each side of the bow of their boats to ward off evil spirits.

MALTA TOURIST OFFICE, NEW YORK.

Ships sailing before city walls.
MALTA TOURIST OFFICE, NEW YORK.

how certain places or practices became what they are today. If you visit a fishing village, you will see that the fishermen of Malta paint an eye on each side of the bow of their boats to ward off evil spirits. Nobody knows how this tradition reached Malta, but the eyes are said to represent the Egyptian god Osiris.

And despite their strong Catholicism, the Maltese have not been in the pocket of the West, either. Dom Mintoff and his Labor Party made Malta a republic, and removed Queen Elizabeth II as head of state. They also joined the nonaligned movement, and have friendly relations with all neighboring countries, including Libya. Malta always seems to be torn between East and West,

Europe and Africa, North and South. Once again, caught in the middle. This microstate even had difficulty deciding who its patron saint would be: St. Paul brought Christianity to the islands and was Malta's first patron. But St. John was the patron of the Knights who were the occupying power in Malta for almost 270 years. Finally, a compromise was reached: the cathedral they built in Valletta, St. John's, was called a co-cathedral, as a counterpart to the one in Mdina, St. Paul's.

Because this microstate is in the middle of everything, a visit to Malta can be a visit to many cultures and many periods all in one place. From its mixture of Mediterranean peoples to its varieties of Italian, English, and Mediterranean cuisines, from its beaches to its auberges, from bustling Valletta to rural Gozo, Malta can provide an inexpensive adventure for anyone. And all in one of the tiniest countries in the world.

Basic Data

Official Name	Republic of Malta
Official Native Name	Repubblika ta' Malta
Nickname	Microstate in the Middle
Origin of Name	Unknown, but formerly called "Melita"
Capital	Valletta
Origin of Name	Named after Knights Grand Master Jean de Vallette
Official Language(s)	Maltese (Malti), English
Motto (in Latin)	*Cenare et perpotare*
Motto in English	To do good works and to think good thoughts
Nationality	Maltese
Area in Square Miles	122

Latitude	35.5° north
Longitude	14.35° east
Time Zone	GMT+1
Big Sister	None, but Britain and Italy had strong influences
Big Sister Guidebooks to Use	Malta, Italy
Convenient Cities	Catania, Syracuse, Palermo, Rome, Livorno
GDP	$6.818 billion (2002 estimate)
GDP per capita	$17,200 (2002 estimate)
Major Exports	Machinery and transport equipment, manufactures, potatoes, onions
Present Currency	Maltese lira
Exchange Rate	2.29 (dollars/lira)
Population	400,420 (July 2003 estimate)
Annual Population Growth	0.73% (2003 estimate)
Type of Government	Republic
Head of State	President Guido de Marco
Head of Government	Prime Minister Eddie Fenech Adami
Name of Parliament	House of Representatives
Date of Constitution	1974
National Holiday	Independence Day
National Holiday Date	September 21
Year of Foundation	None, but Maltese language formed from AD 870 on
Year of Independence	1964
Women's Suffrage	1947
UN Membership	1964

Diocese	1. Malta; 2. Gozo
Patron Saint	St. Paul; St. John is the patron of the Knights
Telephone Code	356
Internet Suffix	.mt
Radio Stations	19
Television Channels	6
Official Web Site	http://www.visitmalta.com/
Wine	Vigne d'Or, Marsovin, Delicata
Flag	A white and a red vertical stripe with the George Cross in canton

SOURCES: U.S. Central Intelligence Agency: *The World Factbook, 2003*; *Worldmark Encyclopedia of Nations*; *Europa World Yearbook*; *Political Handbook of the World*.

National Holidays

New Year's Day	January 1
St. Paul's Shipwreck	February 10
St. Joseph's Day	March 19
Carnival	Before Lent
Good Friday	Friday before Easter
Freedom Day	March 31
May Day (labor)	May 1
Sette Giugno (bread riots)	June 7
Assumption Day	August 15
Victory Day	September 8
Independence Day	September 21
Immaculate Conception	December 8
Republic Day	December 13
Christmas Day	December 25

Major Dates in Malta's History

1000 BC	Phoenicians settle Malta
218 BC	Malta becomes part of Roman Empire as result of Punic wars
AD 60	St. Paul shipwrecked in Malta
533	Malta becomes part of Byzantine Empire
870	Arabs take control of Malta
1090	Norman kings of Sicily seize Malta from Arabs
1520	Holy Roman Emperor Charles V inherits Malta as new monarch of Spain
1530	Charles V grants Malta to Knights Hospitallers
1565	Turks besiege Malta, Knights defeat them
1798	Knights of Malta surrender to Napoleon
1800	British take Malta from Napoleon
1921	Constitution promulgated, limited self-government granted
1936	Malta reverts to crown colony as constitution is revoked due to squabbles on role of Church
1942	Maltese get George Cross for bravery during WW II bombing
1947	Malta given increased self-government
1953	NATO establishes Mediterranean military base in Malta
1956	Malta agrees to political integration with Britain
1964	Malta gains its independence, joins UN
1974	Malta becomes a republic
1979	British military bases closed, forces withdraw from Malta
1987	Malta becomes nonaligned nation
1990	Malta applies to join EU for first time
1996	Labor Party freezes EU application

1998	Nationalist Party reactivates EU application
2003	In referendum, Maltese decide to join EU
2004	Malta becomes full member of EU

Foods

Food Name	Type	English Name	Ingredients
Hobż	General	Bread	Crusty bread
Ġbejniet	General	Cheese	Goat's or sheep's milk cheese
Pastizzi tal-irikotta	General	Ricotta pastry	Savory cheese pasties
Fenkata	Meal	Rabbit Evening	A kind of rabbit banquet
Hobżbiżżejt	Appetizer	Bruschetta	Bread with oil rubbed with tomato and herbs
Minestra	Appetizer	Minestrone soup	Thick vegetable soup
Braġioli	Entrée	Braciola	Spicy beef rolls, with meat, eggs, bacon
Timpana	Entrée	Pie	Pie containing macaroni, ricotta, eggplant, and egg
Torta tal-lampuki	Entrée	Lampuki pie	Lampuki (fish), tomatoes, onions, peas

Ros-fil-forn	Entrée	Pie	Pie containing rice, ricotta, eggplant, and egg
Fenek biz-zalza	Entrée	Rabbit stew	Rabbit, onions, herbs, wine
Mqaret	Dessert	Date pastries	Deep-fried date pastries with aniseed

Places to Visit

Name and Description	City	Island	Architect / Artist	Year
St. George's Basilica, "The Golden Basilica"	Victoria	Gozo	Preti, altarpiece	1673
Gozo Cathedral, with trompe l'oeil fresco dome	Victoria	Gozo	Gafà, di Messina	1697
Ggantija ("gigantic") Temples— Neolithic ruins	Xaghra	Gozo	—	3300 BC
il-Kastell (the Citadel)—city walls of Victoria	Victoria	Gozo	Vittorio Cassar	1600
Xewkija—the Rotunda Church with huge dome	Xewkija	Gozo	—	1951
Xlendi—Resort village with old watchtower	Xlendi	Gozo	—	1658

Ta' Pinu National Shrine of miraculous cures	Gharb	Gozo	—	1925
Church of Assumption— with fourth-largest dome in world, unexploded WWII bomb	Mosta	Malta	Grognet de Vasse	1863
Biblioteca—Knights' Library, with their historical documents	Valletta	Malta	—	1780
National Museum of Archaeology—in Auberge de Provence	Valletta	Malta	Cassar	1571
Grand Master's Palace— president's house	Valletta	Malta	Cassar	1571
St John's Co-Cathedral— baroque, with oratory and museum	Valletta	Malta	Cassar, Preti, Caravaggio	1572
Auberge de Castille— prime minister's office	Valletta	Malta	Cassar	1580
Church of St. Paul Shipwrecked	Valletta	Malta	Cassar, Gafa	1680
Manoel Theater— beautifully restored baroque theater	Valletta	Malta	Francois Mondion	1731
Upper Barrakka Gardens—private gardens of Knights, with view of grand harbor	Valletta	Malta	Laparelli?	1570
Marsa—a huge sporting ground (with horse racing during Imnarja festival)	Valletta	Malta	—	—

Fort St. Elmo—where the Great Siege began	Valletta	Malta	Pedro Pardo	1551
Knights' Hospital, Mediterranean Conference Center	Valletta	Malta	Preti	1574
Hagar Qim and Mnajdra Temples	Zurrieq	Malta	—	3300 BC
St. Paul's Church	Rabat	Malta	Gafà	1692
Mdina Cathedral	Mdina	Malta	Gafà, Preti	1700
St. Paul's Catacombs	Rabat	Malta	—	AD 57

Monaco:
The Aristocrat of Microstates

Who hasn't heard of the casino at Monte-Carlo? Or of Princess Grace? Monaco is far more famous than it deserves to be, as the second-smallest country in the world. This principality packs a lot of elegance and renown into its tiny territory, which is the most densely populated country on earth. But until a century and a half ago, it was a sparsely populated backwater. In 1861, Prince Charles III effectively exchanged most of his territory for a casino, plus the profit, notoriety, and influx of wealthy people that came with it. Today Monaco is entirely urban—the only open spaces are now parks and the like. After reclaiming another one-fifth of its territory from the sea, this microstate is now at the limit of possible expansion. And since there are already enough tall buildings, Monaco has taken to building many of its support facilities underground.

It is really no wonder that hoards of the "beautiful people" have been attracted to Monaco. Its location couldn't be better. Its Mediterranean seashore supplies its mild, sunny climate. You can go skiing in the nearby Alps, and then go boating in the same day. Monaco is built on a bluff over the sea at the foot of the low Mediterranean Alps. The "Rock," as it's sometimes called, is Monaco-Ville, the capital area, containing the princely palace and

Aerial coastal view of Monaco.
MONACO GOVERNMENT TOURIST OFFICE.

the old town. It separates the new Fontvieille section (reclaimed from the sea) in the west from the port section (La Condamine) and the stylish Monte-Carlo section in the east. There is also a Moneghetti area up the hill overlooking the rest of the nation.

Monaco's situation near the Italian-French border gives it a blend of two preeminent cultures and cuisines. Unfortunately, sometimes this binational culture gets smothered by an international one or simply by French dominance. Today most of Monaco's population is "foreign," and only a sixth is native Monégasque. These natives are given priority in housing and employment, but are prohibited from gambling in the casino. Unlike Andorra's, Monaco's foreign-born residents don't come from the surrounding areas, but are mostly well-to-do tax dodgers from just about everywhere. Although many middle-class people work there, these are mostly commuters from just across the border. You may notice an unusually large number of police and

Stairs at Monaco-Ville (in the Old Town).

MONACO GOVERNMENT TOURIST OFFICE.

surveillance cameras on duty to protect Monaco's wealthy residents and honored guests.

Before the casino was built, the situation was reversed—the well-to-do spurned Monaco, and mostly peasants lived there. For a long period, even the princes of Monaco preferred to live in Paris. But unlike the princes of Liechtenstein, the Grimaldi family actually came from the Monaco region, and left the principality for a more interesting French capital. This was just one of several historical periods of Grimaldi rule, which can be distinguished roughly as follows: early medieval struggles to take and hold Monaco, late medieval Spanish rule, Renaissance absentee rule from Paris, the French Revolution and its aftermath, Charles III and Albert I's transformations, Rainier and Grace's revival, and today's uncertainty.

The Lords of Monaco

In the middle of the twelfth century, after the Arabs were driven out of the northern part of the Mediterranean, the Republic of Genoa got control of the area surrounding Monaco and built a fortification on the Rock. Some of this original building still forms the Princely Palace, a must-see on any visit there. Nearly a century after the Genoese arrived, François Grimaldi dressed himself as a monk and got admitted to this castle, and then let his co-conspirators in. They took over from the Genoese, and became the rulers of Monaco, an act commemorated in Monaco's coat of arms, which depicts two monks armed with swords. But the Grimaldis were not easily able to hold on to Monaco during the next decades, and they twice lost it to Genoa, having to buy it back each time. In the meantime, they also purchased the neighboring cities of Menton and Roquebrune. One of this period's Grimaldi lords of Monaco, known as Charles the Great, was a mercenary captain in the employ of France. He participated in the same Mediterranean piracy that Knights Hospitallers carried on from the island of Rhodes: any vessel passing near Monaco would have to pay protection money.

In 1529, a different Charles, Spanish king Charles I, stayed in Monaco for a few days before sailing on to Rome to be crowned Holy Roman Emperor Charles V. Monaco had recently come under the protection of this Spaniard, and thus the region began its years as an independent Spanish protectorate. This period was one of financial difficulty and increasingly direct rule from Spain. Nor was there much stability in the palace, and the lords of Monaco by the name of Jean II, Lucien, and Honoré I all ended their reigns as victims of murder. In fact, murdering his brother Jean was Lucien's way of making the ruling succession happen a little sooner.

The Princes of Monaco

By the middle of the seventeenth century, Monaco was effectively a Spanish dependency, and Honoré II aimed to remedy this situation. But he also wanted to raise his noble ranking from "lord" of Monaco to "prince." So before taking any actions against Spain, he started referring to himself as "prince" in all his correspondences with the Spanish chancery. Eventually, letters coming back from the Spanish were addressed to the prince of Monaco as well. Next, Honoré II made an agreement with France for protection and plotted to get the Spanish soldiers drunk and rout them out of the fortress. The ruse worked, and the French rewarded Honoré with many other noble titles, as well as recognizing him as prince. This marked the beginning of the period when Monaco's rulers preferred life at the French court in Paris and Versailles to life at the isolated fortification on the Mediterranean. Honoré's grandson, Louis I, was even appointed French ambassador to the Vatican. An absentee ruler of the Rock, he was now stationed in Rome. Louis's wife, Charlotte-Catherine, became notorious for her behavior in Paris. In decadent, pre-Revolutionary France, she had been the king's mistress. She went on to many other affairs, including with other women. But Monaco occasionally benefited from the French influence, as when Antoine I built an opera house there, although his extravagance weakened Monaco's finances severely.

With the French Revolution, disaster struck the French royal court and everything associated with it, including Monaco. The Grimaldis were once again deposed, and the Palace was turned into a workhouse. Luckily for them, after the defeat of Napoleon, the Congress of Vienna was in favor of restoring as many monarchies as it could, and in a few years the Grimaldis were back. Unfortunately, much of the wealth remaining after the profligate days before the Revolution had been lost. Monaco was back at square one. But now a different kind of revolution was brewing, one from which Monaco could benefit: the Industrial Revolution, which brought a class of wealthy people who could afford vacations on the lovely French Riviera. With the opening of the coastal railroad came urban lifestyles and the tourist industry.

Although no Monégasque prince had lost his head in the French Revolution, some of the people of the principality acquired democratic ideas. The nearby Kingdom of Sardinia had a liberal constitution guaranteeing more rights and freedoms than Monaco had at the middle of the nineteenth century. When given the chance to decide their fate, the people of the towns of Menton and Roquebrune voted in favor of independence from Monaco, and they joined the Kingdom of Sardinia. Later, this area of the formerly Italian Riviera was annexed to France, but Monaco was given 4.1 million francs in compensation. In addition, a treaty was signed giving Monaco true independence and protection under France. By this time, one of Monaco's greatest princes, Charles III, was on the throne. He would anticipate or at least adapt to the major changes of the nineteenth century, and it was he who would put Monaco on the map.

Charles III used the compensation money to invest in the Société des Bains de Mer (SBM), the holding company for the casino, hotels, and other improvements which made Monaco an attractive place for the wealthy to vacation. Today the SBM still owns about one twelfth of Monaco's surface area. Monte-Carlo, named after the prince who developed it, is Italian for "Mount Charles." Not many years after the postage stamp itself came into existence, Charles foresaw that collectors would pay for interesting

Monte-Carlo Casino at night.
MONACO GOVERNMENT TOURIST OFFICE.

stamps without using them to mail letters, and started issuing Monaco postage stamps, cofounding with San Marino what is now a flourishing industry in several microstates. When Charles died in 1889, he left Monaco a rich and famous microstate.

Charles' son, Albert the Magnificent, was no less a great prince, but also a great scientist. Though somewhat reluctantly, he adopted Monaco's first constitution in 1911. A true renaissance man, Albert traveled around the world on scientific missions, making important discoveries in the areas of biology and oceanography, and justly received several awards for his work. He established various foundations and institutions in Monaco devoted to science. Prince Albert's Exotic Gardens and his Oceanographic Museum and Aquarium are not to be missed on any visit to the principality. He remained on good terms with both the German kaiser and the French president, hoping to negotiate their differences and prevent war. His wife was a patron of the arts, and managed to get Sergei Diaghilev and the Russian Ballet to appear in Monte-Carlo. By the time of his death, Albert had made Monaco a tiny wonder, respected by international communities of all kinds.

Of course, World War I did break out, and Albert's son Louis enlisted in the French army and fought bravely. Louis was not the marrying kind, producing no legitimate heir. His sister married a German nobleman. By the end of the war, France was concerned that the throne of Monaco could pass into the hands of a German, or someone sympathetic enough to allow the enemy to use Monaco as a port in wartime. So the French signed a new treaty with Monaco, promising independence and protection in return for modification of the laws of succession and giving France a say in the government and in the succession itself. The new laws allowed Louis to acknowledge his illegitimate daughter, Charlotte, as his successor. She would later renounce the throne in favor of her son, Rainier III.

Louis II's reign was not marked by any great milestones, except perhaps for the first Monte-Carlo Grand Prix race, held in 1929. Instead, the Great Depression reduced tourism and made the casino less successful, and the SBM corporation began losing money. In addition, France and Italy were allowing casinos in their territories, making Monte-Carlo less unique and less attractive. The Second World War didn't help Monaco's fortunes either: Monaco was bombed and occupied by both the Italians and the Germans. Louis had attempted to remain neutral, whereas his grandson Rainier joined the French resistance. Rainier received the French Croix de Guerre and Bronze Star for his bravery.

Prince Rainier III and Family

Rainer III, the current ruler of Monaco, was the first prince of Monaco to be born within the principality since 1758. His elder sister, Antoinette, would be the first Grimaldi to marry a Moné-gasque. Later, she would try to usurp the throne. Rainier's father, Compte Pierre de Polignac, divorced his mother, Charlotte, in 1929 when the boy was six. This meant a long separation from his father, who was exiled from Monaco by the Grimaldis. In any case, grand-father Louis died in 1949, and in that year, the twenty-six-year-old became Prince Rainier III of a Monaco in serious decline.

One of Rainier's first orders was to allow his exiled father to return. He had secretly become friends again with the count during the war, despite the Grimaldis' displeasure with him. Rainier also signed a convention with France in 1951 for greater cooperation in certain technical fields, including telecommunication, customs, and postal services. But perhaps a more revealing move was Rainier's decision to contest the will of his grandfather Louis II, who had left half of his wealth to the young bride he had married in his old age. Although the other half was to go to him and his sister, Rainier claimed that most of this wealth belonged to the principality, not to his grandfather. He brought the case to a special dynastic court operating in secrecy. As Rainier was practically in total charge of the government, he was not likely to lose, and he didn't.

Rainier then began cultivating a friendship with Aristotle Onassis, the Greek shipping magnate who would later court the opera diva Maria Callas and marry Jacqueline Kennedy. Onassis advised Rainier on reviving the casino and invested heavily in it and other projects of the SBM. Though Rainier had modernized the casino to some degree already, it was Onassis who made it a moneymaker once again. At this time, the state received 95 per-cent of its income from the SBM, so Onassis was not just saving a company, but a country. Soon after, Prince Rainier began a cam-paign to diversify the economy of the principality, encouraging clean, light industry such as pharmaceuticals. Eventually, Monaco also began welcoming "letter-box" companies as well, through its policy of low taxation.

Another friendship that Rainier had cultivated was with Gisèle Pascal, a French actress. She might have become princess of Monaco, but that would have meant giving up her career, and she married another actor instead of a prince. With Rainier's girlfriend now out of the race, the search for a suitable bride for the prince was undertaken in earnest, headed by a local priest and friend of Rainier's. One might say that Monte-Carlo hit the jackpot when the beautiful—and Catholic—American actress Grace Kelly accepted Rainier's marriage proposal at the very height of her career. Not only was she a screen idol, but her wealthy father would pay a $2 million dowry, ostensibly for the lavish wedding that took place in April 1956. Onassis showered gifts on the couple as well, enough to allow most of Grace's dowry to be invested elsewhere. Princess Grace became pregnant on her honeymoon, and would eventually provide three possible heirs to the throne of Monaco.

All was not well in the principality, however. There were disputes between Onassis and Rainier on whether Monaco should remain a playground for the rich or should try to attract middle-class visitors. More seriously, the Precious Metals Society, really a bank holding much of Monaco's reserves, failed, creating a scandal. A certain Jean-Charles Rey headed a commission to investigate the bankruptcy, and he found that the government had improperly concentrated the principality's assets here instead of diversifying. Unbeknownst to Rainier, Rey was his sister Antoinette's lover, and the couple were trying to tarnish the prince's reputation, not clear it. They were hoping to create such a scandal that Rainier would be forced to abdicate in favor of his sister. No such furor arose, but Onassis advised against exiling Antoinette, since a show of such instability could only hurt investment. After all was over, the Precious Metals Society was essentially converted into a broadcasting company called Images and Sound, and the French government was among the investors in the new entity.

This was not the only trouble that Jean-Charles Rey was making for Prince Rainier. He also headed a new, independent political party, until then an unknown concept in Monaco. By 1957 his party was regularly vetoing Rainier's budgets and other measures. The resentment between Rainier and his sister grew when he found out about her affair with Rey, and he expelled her

Monte-Carlo Casino interior.
Monaco Government Tourist Office.

from her rooms in the Palace. Finally Rainier had enough and, in January 1959, the prince suspended the constitution, dissolved the National Council, and forbade any street demonstrations. Princess Grace assured her American family that Rainier was no dictator, that this was a temporary measure. But rule by fiat lasted for three years.

During these years, Monaco prospered, and Rainier made it public policy that the government would depend on the casino for no more than 4 percent of its income. One source of income was getting on the nerves of the French, who were losing masses of corporate taxes from companies moving to "letter-box" headquarters in Monaco. Perhaps not coincidentally, the French government was buying up a majority stake in the Images and Sound company, which now ran the Monaco radio station. When Rainier saw that it was being bought out from under him, he suspended trading of its shares on the Paris Bourse. He also dismissed his minister Émile Pelletier, a former interior minister of Charles de Gaulle, with some very harsh words for the French, which the *New York Times* reported as "unprintable."

This was the beginning of a war of wills between the princes of two microstates: Prince Rainier III of Monaco versus General de Gaulle, president of France and coprince of Andorra. Apparently, former war hero Rainier assumed he could call the bluff of former war hero de Gaulle, and he ignored French demands that Monaco impose a corporate tax about as high as that of the republic, namely 40 percent. In March 1962, de Gaulle upped the ante, demanding the right to countersign (or veto) all of Rainier's decrees. Rainier rightly retorted that this would amount to annexation. Soon Rainier was calling for a bilateral commission to work out the differences between the two nations. In order to keep Monégasque public opinion on his side, he also restored the constitution and the National Council. But as Monaco was making no concessions on the issue of taxation, de Gaulle declared that the convention of 1951 was abrogated, to take effect in six months, as required by the treaty. Over the next few months, de Gaulle ended agreements on customs, pharmaceuticals exportation, postal exchange, telegraph, and telephone service.

On October 12 the first of the announced abrogations went into effect—the customs convention—and France blocked the road to Nice with customs inspectors. No problems were created within the tiny principality, but anyone trying to get in or out was delayed sometimes for hours for customs inspections. Rainier and Grace were in Paris at the time, apparently confident that the French would not follow through with the threat. They rushed home, and Rainier addressed his subjects, cajoling them to ignore these inconveniences. But Rainier could see the writing on the wall: his country was too dependent on France and too tiny to assert itself militarily. Besides, real estate values were already falling due to the inconveniences and the likelihood that Monaco would no longer be a tax haven. By February 1963, he agreed to the French demands and planned to raise corporate taxes in stages to levels very close to the French ones. Eventually, Monaco and France signed new conventions and recovered their friendly relations. The Monégasque people benefited from the struggle, too, getting an improved constitution that guaranteed the right of women to vote.

However there was one more struggle left, and that was with Aristotle Onassis, concerning control of SBM. In his plan to oust Onassis from SBM, Rainier had the support of the French government. He created six hundred thousand new shares of stock, all to be owned by the state of Monaco. This gave Rainier absolute control, and he forced Onassis to sell most of his stock at a price well below market value. An appeal to the Supreme Court of Monaco of course fell on deaf ears. Onassis sailed away from Monte-Carlo on his yacht, never to return.

Monaco prospered in the 1960s and '70s, helped in part by the publicity surrounding the children, Caroline, Albert, and Stephanie. Their lives seemed to consist of nothing but fast living, brief marriages, scandal, and tragedy.

In 1981, the hereditary prince, Albert, laid the cornerstone for the Fontvieille section, and work began on reclaiming new land from the Mediterranean. This is now considered the light industry area, although it contains some beautiful parks and a new sports stadium. Twelve years later, Albert was on the scene in New York as Monaco was welcomed as the newest member of the United Nations. He is also a perennial participant in the winter Olympics bobsledding event. But there is still much uncertainty about whether Albert will marry and produce an heir, and about what he can do to keep the principality in the public eye and keep the tourists coming.

Visiting Monaco

Coming to Monaco is easy. By car, you reach it on the Mediterranean highway in southern France between Nice and the Italian

The Changing of the Guard takes place daily at the Palace Square at 11:55 A.M.
MONACO GOVERNMENT TOURIST OFFICE.

border. The railway parallels the roadway. There is an international airport at Nice, only minutes away from the principality. There is also plenty of bus transportation to and within Monaco. The country is so small that you can walk across it, although some places this requires climbing. As a matter of fact, when you arrive, it could be helpful go up to the heights of Moneghetti to get a bird's-eye view of the whole country. The tourist office will provide maps and other pamphlets free of charge.

If you have a lot of money to spend, you'll want to stay in one of the innumerable luxury hotels and eat in the upscale restaurants. If you don't, there is still some inexpensive accommodation, including a youth hostel. Alternatively, you could stay in a small neighboring French town or in Nice and make day trips to the principality. Less expensive dining can be found around the railway station or the port.

Monégasques must bore easily, because the entire country is a kind of resort, equipped to amuse the idle rich year round. If you grow tired of the beach or yachting, you can go dancing at the chic Jimmy'z discotheque, or else spend some money at the casino. Monaco has a resident ballet company, a symphony orchestra, and an opera house; if it's not the opera season or the ballet season, then it must be the theater season. In other words, you could spend the rest of your life in Monaco without lacking for things to do. Get a list of what's happening now from the tourist office.

If you don't have that much time, you still will need a day or two to see the sights. Monaco has some unusual museums, such as the Prince's car collection and the museum of antique dolls and automatons, which are still in working order. On your visit to the princely palace and its art collection, you'll want to see the changing of the guard just before noon. And don't leave without seeing some of the legacy left behind by the scientist Prince Albert, such as the Oceanographic Museum and the Exotic Gardens.

Monégasque Culture

If you're looking for quaint local culture, you've come to the wrong country. In some ways, you'd be better off looking just outside Monaco to find native Monégasque culture. Attempts have been made to preserve or revive the Monégasque language and local craftmaking, but Monaco really specializes in the kind of high culture that is enjoyed the world over. As a matter of fact, if you'd like to see what Monaco could have been like if it hadn't been for the casino and everything that followed, you might want to visit Seborga, just across the border in Italy. Seborga claims to be the eighth European microstate, with its own flag flying everywhere in town. You might even meet the "prince of Seborga." Just don't expect to find a place to stay the night.

Church of St. Devota, patron saint of Monaco.
MONACO GOVERNMENT TOURIST OFFICE.

Perhaps you're familiar with *salade niçoise*, with its distinctive olives, anchovies, tuna, and olive oil. *Niçoise* simply means "from Nice," the closest city to Monaco. Any dish *à la niçoise* is likely to contain some of those ingredients and can be considered Monégasque as well. In fact, one of the most popular foods in Monaco is *Pan-bagnat*, a *niçoise* salad in a roll. Monégasque or Niçoise cuisine is a blend of Italian, southern French, and Mediterranean cooking. But if you don't specifically seek out Monégasque cooking, in Monaco you are just as likely to be served high French cuisine or Italian dishes or food from anywhere else in the world.

One way in which Monégasque traditions differ from others is their interpretation of St. Nicholas. The children believe that Santa Claus lives in the mountains above Monaco and, on the night of December 6, he sends a cloud of doves to deliver presents to good children. On their national religious holiday, January 27, all people of the principality, young and old, participate in the commemoration ceremony led by the monarch. This is the feast of St. Devota, who was martyred in Corsica and whose body was placed in a boat by a priest and a sailor. Intended for Africa, the boat was blown north to Monaco. It was found by Monégasques, and they began venerating Devota as their patroness. When later her relics were stolen, the thief's escape boat was burned on the beach. So each year, the whole population of Monaco gathers at the valley of Gaumates to burn a fishing boat in Devota's memory.

Basic Data

Official Name	Principality of Monaco
Official Native Name	Principauté de Monaco
Nickname	Aristocrat of Microstates
Origin of Name	Perhaps from the Ligurian tribe of the Monoïkos; or from "Monoïkos," a Greek name ancient writers associated with Hercules
Capital	Monaco-Ville
Origin/Meaning of Name	Monaco City
Official Language(s)	French
Motto	*Deo juvante*
Motto in English	With God's help
Nationality	Monégasque
Area in Square Miles	0.76
Latitude	43.44° north

Longitude	7.24° east
Time Zone	GMT+1
Big Sister	France
Big Sister Guidebooks to Use	France, French Riviera
Convenient Cities	Nice, Genoa
GDP	$870 million (1999 estimate)
GDP per capita	$27,000 (1999 estimate)
Major Exports	Glassware, electrical goods, cosmetics, precision instruments, and pharmaceuticals
Present Currency	Euro
Currency before Euro	French franc
Exchange Rate / Dollar	1.19
Population	32,130 (July 2003 estimate)
Annual Population Growth	0.44% (2003 estimate)
Type of Government	Constitutional monarchy
Head of State	Prince Rainier III
Head of Government	Minister of State Patrick Leclercq
Name of Parliament	National Council
Date of Constitution	1962
National Holiday	St. Rainier's Day
National Holiday Date	November 19
Year of Foundation	1215—Grimaldi dynasty began in 1297
Year of Independence	1861
Women's Suffrage	1962
UN Membership	1993
Diocese	Monaco
Patron Saint	St. Devota
Telephone Code	377

Internet Suffix	.mc
Radio Stations	9
Television Channels	5
Official Web Site	http://www.visitmonaco.com
Flag	Two equal horizontal bands of red (top) and white

SOURCES: U.S. Central Intelligence Agency: *The World Factbook, 2003*; *Worldmark Encyclopedia of Nations*; *Europa World Yearbook*; *Political Handbook of the World*.

National Holidays

New Year's Day	January 1
Feast of St. Devota	February 26
Good Friday	Friday before Easter
Easter Monday	Monday after Easter
May Day (labor)	May 1
Ascension	40 days after Easter
Whit Monday	Monday after Pentecost
Corpus Christi	Late May/Early June
Assumption	August 15
All Saints' Day	November 1
National Day	November 19
Immaculate Conception	December 8
Christmas Day	December 25

Major Dates in Monaco's History

700 BC   Phoenicians settle Monaco
122 BC   Romans settle in Provence; later, Julius Caesar sails
         from Monaco

271

AD 304	St. Devota's body arrives in Monaco
600	Monaco is part of kingdom of Lombards
700	Monaco is part of kingdom of Arles
1215	Ruling families from Genoa build first fort in Monaco as their new colony
1297	Grimaldis take over, first alliance with Spain
1346	Menton and then Roquebrune (1355) purchased, added to Monaco
1505	Jean II murdered by his brother Lucien—Lucien later murdered by relative
1524	Spanish protection for Monaco
1604	Prince Honoré I drowned by subjects in revolt
1641	French protection for Monaco—Treaty of Péronne
1793	Monaco annexed to France
1814	Treaty of Paris restores rights of Grimaldis
1815	Congress of Vienna grants Monaco Sardinian protection
1848	Menton and Roquebrune declare themselves free cities, join Sardinia (later France)
1861	Independence restored, French protection, loss of territory confirmed
1865	Customs union with France, casino opened
1911	Monaco gets constitution, prince is no longer absolute ruler
1918	Royal succession and French protection treaty written into Treaty of Versailles
1941	Monaco occupied by Germans
1962	New constitution: votes for women, death penalty abolished
1993	Monaco joins UN

Foods

Food Name	Type	English Name	Ingredients
Beignets de fleurs de courgette	General	Zucchini flower fritters	Deep-fried zucchini flower fritters in tomato sauce
Pissaladière	General	Provençal onion tart	Pizza dough with onion, olive, anchovy, and herb filling
Socca	General	Chickpea crepes	Chickpea flour, olive oil
Anchoiade	Condiment	Anchovy paste	Anchovy paste, oil
Tapenade	Condiment	Olive paste	Paste of oil, olives, and capers (anchovies)
Soup aux moules	Appetizer	Mussel soup	Mussel soup with herbs and vermicelli
Soupe de pistou	Appetizer	Pesto soup	Vegetable soup with basil and olive oil
Barbagiuan	Entrée	Stuffed fritters	Fried dough pocket with a rich filling of zucchini and eggs.
Pan-bagnat	Entrée	Niçoise sandwich	*Salade niçoise* served on country bread dipped in olive oil, vinegar, garlic, and basil.

Rougets à la Niçoise	Entrée	Red mullet, Nice style	Sautéed red mullet (snapper) with olives, anchovies, capers, and tomatoes
Stocafi	Entrée	Stockfish	Fish casserole with white wine, cognac, and tomatoes
Tourte de blette	Entrée	Swiss chard pie	Pastry filled with Swiss chard, Parmesan cheese, parsley, eggs, onions, and rice
Fougasse	Dessert	Focaccia	Small, sweet bread flavored with oranges and decorated with nuts, raisins, and anise
Fraises de bois au vin rouge	Dessert	Wild strawberries	Wild strawberries in red wine
Tarte au citron	Dessert	Lemon tart	Lemon butter tart

Places to Visit

Name and Description	Neighborhood
Exotic Gardens, Observatory Caves, and Museum of Prehistoric Anthropology	Moneghetti
Naval Museum—scale models of famous sea vessels	Fontvieille

Museum of the Prince's Antique Car Collection	Fontvieille
Museum of Stamps and Coins	Fontvieille
Fontvieille Park and Princess Grace Rose Garden	Fontvieille
Aquavision boat trips with underwater windows	La Condamine
Church of St. Devota	La Condamine
Port of Monaco with yachts	La Condamine
The Museum of Old Monaco	Monaco-Ville
Palace Princier (Prince's Palace)	Monaco-Ville
Place du Palais (Palace Square) with changing of the guard	Monaco-Ville
Napoleonic Museum and Historic Archives	Monaco-Ville
Oceanographic Museum and Aquarium	Monaco-Ville
Old Town—a taste of pre-high-rise Monaco	Monaco-Ville
Monaco Cathedral	Monaco-Ville
Casino de Monte-Carlo	Monte-Carlo
Salle Garnier—opera house and theater	Monte-Carlo
Café de Paris—gaming rooms and brasserie	Monte-Carlo
Casino gardens and terraces	Monte-Carlo
National Museum: Automatons and Dolls of Yesteryear	Monte-Carlo
Japanese Garden	Monte-Carlo
Jimmy'z—discotheque	Monte-Carlo
Seborga—aspiring Italian microstate	Just across Italian border

San Marino:
The Freedom Microstate

The Latin word *libertas*, "freedom," appears on the shield in the middle of every San Marino flag, but not as an empty phrase. Freedom is what San Marino is all about. The world's oldest surviving republic, San Marino was an island of democracy on an undemocratic Italian peninsula for almost a millennium. The Sammarinese admired Abraham Lincoln so much for freeing the American slaves that they made him an honorary citizen. San Marino also has a long tradition of taking in refugees from conflicts all around it, most recently during World War II. As a matter of fact, this microstate takes democracy so seriously that it pays 75 percent of the airfare to fly its citizens living abroad back to the fatherland to vote in its general elections. About half of those eligible take advantage of the offer, and of course almost every adult citizen who is already there casts a ballot. When you visit the city of San Marino, it's hard not to notice the Statue of Liberty in the Palazzo Publico, marching forward with flagpole in hand. Her crown has the shape of the three towers that have defended this bastion of liberty through the ages.

Dominated by triple-peaked Mount Titano, San Marino is a tiny enclave in northeastern Italy, near the Adriatic Sea and the eastern coastal town of Rimini. Because of the tilt of Italy's boot, it is actually about 120 miles due north of Rome. Rome, Venice, and Milan are the nearest cities with airports—from them you can get to San Marino by train, car, or bus. But if you're going by train, you must stop first at Rimini and then take the highway the rest of the way, because there is no rail connection to this microstate. The town of Urbino is south of San Marino, and the ancient duchy of Montefeltro was located just to the west. The names Montefeltro and Malatesta are often heard in this region, because they were the ancient rulers of the towns of Urbino and Rimini during the Middle Ages.

Legends and Early History

San Marino's history actually goes back to before the Middle Ages, and it begins with the story of St. Marinus, founder of the nation. As with many early saints, it is difficult to separate history from legend, but there doesn't seem to be any better explanation for how the country got its name. Marinus and his friend Leo were stonecutters from the Croatian island of Arbe, who sailed across the Adriatic to escape the persecution of Christians by the Roman emperor Diocletian. They landed in Rimini, and each became a hermit on separate mountains further inland. Marinus chose Mount Titano, a titanic cliffside known for its isolation. Soon Marinus built up a group of followers, whom he baptized, and with whom he formed a monastery. Eventually Marinus's fame aroused the jealousy of Verissimo, the son of Felicissima, the rich owner of the mountain. When he went up to challenge Marinus, Verissimo was mysteriously struck down and was left paralyzed. Knowing that Marinus was a pious man, Felicissima offered him any reward he might ask for if he would cure her son. Marinus asked only for her to be converted and for enough land to be buried in. When her son was miraculously cured, Felicissima gave him the whole mountain.

It is quite appropriate that a stonecutter should be the patron saint of the microstate, since stonecutting is its most traditional craft, and many of its buildings are made from sandstone mined there. Another legend about the founder explains why he sought the solitary life of a hermit. Some time after Marinus landed in Rimini and began spreading the Gospel, a woman arrived from Dalmatius, claiming to be his abandoned wife. He took refuge on the slopes of Mount Titano to escape her accusations. Eventually she found him, but Marinus prayed alone in a cave for six days until she recovered her senses and returned to Rimini. There she confessed her guilt and died. In various places around the Republic, you may also see St. Marinus depicted with his tame bear. According to another legend, this is the bear that tore Marinus's donkey to shreds during his trip to receive a deconship in Rimini. When Marinus encountered the bear at the scene of this crime, miraculously the bear became his servant for the rest of his life. On his deathbed, the patron of the world's only country to be founded by a saint is supposed to have said to his countrymen: "I leave you free from domination by other men."

Guelfs versus Ghibellines

After St. Marinus's death in 366, the monastery and the community around it continued to grow. There are a few historical documents that prove San Marino was inhabited by a religious community as early as AD 885. But San Marino's early history of troubles begins in the Middle Ages, during the struggle between the Guelfs and the Ghibellines. For a large part of its history, San Marino was at or near the border of the Papal States, an often-disputed area. The Guelfs were the supporters of the popes, and the Ghibellines supported the idea of secular government, as embodied by the Holy Roman Emperor. Of course, Catholic clergymen were expected to be Guelfs, and when Pope Innocent IV heard that Bishop Fretrano Ugolino was not only a friend of San Marino but also a proud Ghibelline, he excommunicated Ugolino along with the whole population of San Marino. Two years later, in 1249, the excommunication was lifted, and it did not dissuade

Two views of San Marino, founder of the country, here and opposite.

San Marino from allying itself with the Ghibelline Guido da Montefeltro, against the tyrannical Malatesta family in Rimini. Guido appears in Dante's epic poem, *Inferno*, in the eighth circle of hell, as punishment for giving deceitful advice. Dante, the father of Italian literature, was a Guelf.

The first attempt to place San Marino under papal administration occurred in 1291, when a priest named Teodorico tried to make the Sammarinese pay taxes to the pope and acknowledge his sovereignty. Instead, San Marino appealed to a famous judge in Rimini by the name of Palamede, who ruled that the country was free and independent. Soon after that, Rimini was taken over for the first time from the Ghibellines by the Guelf Malatesta family in 1295. This was the beginning of a century-and-a-half struggle between them and the Montefeltros, in which San Marino was often involved.

The son of the first Malatesta ruler of Rimini, Gianciotto, married the beautiful Francesca of Ravenna. He discovered her dulterous relationship with his brother, Paolo, and killed them th. Francesca is immortalized in the *Inferno* and numerous er literary and artistic works as Francesca da Rimini. An ring of peace, a pardon from the Church, and exemption from ion was made by the Malatestas to the Sammarinese in 1322, v they would break their alliance with the Montefeltros, but s rejected. Though they were Ghibellines, in the early fif- entury the Montefeltros began making peace and alliances popes. For example, Guidantonio Montefeltro married apal-related Colonna family. And Guidantonio's illegit- Federico would actually captain the papal army, which nst Sigismondo Pandolfo Malatesta.

ndo Malatesta is often considered a paradigm of the ssance prince because he had great military talents on of the arts. Unfortunately, he was also a merce- his talents to all sides during the wars. Perhaps this hatred of Pope Pius II as well as that of San rico II da Montefeltro, who would defeat Sigis- rom Sigismondo San Marino took the towns of

Fiorentino, Montegiardino and Serravalle and incorporated them into its territory. The city of Faetano voluntarily joined the microstate, completing the last expansion of its territory. War was ended in 1463, and the Sammarinese lived in peace for another forty years. With the demise of Sigismondo, the Malatestas lost most of their territory except for Rimini. The Ghibelline Montefeltros held on for another half century.

Another paradigm of the Renaissance prince was Cesare Borgia, at least in the eyes of another famous Italian author, Niccolò Machiavelli. Borgia was actually a Catalan immigrant to Italy, who, like Sigismondo, was born illegitimate and was legitimized by the pope. Unlike Sigismondo, Borgia was lucky enough to see his father become pope, as Alexander VI. But like Sigismondo, Borgia was ruthless. Among his many misdeeds, he murdered his sister Lucretia's husband, Alfonso. His Romagna campaign was one of his most brutal, in which he conquered San Marino in the year 1503. Already a cardinal, he was hoping to become an important Italian prince before his father died and the papal money ran out. Luckily for San Marino, Pope Alexander VI died a few months after his son arrived. The new pope, Julius II, was a member of the della Rovere family, bitter enemies of the Borgias, and Cesare had to flee to exile in Spain.

Cesare Borgia also had conquered Urbino, taking it from its Duke Guidobaldo Montefeltro. After Borgia's fall, Guidobaldo got his territory back, but because he had no heirs, after his death the duchy went to his adopted nephew Francesco Maria della Rovere. The former domain of the Montefeltros was ruled for another 130 years by the Guelf della Rovere family as dukes of Urbino. Urbino flourished until 1631, when the last of the Dukes died, and control of the territory passed on to the Papal States. San Marino was now surrounded by Guelf lands, but fortunately it had signed a treaty of protection with the pope some thirty years earlier.

San Marino then fell into of a century of decay and apathy, with many notable citizens emigrating to seek work and fortune. This period almost ended in disaster, when Cardinal Giuliano Alberoni arrived in San Marino in 1739 with a company of troops on the pretext of arresting a couple of criminals holed up in a church. Indeed, San Marino had acquired a reputation as a haven for smugglers, but Alberoni's true motive was to incorporate the republic into the Papal States. Like Cesare Borgia, Alberoni had no respect for the Sammarinese people, cruelly looting their houses. And once again, San Marino appealed for arbitration from a third party, this time through secret messages to the pope. The pope sent Monsignor Enrico Enriquez, whose investigation found that Alberoni had exceeded his authority. San Marino was liberated on February 5, 1740, St. Agatha's feast day, still commemorated as a national holiday.

Modern History

San Marino was never invaded again. Napoleon could hardly conquer the birthplace of modern democracy and retain any pretenses of being a republican. In the nineteenth and twentieth centuries San Marino took in war refugees, from the Risorgimento and during World War II. The Second World War took a severe toll on San Marino, even though it remained neutral. It's not easy to maintain one hundred thousand refugees when your native population is less than a third of that. Furthermore, San Marino and its rail link to Rimini were both bombed by the Allies.

When the war was over, the economy of the region improved only very slowly, so the Sammarinese began looking for ways to improve their lot. San Marino had already followed Liechtenstein's example of allowing foreign companies to incorporate there on easy terms, but this scheme had failed because there was no stable banking system in the region. Liechtenstein had the reliable Switzerland banking system on its border, whereas San Marino had Italy and its unstable currency. Another example that San Marino might follow seemed to be the American state of Nevada, attracting many visitors through its easy marriage and divorce laws and through its gambling casinos. In 1949, San Marino opened a casino and began permitting civil marriage and divorce. The conservative Italian government was not pleased,

Procession commemorating liberation from Cardinal Alberoni.

STATE TOURIST BUREAU OF THE REPUBLIC OF SAN MARINO.

and began withholding its customs contribution rebate. These payments represent San Marino's part of the tariffs on goods that must be imported through Italy, and they make up a good portion of the government's budget. The Italians also prohibited their own citizens from gambling in the new casino. This was somewhat hypocritical, since the San Marino casino really amounted to competition with the Italian one in San Remo. In any case, Italy began stopping all vehicles at the border to be sure Italians were not entering San Marino. Although non-Italian tourists could still enter, long delays discouraged tourism. Furthermore, a large part of San Marino's economy was traditionally based on Italian tourists buying transshipped goods with lower taxes than in Italy. After two years of hardship, San Marino capitulated and negotiated an agreement with Italy, which was signed another two years later in 1953: it limited its marriages and divorces to its own citizens, closed the casino, and agreed not to build a radio or TV station. For its part, Italy agreed to increase the customs rebate, pay an indemnity for the broadcasting ban, and rebuild the railway line destroyed during the war. In 1957 the two countries decided to build a highway between Rimini and San Marino instead, and this remains the only way to get to San Marino. Perhaps France took Italy's actions a model for its bullying behavior in 1962 with Monaco.

During the late 1940s and early 1950s, San Marino was ruled by an elected coalition government of communists and socialists. With the aid of Italy, the communists were overthrown and some were imprisoned. The coalition returned to power in the late 1970s. Now, you may not associate the communist party with freedom, and it might strike you as ironic that San Marino was for years the only Western European country with a communist government. However these were not the undemocratic communists of the Soviet Union, and they often broke with their Eastern brothers, as when Czechoslovakia was invaded in 1968. It is now known that, during the cold war, the CIA funded right-wing parties in Italy to keep communists from coming to power. They were apparently uninterested or unable to do so in San Marino.

Government

San Marino's government is its pride and joy. Its form is unique yet familiar, ancient yet modernized. San Marino was never ruled by a monarch, and its earliest known government may have been modeled on the ancient Roman consuls. A document from 1244 says that at that time there were two consuls, now called the captains regent, plus the Arengo, an assembly of all the heads of families in the nation. These are two of the five bodies that make up today's government. Eventually the Arengo delegated its powers to a Grand and General Council, because there were getting to be too many heads of fam-ilies to run a government smoothly. Today the Arengo is largely a symbolic institution. On March 25, 1906, the Arengo made the important decision that the Grand and General Council would be democratically elected every five years. This day is still celebrated every year as Arengo Anniversary Day.

The sixty-member Grand and General Council and the two captains regent are now the most powerful and important institutions of government in San Marino. The Grand and General Council appoints all the other bodies, including the captains regent themselves. The members of the other bodies are selected from members of the Grand and General Council. Conversely, the captains regent convene and preside over all the other bodies. The Grand and General Council is a legislature and the captains regent are coheads of state. The other two bodies are the State Congress, a group of ten ministers of executive government, and the Council of Twelve, a sort of ombudsman body. You must apply to the Council of Twelve if you wish to purchase land or reside in this microstate. San Marino seems to be unique in having so many divisions of government. This system has slowly evolved to fit the needs of the country, with little regard to what the rest of the world was doing.

The Grand and General Council is an unusually powerful legislature with duties usually reserved for heads of state. For example, it appoints and dismisses the government and grants amnesties and pardons. The captains regent are appointed every six months and they cannot be reelected for another three years. Regency Exchange Day of course happens twice a year, on April 1 and October 1, and these days are holidays of great pomp and ceremony. The inauguration takes place in Valloni Palace, on the walls of which the names of all the captains regent are recorded back to the year 1360. There, dressed in a special uniform including a velvet cape and a beret, the newly inducted captains regent formally receive all people who hold high office in the country. These would be ideal days for a visit.

Visiting San Marino

Staying in the Most Serene Republic of San Marino can be expensive, so you might want to find accommodations in Rimini, which you must pass through anyway. If you spend only a day there, you could see most of the sights in the mountainous capital city, also called San Marino. With more time, you could venture down the cable car to Borgo Maggiore or go further afield to Faetano and its tiny lake. If you don't have your own transportation, you can use local buses. The city of San Marino is full of narrow medieval streets, winding their way up the three peaks of Guaita, Cesta, and Montale. Unfortunately, much of the medieval-style architecture has been rebuilt, including the three castles atop the peaks. If you have time to visit only one castle try Cesta, for it contains an impressive collection of ancient weapons and armor. The fortresses are certainly worth visiting, if only for their spectacular views of all of San Marino, the surrounding area of Italy, and the beautiful Adriatic coastline.

Everyone who comes to San Marino visits the Palazzo Publico, the seat of government, which has a beautiful interior, including a double throne for the two captains regent. In summer you can witness the changing of the guard ceremony in its plaza. The Basilica to St. Marinus is done in a beautiful neoclassical style, but unfortunately it replaced a pre-Romanesque relic. There are numerous outdoor statues adorning the capital, including the

Guaita Tower, the first of three defensive fortifications on Mount Titano.
THOMAS M. ECCARDT.

first monument to Italian Risorgimento hero Garibaldi, who took refuge in San Marino. For indoor art, you can visit the San Francesco Church and Museum. Valloni Palace contains more art, and also some of the earliest documents of San Marino. There are some new, privately owned, rather kitschy museums, such as the Museum of Torture, but there is also the unique Museum of Emigration, a kind of counterpoint to Ellis Island in New York. The

Stamp and Coin Museum in Borgo Maggiore will give you an idea of the history of the stamps that created a microstate industry. Outside San Marino, and in addition to the resort town of Rimini, you might want to visit San Leo, whose castle and churches are dedicated to St. Leo, friend and fellow hermit of St. Marinus. They are smaller but somewhat more authentic than the monuments in San Marino.

Culture and Recreation

Sammarinese people eat like their neighbors in the Romagna province of Italy. They often make their own pasta, including tagliatelle, ravioli, tortellini, and lasagna. Because San Marino is not far from the gastronomic heart of Italy, Bologna, you can always find something delicious to eat there. Like most Italians, the Sammarinese eat pasta as a first course, and then some kind of meat, cheese, or salami as a second course. One of the few things grown in large quantities in San Marino is grapes. They are used to produce excellent local wines such as Muscato San Marino and Sangiovese.

Sammarinese people are also good at sports. They can easily reach the nearby Italian beach for swimming, and they also enjoy the international sports of tennis, basketball, and soccer. San Marino also hosts a Grand Prix auto race, which is counted in the World Formula One championship. Unfortunately, there aren't enough suitable roads for this race inside the microstate, so it's held in the nearby Italian town of Imola. San Marino participates in the international Olympic Games, and also in the Games of the Small States, which they hosted in 2001. One traditional sport enjoyed by many in San Marino is archery. There are archery contests during the many festival days, especially in summer. Other medieval skills such as crossbowmanship and flag-waving are demonstrated at these *festas*. In July, a special "Medieval Days of San Marino" festival is held in the appropriately styled old town. Perhaps all this flavor of the Middle Ages reminds the Sammarinese of their glory days in the fifteenth century when they took territory away from the Malatesta family and made their microstate just a little bigger.

Basic Data

Official Name	Most Serene Republic of San Marino
Official Native Name	Serenissma Repubblica di San Marino
Nickname	Freedom Microstate
Origin of Name	Presumably from a Christian stonemason named Marinus, who was hiding in the local mountains from the anti-Christian Roman emperor Diocletian
Capital	San Marino
Origin/Meaning of Name	St. Marinus
Official Language(s)	Italian
Motto	*Libertas*
Motto in English	Freedom
Nationality	Sammarinese
Area in Square Miles	24
Latitude	43.56° north
Longitude	12.25° east
Time Zone	GMT+1
Big Sister	Italy
Big Sister Guidebooks to Use	Italy, Umbria
Convenient Cities	Rimini
GDP	$940 million (2001 estimate)

GDP per capita	$34,600 (2001 estimate)
Major Exports	Building stone, lime, wood, chestnuts, wheat, wine, baked goods, hides, ceramics
Present Currency	Euro
Currency before Euro	Italian lira
Exchange Rate / Dollar	1.19
Population	28,119 (July 2003 estimate)
Annual Population Growth	1.38% (2003 estimate)
Type of Government	Republic
Heads of State (captains regent)	Mr. Mauro Chiaruzzi and Mr. Giuseppe Maria Morganti
Heads of Government	same
Name of Parliament	Grand and General Council
Date of Constitution	1600
National Holiday	Foundation of Republic
National Holiday Date	September 3
Year of Foundation	AD 301
Year of Independence	AD 301
Women's Suffrage	1959
UN Membership	1992
Diocese	San Marino-Montefeltro
Patron Saints	St. Marinus and St. Agatha
Telephone Code	378
Internet Suffix	.sm
Radio Stations	3
Television Channels	1
Official Web Site	http://www.omniway.sm/ (Italian)
Wine	Brugneto (red), *biancale* (dry white), Grilet (sparkling)

Flag   Two equal horizontal bands of
                                        white (top) and light blue with
                                        the national coat of arms
                                        superimposed in the center

SOURCES: U.S. Central Intelligence Agency: *The World Factbook, 2003*; *Worldmark Encyclopedia of Nations*; *Europa World Yearbook*; *Political Handbook of the World.*

National Holidays

New Year's Day	January 1
Epiphany	January 6
St. Agatha's Day / Liberation from Alberoni	February 5
Arengo Anniversary Day	March 25
Regency Exchange Day	April 1
Good Friday	Friday before Easter
Easter Monday	Monday after Easter
May Day (labor)	May 1
Corpus Christi	Late May / Early June
Fall of Fascist Government	July 28
Assumption Day	August 15
San Marino National Holiday	September 3
Regency Exchange Day	October 1
All Saints' Day	November 1
All Souls' Day	November 2
Immaculate Conception	December 8
Christmas Eve	December 24
Christmas Day	December 25
St. Stephen's Day	December 26
New Year's Eve	December 31

Major Dates in San Marino's History

298 BC	Area of future San Marino is known to have been Roman territory
AD 301	Stonecutter St. Marinus, fleeing anti-Christian emperor Diocletian, founds San Marino
450	A community forms in San Marino
1243	Captains regents established as joint heads of state
1463	Peace is made after San Marino defeats lord of Rimini (1461); the pope gives cities to San Marino
1503	Cesare Borgia occupies San Marino for a few months
1631	The pope recognizes San Marino's independence; later popes protected San Marino from the Italians
1739	Cardinal Alberoni occupies San Marino; the country send secret notes to the pope; the pope liberates San Marino
1797	Napoleon offers expansion territory to San Marino, which refuses it
1849	San Marino gives refuge to Garibaldi
1862	San Marino in treaty with Italy, when a united kingdom of Italy is formed
1944	Allies bomb San Marino, officially neutral but with fascists in control of the government
1992	San Marino joins UN

Foods

Food Name	Type	English Name	Ingredients
Pasta casalinga	General	Pasta	Homemade noodles
Coniglio al finocchio selvatico	General	Roast rabbit	Fennel-flavored rabbit

Tagliatelle	General	Pasta	Thin strips of pasta
Piadina	General	Flatbread	Flour, lard, fine salt
Fagioli con le cotiche	Appetizer	Bean soup	Thick, dark bean soup with bacon
Pasta e ceci	Appetizer	Chickpea soup	Chickpea and pasta soup with rosemary
Passatelli in brodo	Appetizer	Dumplings in broth	Dumplings of bread crumbs, cheese, and egg pasta in chicken broth
Cappelletti in brodo	Entrée	Cappelletti	Small hat-shaped ravioli in broth
Cutlets Bolognese	Entrée	Cutlets	Veal cutlets
Lasagne al forno	Entrée	Lasagna	Flat pasta baked with sauce, cheeses, meat
Nidi di rondine	Entrée	Swallows' nests	Noodles filled with ham, cheese, meat baked in white sauce
Ravioli	Entrée	Ravioli	Square noodle pockets filled with meat, cheese, etc.
Bustrengo	Dessert	Carnival cake	Bread crumbs, corn flour, milk, eggs, sugar and raisins

Cacciatello	Dessert	Crème caramel	Mixture of milk and eggs eaten cold
Torta di Titano	Dessert	Mount Titano cake	Chocolate-covered torte with liqueur and milk
Torta di San Marino	Dessert	San Marino cake	Chocolate-covered torte
Zuppa di ciliege	Dessert	Cherry soup	Cherries stewed in wine

Places to Visit

Name and Description	Neighborhood	Region
Campsite	Cailungo di Sotto	North
Maranello Rosso collection / Ferrari Museum—expensive cars on display	Falciano	North
Malatesta Castle	Serravalle	North
Firearms Museum	Borgo Maggiore	Mid
Museo Filatelico e Numismatico—Stamp and Coin Museum	Borgo Maggiore	Mid
New sanctuary of the Blessed Virgin with rippled side	Borgo Maggiore	Mid
Cable car between San Marino and Borgo Maggiore	Borgo Maggiore	Mid
Basilica of San Marino and little church of St. Peter	San Marino	Mid
San Francesco Church, Museum and Art Gallery	San Marino	Mid
Palazzo Publico—Gothic government house	San Marino	Mid

Montalbo Cemetary	San Marino	Mid
Valloni Palace—with art, library, and archives—restored after WWII bombing	San Marino	Mid
Museum of Ancient Weapons— in la Cesta Tower	San Marino	Mid
Statue of Liberty and Piazza della Libertà	San Marino	Mid
Three mountain peaks with fortress towers— Guaita, Cesta, and Montale	San Marino	Mid
Museum of Emigration	San Marino	Mid
Gate of San Francisco— Main entrance to San Marino City	San Marino	Mid
Changing of the guard at Palazzo Publico	San Marino	Mid
Church and Convent of the Servants of Santa Maria	Valdragone	Mid
San Marino's lake, where trout and carp can be caught	Faetano	East

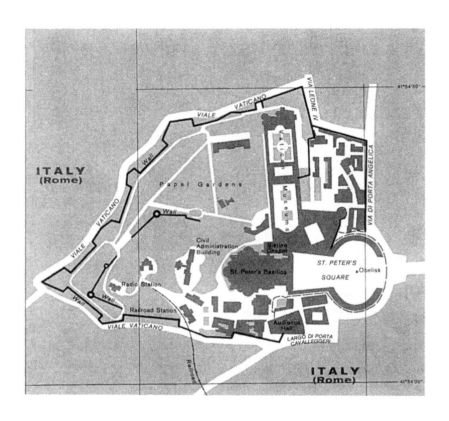

41°54'30"

ITALY
(Rome)

VIA LEONE IV

VIALE VATICANO

VIALE

Wall

VATICANO

VIALE

Wall

Wall

Wall

Papal Gardens

Vatican Museum

VIA DI PORTA ANGELICA

Civil
Administration
Building

Sistine
Chapel

St. Peter's Basilica

ST. PETER'S
SQUARE

Obelisk

Radio Station

Railroad Station

VIALE VATICANO

Audience
Hall

LARGO DI PORTA
CAVALLEGGERI

Railroad

ITALY
(Rome)

41°54'00"

Vatican City:
The Papal Microstate

Vatican City may be the most unusual country in the world. It truly is the papal microstate, since everything revolves around the pope—very few countries put such a concentration of power and influence in the hands of a single person. The State of the Vatican City, as it is officially known, in fact was created specially for the pope. The Vatican is surely one of the most influential countries as well. Its flag is displayed in Roman Catholic churches around the world. Though its territory is the smallest in the world, if all its constituents—Roman Catholics—were counted as its citizens, the Vatican would be the second most populous country on earth. And speaking of territory, it is the only country whose every square inch is owned by a single person or entity, namely, the Holy See.

So far, you've seen three names associated with this microstate, the latest being the Holy See. The word *see* simply means "seat" or "headquarters." The Holy See can be thought of as simply being the management of the Church. The Vatican is really the wall-enclosed complex of buildings including St. Peter's Basilica, several museums, residences, office complexes, and the Vatican Gardens. And Vatican City is the proper name for the

Der Vatican in Rom. *Originally published for Hermann J. Meyer, 1852.*
PICTURE COLLECTION, THE BRANCH LIBRARIES, THE NEW YORK PUBLIC LIBRARY, ASTOR,
LENOX AMD TILDEN FOUNDATIONS.

country, which includes the walled complex, plus a few other
churches and buildings scattered around Rome. The buildings
outside the walls, however, are not strictly considered Vatican
City territory, although they are Vatican property, and Vatican citizens are exempt from Italian law enforcement while within these
buildings.

The Holy See and the Vatican City are considered two separate entities or "persons" in international law. If this seems mysterious to you, consider the explanation given by the *Catholic
Encyclopedia*: "The Vatican City and the Holy See are distinct
entities, but indissolubly united in the person of the pope, who is
at once the ruler of the state and head of the Roman Catholic

Church." When dealing with the outside world, it is always the Holy See that speaks for the Vatican. The Holy See is a permanent observer at the United Nations, the Vatican is not. The Holy See signs all treaties, and even in the rare event that the Holy See chooses to make Vatican City a member of an international organization, the Holy See signs for the Vatican. Again in the words of the *Catholic Encyclopedia*, the Vatican City is an *instrument* of the Holy See.

Occasionally there has been some confusion as to which entity—Vatican City or the Holy See—is supposed to be under consideration, and not merely among foreigners, but even by the Vatican bureaucracy itself. One reason may be the fact that the Holy See seems to be more like a religion, while Vatican City is more like a state. Naturally, foreign governments want to deal with another state, not a religion, not even if it is a firmly established state religion. Why should a country be created for a religion? And why such careful differentiation between these two entities? Some of the mystery may be cleared up when you consider the origins of Vatican City.

Officially, the State of the Vatican City goes back only to 1929, when Mussolini and Pope Pius XI agreed to settle the "Roman Question." That was when their representatives signed the Lateran Treaty, establishing Vatican City as a new country independent of Italy. Essentially, the treaty gave the Holy See its own tiny territory. Sixty years before that, the Holy See had lost this territory, plus an area thousands of times bigger called the Papal States. The Roman Question arose when Italian nationals took central Italy, uniting their northern and southern regions into the country we know today. For more than a millennium, popes had been accustomed to ruling this area, and they were also used to possessing a large diplomatic corps, and maintaining relations and missions in countries all over the world. Although few countries broke diplomatic relations with the Holy See when it lost its territory, it felt that it needed its own territory in order to be considered a state. But thanks to the technical distinction between the

Holy See and the Vatican, Vatican City is not officially considered the successor to the Papal States. A temporary interruption of the independence—or even the existence—of a country is not unknown to history, and would not normally break a chain of successor states. Yet because the Holy See is technically not the government of Vatican City, the Papal States and the Vatican are officially considered two different historical countries that hosted the Holy See at different times. A third country, Italy, theoretically hosted the Holy See during the interregnum, but at that time the popes shut themselves up in the Vatican and Italy did not exercise much authority there.

The Papal States

The unofficial predecessor of the Vatican has an appropriate enough name, although the Holy See refers to the Papal States as the "States of the Church." For hundreds of years, the pope was Rome and Rome was the pope. But before there were popes, there were Roman emperors. Ironically, it was at the Vatican Hill that Emperor Nero built a stadium in which the earliest Christians were put to death. And the first pope, St. Peter, was martyred here as well. In fact, Church archaeologists believe they have found Peter's bones in a crypt in the Vatican, whose excavation you can visit by appointment. In any case, for the first seven hundred years or so following the birth of Christianity, the successors of St. Peter had no official territory as such. You could call this the prehistory of the Papal States.

Despite the pomp and splendor of the papacy, papal rule has never been very stable. Popes had to flee their headquarters innumerable times, due to invasions and popular uprisings. There have been several antipopes—false pretenders to the papal throne—in history, and at least one sale of the papacy. But everything usually ended happily when a council was called and the outstanding issues were settled. As the spiritual heads of the world's Catholics, popes

Old St. Peter's in Rome. Atrium and façade. From a drawing by Giovanni Battista Falda.

GENERAL RESEARCH DIVISION, THE NEW YORK PUBLIC LIBRARY, ASTOR, LENOX AMD TILDEN FOUNDATIONS.

crowned and legitimized several emperors, as well as undergoing coronations themselves. Some of these coronations have had some surprises as well.

The earliest popes were not called popes at all, but were merely bishops of Rome. Before these bishops had any official territory, they accumulated lands around Rome donated to them by pious Christian rulers. As the Roman Empire declined, these areas were no longer under the control of the emperors. During this period, the power of the emperors also declined, while the proto-popes consolidated their powers as the chief bishop of the Church. In the early fourth century, Emperor Constantine became a Christian and ended the persecution of Christians in Rome.

Constantine built the first St. Peter's Basilica—later replaced by today's monumental construction—and gave the Church of St. John Lateran to the bishop of Rome. He recognized the bishop of Rome as the head of all churches, and he moved the capital of the Roman Empire away from Rome to Byzantium, now named after him as Constantinople. All this weakened the power of the emperor over Rome and strengthened the bishops of Rome.

By the middle of the fifth century, Rome was constantly being invaded and sacked by barbarians from the north. But one bishop of Rome, Leo the Great, was not afraid. When Attila the Hun was about to invade Rome, Leo met with him and convinced him not to enter the city. "St. Leo halting Attila" is a bas-relief carving on the altar of St. Leo that can be found in the left nave of today's St. Peter's. Perhaps emboldened by his success, Leo took for himself the title Pontifex Maximus, literally, "chief bridge-builder," which had been reserved for the Roman emperor. He also proclaimed that the bishop of Rome was the successor to St. Peter. These precedents are now doctrinal beliefs about all popes.

Eventually the Romans had had enough sackings, and since most of the Germanic invaders were Christians anyway by then, the popes began to make deals with them to protect themselves. When the Lombards were threatening to invade, Pope Stephen II made an alliance with another tribe, the Franks. He consecrated Pepin the Short as king of the Franks in return for protection from the Lombards, plus new territories. Thus, in 754, the Papal States were born, with official recognition by the king of the Franks. Forty-six years later, Pepin's son and successor Charlemagne, drove the Lombards out of Rome again. In a Christmas Day celebration, Leo III, the successor of Stephen's successor, set an imperial crown on Charlemagne's head. This first coronation of a Holy Roman Emperor by a pope set a precedent, giving future popes a say in the temporal empire. It led to the mixing of spiritual and temporal powers among the emperors as well. The spot where Charlemagne's coronation took place in the old St. Peter's Basilica is clearly marked near the main entrance of the new one.

During the next six hundred years, popes had difficulty maintaining control of their States, which largely ruled themselves. A controversy on who could appoint bishops, pope or emperor, was settled in a compromise at the Diet of Worms in 1122. However, corruption in the Church was growing and so were the liberal ideas that would later spawn the Reformation. Several popes were poisoned to death. A long-standing power struggle with French king Philip the Fair ended in the kidnapping of the pope in the early fourteenth century, and the removal of the papacy to Avignon, France. The next pope, Clement V, was crowned in Lyon, France. During the ceremony the crown was knocked off his head. Perhaps this action was intended as a symbol of the powerlessness of the popes at this time of the "Babylonian Captivity."

When in 1377 Gregory XI returned the papacy to Rome, he found his Lateran Palace in ruins. So he moved into a palace near St. Peter's in the Vatican area of Rome. Despite the shocks they received during the Reformation, the Papal States and the popes prospered during the Renaissance. Julius II commissioned the rebuilding of St. Peter's Basilica into the enormous structure it is today. The famous Sistine Chapel, where papal elections are held, was commissioned by and named after Julius' uncle, Pope Sixtus IV. Later, Michelangelo painted his masterpiece murals of the *Creation* and the *Last Judgment* on its ceiling and walls. St. Peter's and the Sistine Chapel are the high point of many people's visit to the Vatican, and some historians say their construction was the high point of the Papal States. The popes' lands also benefited from the conquests of Cesare Borgia, the son of one of Julius II's predecessors. Borgia was eventually imprisoned in Borgia Room number one, now part of the Vatican's museums.

The Council of Trent attempted to reform the Church in order to counter the criticisms of the Reformation. It also consolidated much more power in the hands of the Pope, and away from the national churches. But as it made the Church more of a catholic faith and less of a temporal kingdom, it raised the question in many people's minds as to why—in a world no longer governed by religious leaders—the pope needed to rule central Italy. Napoleon seems to have been of two minds on this issue. He summoned the pope to Paris to have himself crowned as the new Holy Roman Emperor. But just before the pope set the crown on his head, Napoleon snatched it away from him and crowned himself, saying that God had given the crown to him, and warning others not to try to take it away. And so a third coronation went awry in the history of the Papal States. Four years later, Napoleon invaded the Papal States, took the pope prisoner, and set his stepson up as viceroy.

After this ignominy, nineteenth-century popes became more conservative. Partly through the diplomatic skills of Secretary of State Cardinal Consalvi, the Congress of Vienna returned the Papal States to the pope after the defeat of Napoleon. Consalvi also helped write a constitution for the Papal States. On the other hand, he conspired with Metternich to repress the Roman people. At the same time, Italy was undergoing its Risorgimento, a rising of the Italian spirit with aspirations of unifying the peninsula into a single country. By midcentury, the new pope, Pius IX, was doing everything he could to quash the Risorgimento, including excommunicating all Italian Catholics who participated in free elections. Despite his efforts, when given the chance, region after region voted overwhelmingly against remaining part of the Papal States and in favor of annexation to Italy. Finally, it was only French troops who were keeping the pope in power, and only in Rome, for that matter. When the troops were called away to more pressing duties, the Italians marched in, and Pius locked himself in behind the walls of the Vatican.

In less reverent circles, Pius IX might be called a sore loser. He denounced much of the liberal thinking of his time. He summoned the First Vatican Council—where else could he hold it?—and had himself declared infallible. Having lost his temporal power, Pius was now invincible in his spiritual power. His reign was one of the longest in history, but also one of the bitterest. At his funeral, indignant Romans almost threw his casket into the Tiber River. Pius's successors were more liberal in their thinking,

Image of Pius IX. Illustrated London News. *Feb. 18 1878.*
GENERAL RESEARCH DIVISION, THE NEW YORK PUBLIC LIBRARY, ASTOR, LENOX AMD TILDEN FOUNDATIONS.

but the anticlerical feeling he caused among Italians kept the Roman question unanswered for another sixty years.

Vatican City

The long papal "captivity" and the walled-in nature of the country have given the Vatican an air more of a monastery than of a country. Tight secrecy in policy-making and finances also contribute to this impression. There are few human rights for Vatican citizens—no freedom of speech, press, or religion. But as everyone has dual citizenship, anyone is free to leave who finds this objectionable. And the so-called "Secret Archives" of the Vatican are really no secret—any serious scholar can get permission to use them. On the other hand, there is no freedom to set up a business, there is no economic competition, and you will see little or nothing that might be considered advertising. Ironically, in its top-down style of management, the entire Vatican is run more like a business than a country. In fact, the Vatican lacks two of the five criteria for statehood. The Vatican was given minimal territory and independence in 1929 by the Lateran Treaty that created it. The pope is the head of its government. However Vatican City has no permanent population, and all its residents are there by the grace of the Holy Father. Finally, although many countries recognize the Holy See, because of the technical distinction between the two entities, Vatican City does not benefit from this diplomatic recognition.

The Second World War broke out just ten years after the Vatican was founded. As the Holy See had done during the First World War, Vatican City remained scrupulously neutral—too neutral, in the opinion of many. The Vatican has been accused of not speaking out during the killing of millions of Jews, Romany people (Gypsies), and others. Throughout the reign of the wartime pope, Pius XII, the explanation was always that the Church could do more behind the scenes and that to speak out would have been suicidal. This monolithic posture was characteristic of the Vatican in all matters until the election of Pope John XXIII. He called the Second Vatican Council, which was almost the opposite of the first. The Church modernized in many ways, including saying the Mass in the vernacular language, instead of Latin. But the reign of the pope who advocated reform in so many areas, both religious and social, lasted only five years.

Although the momentum for fundamental reform in the Church disappeared with the death of John XXIII, the Vatican continued to streamline its style, if not its substance. Because of the pace of changes that John XXIII had set, many were sadly disappointed that his successor, Paul VI, did not relent and allow Catholics to practice any form of artificial birth control. But Paul began a series of trips to foreign countries, including the United States, where he spoke to the United Nations. He became the first pope to leave Italy in 150 years, and his visits were enormously popular. He also improved relations with communist countries, although he held to the traditional doctrine on priestly celibacy, divorce, and the role of women. Paul VI also ended the tradition of papal coronation.

The next pope took the name John Paul I as a tribute to his two greatly admired predecessors. Unfortunately he died only a month after his election, and the cardinals had to be recalled to the Vatican for a second time in 1978 for another election. This time, yet another tradition was broken, and the first non-Italian was elected since 1522. The Polish pope, John Paul II, turned out to be a revolutionary conservative, if such a thing is possible. He broadened the concept of the traveling pope, spending more time on the road than ever before. He even took vacation trips. Yet he was staunchly anti-Communist, and strictly forbade "liberation theology," that is, any kind of pro-socialist preaching on the part of his priests, particularly in Latin America. On the one hand, he reached out to many religions, notably in repudiating anti-Semitism, but on the other hand, he reserved the right to send missionaries to convert Orthodox Christians to Roman Catholicism. After the scandal and fall of the Ambrosino bank, the Vatican became more open with its finances. John Paul II greatly increased the number of nations with which the Vatican maintains diplomatic relations. He also vastly increased the size of the college of cardinals. Some say that this was part of a strategy to guarantee a conservative successor, but John Paul's reign has been so long that he would have had a large number of appointments to make due to attrition alone. Of course, the college of cardinals is unpredictable

Pope John Paul II on a visit to Liechtenstein is welcomed by Prince Franz Josef II.
LIECHTENSTEIN TOURISM.

and the projected front-runner in a papal election never seems to win. But surely this pontiff's influence will last for decades beyond his term.

Visiting the Vatican

If you feel you haven't visited a country unless you've stayed there overnight, you're probably out of luck with Vatican City. There are no hotels, and unless you are the honored guest of the pope, you will not be permitted to sleep there. But the news is not all bad. The Vatican has recently opened a cafeteria for visitors, near the museums, so at least you can eat in the smallest country in the world. The Vatican may be the country with the biggest proportion of its territory closed to unescorted visitors, but you can see more of it if you plan carefully. Several areas are accessible only by guided tour, and these tours must be booked in advance, so get in touch with the Vatican tourist office before you arrive, if you desire to see them. But if like most people you only want to see St. Peter's and the museums, then you don't need to make reservations.

One way to view all of the Vatican—from some distance—is by climbing to the top of the dome of St. Peter's Basilica. From there you will see all of Vatican City and most of Rome as well. You can even get a bird's-eye view of the inside of St. Peter's from the interior gallery. Outside, the park-like areas to the west and northwest are the Vatican Gardens, which actually make up most of Vatican City's area. Surrounding them is the Leonine wall, built originally by Pope Leo IV in AD 846 to prevent further sacking by the invading Saracens. The wall is mostly a Renaissance construction, however. Beyond the wall—what could be called "abroad"—you will see mostly unappealing Roman apartment blocks. Within the walls and among the trees, you can see various roads and footpaths leading to office buildings, the radio station studios, the Academy of Sciences building, and the little-used railroad station. Directly west, in a far corner, is the pope's heliport. Besides the tree-filled areas, there are gardens that you can tour, plus the pope's kitchen garden, which actually does supply him with fresh vegetables. Who says microstates don't engage in agriculture?

Directly north of the dome are the museums and the Pigna and Belvede courtyards, all of which you will see up close as you follow the hoards of tourists around on the ground level. "Pigna" means pinecone and, sure enough, there is an ancient Roman statue of a pinecone standing outside in the courtyard. There is also a modern bronze "sphere within a sphere" by Arnoldo

Pomodoro, another of which stands on the grounds of the United Nations in New York. The museums have their own special wall entrance in the Viale Vaticano and are not accessible through St. Peter's. Looking northeast, in the foreground is the Sistine Chapel, and a little beyond it are the pope's quarters, known as the Apostolic Palace. From one of his windows he addresses the crowds in St. Peter's Square, usually at noon on Sundays. Beyond the palace and a little north of it, you will see a few buildings and the tiny part of Vatican City that resembles a city, with actual streets. In this "urban" area are the offices of the Vatican's newspaper, *L'Osservatore Romano*, and its printing press; the post office; the garage; the Church of St. Anne, with its own wall entrance; and the barracks of both the Swiss Guards and the Vatican police force.

Directly east is the most spectacular view, although less of it is Vatican City proper. In the foreground is the roof of the nave of the basilica. Beyond the church is the main entrance and the Vatican's front yard, St. Peter's Square. It is a huge oval plaza, surrounded by a colonnade with statues of various saints above the columns. In the center is the famous Egyptian obelisk. Beyond the plaza is Pius XII plaza and the main entrance to Vatican City. The avenue that leads away from the Vatican is the Via della Conciliazione, built by Mussolini to commemorate the Lateran Treaty. Where this road reaches the Tiber River stands Castel Sant'Angelo, one of the extraterritorial possessions of the Vatican. Across the Tiber is central Rome. The Castel Sant'Angelo was a fortification built originally as a mausoleum for the Emperor Hadrian. More than one pope has used the passageway in the extension of the Leonine wall to flee to this refuge from a Vatican under attack. The fictional opera character Tosca jumped from the roof of the castle to her death, escaping the Roman police, during the time of the struggles of the Risorgimento.

Southeast of the dome in the distance is the Roman Coliseum, and beyond it on the other side of Rome is St. John's Lateran, the pope's cathedral as bishop of Rome. The view directly south is closest to the international boundary with Italy, and it contains only a few official business palaces, a sacristy, plus the new papal audience hall. You can meet the pope on Wednesday mornings in this audience hall.

If all roads lead to Rome, then they lead to Vatican City as well. You can get to Rome by car, bus, boat, or train from anywhere in Italy. You can fly there from anywhere in the world. Unlike much of tourist Rome, the Vatican is not far from one of the two subway lines. However, unless you are a dignitary on an official visit, you will have to use your feet to get around inside the Vatican.

Like Monaco, the Vatican is populated by people from all over the world. Unlike Monaco, the Vatican does not retain even the tiniest minority of natives, and it could not attempt to revive an indigenous language or culture, which has been lost for millennia. The Vatican more than makes up for this loss of culture with its architecture and the extensive art holdings in its museums. In fact, every building has been recorded in the International Register of Cultural Property under Special Protection. Because Rome, too, has been the headquarters of a huge international bureaucracy for even longer than the Vatican, rich Romans have eaten foods from far and wide for millennia. True indigenous Roman cooking often employs parts of the slaughter that the upper class was accustomed to throwing away.

St. Peter's Basilica and the Vatican Museums are the most important places to visit on any trip to the Vatican. St Peter's is a mixture of styles, with the interior mostly designed by Bernini, and the dome by Michelangelo. Michelangelo sculpted the famous *Pietà* located near the entrance, and painted the ceiling and walls of the Sistine Chapel. In addition to other important artwork, in the rear of the basilica sits the Chair of St. Peter, or the pope's throne. From the basilica, you can also reach the Vatican Grottos, the Necropolis, and the tomb of St. Peter.

There is so much art on display in the Vatican museums that you can hardly do it justice in a few hours. Predictably, given their prudish curators down through the ages, many of the paintings have been retouched to add loincloths and many of the statues have been supplied with fig leaves. There are museums of ancient Greek, Roman, and Etruscan art, housing some famous statues such as the Apollo Belvedere and the Loacoön, and there are museums dedicated to painting of various periods, notably the Raphael rooms, which include his *Transfiguration* and *School of Athens*. Da Vinci and Caravaggio are also represented. There is also a library and a tapestry room.

Outside the Vatican you might like to visit some of the churches that belong to this microstate. St. John Lateran is the seat of the diocese of Rome, and Santa Maria Maggiore is dedicated to the mother of Jesus. These two churches and San Clemente, with its strange mixture of architectural periods, are located on the other side of town from the Vatican. If you're interested in quasi microstates, visit the world headquarters of the Knights of Malta in Palazzo Malta, 68 Via Condotti. You can read more about the Knights in the chapter on Malta.

Basic Data

Official Name	State of the Vatican City / The Holy See
Official Native Name	Stato della Citta del Vaticano / Santa Sede
Nickname	Papal Microstate
Origin of Name	Origin uncertain; perhaps from the name of an ancient Etruscan town; in any case, Vatican City was established on Vatican Hill
Capital	Vatican City
Origin/Meaning of Name	Vatican City
Official Language(s)	Latin, Italian

Motto	—
Nationality	—
Area in Square Miles	0.2
Latitude	41.54° north
Longitude	12.27° east
Time Zone	GMT+1
Big Sister	Italy
Big Sister Guidebooks to Use	Italy, Rome
Convenient Cities	Rome
GDP	$209.6 million
GDP per capita	257,810.58
Major Exports	exports prohibited by law
Present Currency	Euro
Currency before Euro	Italian lira
Exchange Rate / Dollar	1.19
Population	911 (July 2003 estimate)
Annual Population Growth	1.15% (2003 est.)
Type of Government	Monarchical-sacerdotal state
Head of State	Pope John Paul II
Head of Government	Secretary of State, Cardinal Angelo Sodano
Name of Parliament	Pontifical Commission
Date of Constitution	1967
National Holiday	Installation of Pope John Paul II
National Holiday Date	October 22
Year of Foundation	AD 750
Year of Independence	1929
Womens' Suffrage	—
UN Membership	—
Diocese	Rome

Patron Saint	St. Peter
Telephone Code	39
Internet Suffix	.va
Radio Stations	7
Television Channels	1
Official Web Site	http://www.vatican.va/
Flag	Two vertical bands of yellow (hoist side) and white with the crossed keys of St. Peter and the papal miter centered in the white band

SOURCES: U.S. Central Intelligence Agency: *The World Factbook, 2003*; *Worldmark Encyclopedia of Nations*; *Europa World Yearbook*; *Political Handbook of the World*.

National Holidays

New Year's Day	January 1
Epiphany	January 6
Good Friday	Friday before Easter
Easter Monday	Monday after Easter
Liberation Day (from German WWII occupation)	April 25
May Day (labor)	May 1
Sts. Peter and Paul's Day	June 22
Coronation Day of Pope John Paul II	October 22
All Saints' Day	November 1
Immaculate Conception	December 8
Christmas Day	December 25
St. Stephen's Day	December 26

Major Dates in the History of the Vatican and the Papal States

AD 50   Vatican Hill used by Nero for public gardens and circus

100   St. Peter buried in Vatican tomb

400   Papal residence St. Peter's Basilica built

754   Pepin the Short gives "patrimony of St. Peter" (Papal States) to the popes

1250   Papal States undergo greatest expansion

1300   "Babylonian captivity" in Avignon, France

1377   The pope returns to Rome

1500   New St. Peter's built on site of old St. Peter's

1503   Cesare Borgia dies and his land goes to the pope; true papal control of Papal States

1796   Napoleon conquers Papal States

1809   Napoleon annexes Papal States, Pius VII made prisoner

1815   Congress of Vienna returns Papal States to the pope under Austrian protection

1846   Pius IX becomes pope, gives Papal States their constitution

1870   The pope loses control of Papal States, retreats within the Vatican

1929   Lateran Treaty with Mussolini creates Vatican City

1947   Lateran treaty incorporated into the Italian constitution

1985   Revised Lateran Treaty, end of Catholic religious privileges in Italy

Foods

Food Name	Type	English Name	Ingredients
Carciofi alla giudia	General	Artichokes	Deep-fried artichokes
Carciofi alla romana	General	Stuffed artichokes	Artichokes stuffed with mint and garlic
Fave with pecorino romano	General	Beans	Broad beans with a slice of pecorino cheese
Fiori di zucca	General	Zucchini flower fritters	Deep-fried zucchini flowers stuffed with mozzarella and anchovies
Pecorino Romano	General	Grated cheese	Grated cheese made with sheep's milk
Puntarelle salad	General	Chicory salad	Catalonian chicory with garlic, olive oil, and anchovy
Abbacchio al forno	Entrée	Roast lamb	Roast lamb with rosemary and garlic
Baccalà	Entrée	Codfish	Deep-fried salted codfish
Coda	Entrée	Oxtail	Oxtail
Gnocchi	Entrée	Potato dumplings	Dumplings made of potato or pasta

318

Pizza margherita	Entrée	Pizza	Plain pizza with tomato sauce and cheese
Saltimbocca alla Romana	Entrée	Filet of veal	Filet of veal with prosciutto
Spaghetti al cacio e pepe	Entrée	Spaghetti	Spaghetti with cheese, pepper, and olive oil
Spaghetti alla gricia	Entrée	Spaghetti	Spaghetti with cheese, pepper, olive oil, and pancetta
Trippa	Entrée	Tripe	Tripe

Places to Visit

Name and Description	Location
St. Peter's Basilica	Basilica
Pio-Clementine Museum	Museums
Etruscan Museum	Museums
Raphael Rooms	Museums
Borgia Apartments	Museums
Sistine Chapel	Museums
The Pinacoteca	Museums
Vatican Gardens	Gardens
Castel Sant'Angelo	Rome
Knights of Malta world headquarters	Rome
St. John Lateran Church	Rome
Audience with pope	Audience Hall

PART III

Touring the Microstates

Would you like to rub shoulders with nobility? Are you looking for a new place to start or extend a business? Do you enjoy walking or hiking or skiing? Do you enjoy shopping and getting a bargain? If so, a European microstate would be a enjoyable place for you to visit. If you enjoy history, you'll enjoy two of the microstate capitals—Valletta on Malta and Luxembourg-Ville—have been declared UN World Heritage Sites. On the other hand, some people visit the microstates just because they are microstates—in this chapter you will learn how and why they do. Though it is a little complicated, you can even tour all or most of the microstates in one trip.

Niche Sovereignties

The microstates are known as "niche sovereignties," tiny notches of territory not subject to the laws and customs of the surrounding region. As noted earlier, most of them do not have their own currencies, but legally issue their own versions of other countries' coins. These coins are so collectable that they are often difficult to find in everyday circulation. You can try a bank, but it may be best to inquire at the tourist office in the capital city, where you may be able to purchase them. A commemorative set of Vatican euros was so prized that police had to break up scuffles among people waiting overnight to buy them on the date of issue. The tourist office is the first place to ask about having your passport stamped, as well. These days, there are no customs controls between most counties in Western Europe thanks to the EU and other organizations, so you will not find any customs offices at the international frontier. The tourist office may collect a small charge for a souvenir customs stamp.

Postage stamps are another attraction to the microstates of Europe, where the issuing of commemorative stamps can be an important industry. For more than a century, this has been a profitable way for the microstates to take advantage of their niche sovereignties, but the appeal may be waning, as faxes and e-mails replace letters. Of course, the post office is the place to buy stamps to collect or to send postcards home from an exotic country. In addition, almost every microstate has a museum of stamps and coins where you can view the stamps and coins that you have missed. The first European microstate to issue a postage stamp was Luxembourg, in 1852, but San Marino apparently was the first to issue a commemorative stamp, hoping to tempt collectors. In 1894, San Marino issued a stamp commemorating the opening of a new government—two decades later, Monaco, Liechtenstein, and Luxembourg began cashing in on this idea.

Another kind of institution is common to almost all the microstates is an automobile museum. Even the Vatican has a coach museum. But you won't find a museum of antique trains or mass transportation. This is not surprising, since there is little rail transportation to—and even less within—the microstates of Europe. Except for Luxembourg, you typically need to get around the microstates by foot, bike, bus, or car. You cannot even reach Andorra, Malta, San Marino, or the Vatican directly by train, but all the microstates are accessible by car, including Malta, if you take your car onto the ferry.

Automobile museum.
MINISTRY OF TOURISM OF THE GOVERNMENT OF ANDORRA.

Traveling between the Microstates

The problem with touring multiple microstates is distance—no two microstates are closer than 150 miles apart, so you would spend much of your time traveling rather than sightseeing. Most people stop in on a European microstate as part of a trip to somewhere else. Typically, if you're in a nearby city, such as Barcelona, you might take a side trip to a microstate such as Andorra. Certainly, if you're in Rome, you will want to visit the Vatican. The microstates are a convenient way to add a country to list of those you've visited. Microstates are especially valuable to aspiring Century Club members, who must visit one hundred countries before they can join this exclusive group.

It happens that most of the European microstates cling to the bor-ders of just a couple of countries, France and Italy. France shares a border with Andorra, Monaco and Luxembourg. Italy is neighbors with Malta, Vatican City, and San Marino, and is very close to Monaco. Only Liechtenstein does not touch either France or Italy. When doing a grand tour of either of these big sisters, you could easily take in several of their microstate neighbors. This is linguistically important as well, since you can get along in French or Italian in all the microstates but, again, Liechtenstein. Consult the individual microstate chapters for details on getting to the microstates from their neighbors.

There is no regular rail service directly between the micro-states, so you must change trains between any two. Basel in Switzerland can be your hub between Luxembourg, Liechten-stein, and Monaco. There is a railway along the Mediterranean that runs from Barcelona through Monaco, Genoa, Rome, and Naples all the way to Catania, Sicily, where you can get a ferry to Malta. Rimini is the railway stop for San Marino, and it is acces-sible from Rome and Milan. It may be useful to get a railway pass that can be validated on a day to day basis.

Rail Transportation between the Microstates.
THOMAS M. ECCARDT.

As yet there is very little international bus service to help you travel between the microstates, but renting a car is probably the most practical way to do a grand tour of the microstates of Europe. The roads generally match the railways, but Zurich may be a better connecting city than Basel for road trips between Luxembourg, Liechtenstein, and Monaco. You can take the same route as the train from Barcelona to Catania, passing the same delicious Mediterranean scenery. Be aware that roads can be narrower and drivers less courteous than you may be accustomed to.

Only Luxembourg and Malta have airports, but Monaco and Vatican City are close to the Nice and Rome airports, respectively. Any of these places could serve as the start or end of your microstate tour. It is probably not advisable to use air transportation between the microstates, except for Malta. Nowadays it is often cheaper to fly than to take a ferry, so a plane from Rome may be your best bet when traveling to and from this island microstate. Also be aware that the train or car route to Catania is slowed by another ferry crossing from the Italian mainland to Sicily. Another useful hub is the northern Italian city of Milan, with its international airport, central location, and rail connections to Rome, Rimini, Monaco, and Basel.

Given that most of them are landlocked, it is surprising how many European microstates are accessible by boat. The Vatican is close to the Tyrrhenian Sea and San Marino is close to the Adriatic. Liechtenstein is on the Rhine River and Luxembourg is on the Moselle. These two rivers meet at Koblenz, Germany. Of course, Malta and Monaco are on the Mediterranean. The only microstate totally inaccessible by boat is Andorra. So with a boat suitable for the high seas and river navigation, it is possible to visit all but one of the microstates of Europe. But this journey would be very time consuming indeed, because you'd have to sail from the North Sea all the way around Europe and into the Mediterranean. More practical trips would be river cruises to Liechtenstein or Luxembourg or sailing between Monaco, Malta, and Rome.

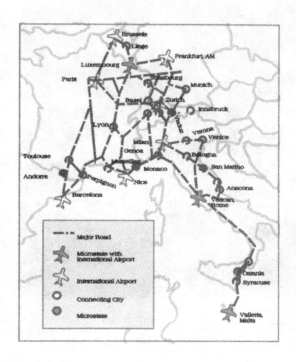

Road Transportation between the Microstates.
THOMAS M. ECCARDT.

Malta International Airport.
MALTA TOURIST OFFICE, NEW YORK.

Setting Off for the Microstates

You have already read about some celebrations of microstate holidays, which are ideal times to visit. So it is to your advantage to time any trip carefully. For a tour of several European microstate festivals, the month of September and environs is best. August 15 is the national holiday (Prince's Day) of Liechtenstein. September 1 is Kermesse, the festival of the City of Luxembourg. Andorra's patron saint, Our Lady of Meritxell is commemorated on September 8. September 21 is Malta's Independence Day, and October 1 is one of two annual celebrations in San Marino called Regency Exchange Day, when the captains regent take office. Finally, October 22 is Coronation Day in Vatican City, commemorating the date that Pope John Paul II took office. June contains at least three microstate holidays and sometimes Corpus Christi. February has several microstate religious holidays. Although February is still a bit cold in the microstates, June and September usually produce fairly moderate weather and avoid the peak of the tourist season.

Tourism is a major industry in all of the microstates, and it is well managed by their governments. That means there are plenty of tourist offices to help you get around. It also means that you may be only one of many people asking for help in the height of the tourist season. But your genuine interest and understanding of the exotic country you are visiting may make you stand out and earn you the respect and support of civil servants and natives alike. Bon voyage, *buon viaggio*, and *glückliche Reise*!

Select Bibliography

Accattoli, Luigi. *Life in the Vatican with John Paul II*. New York: Universe Publishing, 1998.

Aquilina, Joseph. *Maltese: A Complete Course for Beginners*. Lincolnwood, IL: Teach Yourself Books, 1965.

Baker, Randall, ed. *Public Administration in Small and Island States*. West Hartford, CT: Kumarian Press, Inc., 1992.

Banks, Arthur and Thomas Muller. *Political Handbook of the World*. Binghamton, NY: CSA Publications, 1999.

Barnes, Ian and Robert Hudson. *The History Atlas of Europe*. New York: Macmillan, 1998.

Boswell, David M. and Brian W. Beeley. *Malta: World Bibliographical Series*. Oxford: Clio Press, 1998.

Boulton, Suzie. *Passport's Illustrated Guide to Malta and Gozo*. Lincolnwood, IL: Passport Books, 2000.

Brosnahan, Tom et al. *Mediterranean Europe on a Shoestring*. Melbourne, Australia: Lonely Planet Publications, 1997.

Bunting, James. *Switzerland including Liechtenstein*. New York: Hastings House, 1973.

Cardinali, Marino. *San Marino e la sua storia*. Milano: La Souvenir [Kina Italia], 1982.

333

Carrick, Noel. *Andorra*. New York: Chelsea House Publishers, 1988.
————. *Let's visit Liechtenstein*. London: Burke Publishing, 1985.
————. *San Marino*. New York: Chelsea House Publishers, 1998.
Catholic University of America. *New Catholic Encyclopedia*. New York: McGraw-Hill, 1967.
Cavalli-Sforza, Luigi L. *Genes, Peoples, and Languages*. New York: North Point Press, 2000.
Center for Comparative Political Research of the State University of New York. *Political Handbook of the World*. New York: McGraw-Hill, 2002.
Central Intelligence Agency. *The World Factbook, 2003*. Washington, DC: Imaging and Publishing Support, 2003.
Christophory, Jul and Emile Thoma. *Luxembourg*. World Bibliographical Series. Oxford: Clio Press, 1997.
Columbia University Press. *Columbia Encyclopedia*. New York: Columbia University Press, 1975.
Conry, Kieran. Let's Visit the Vatican. London: Burke Publishing, 1984.
DeLaite, Alexandra, ed. *Let's Go Italy*. New York: St. Martin's Press, 1999.
Dubin, Marc. *The Rough Guide to the Pyrenees*. London: Rough Guides, Ltd., 2001.
Dunford, Martin and Phil Lee. *The Rough Guide to Belgium and Luxembourg*. London: Rough Guides, Ltd., 2001
Duursma, Jorri. *Fragmentation and the International Relations of Micro-States: Self-Determination and Statehood*. Cambridge: Cambridge University Press, 1996.
Edwards, Adrian. *San Marino*. World Bibliographical Series. Oxford: Clio Press, 1996.
Encyclopaedia Britannica, 2003. Chicago: Encyclopaedia Britannica, 2003.
Europa Publications Ltd. *The Europa World Year Book*, 44th ed. London: Europa Publications Ltd., 2003.
Facaros, Dana and Michael Pauls. *Rome, Padua, Assisi*. London: Cadogan Guides, 1999.

Financial Times of London. "Luxembourg Survey." London: Financial Times, 6 June 2002.

Gall, Timothy L. *Worldmark Encyclopedia of the Nations: Europe.* Detroit: Gale Group, 2004.

Glatt, John. *The Royal House of Monaco.* New York: St. Martin's Press, 1998.

Gillman, Helen. *Lonely Planet Rome.* Victoria, Australia: Lonely Planet Publications, 1999.

Hindley, Geoffrey. *The Royal Families of Europe.* New York: Carroll & Graf Publishers, 2000.

Hitzelsberger, Franz, Jochen Reuter, Wolfgang Steinle. *Scientific Report on the Mobility of Cross-border Workers within the EEA.* Munich: MKW Wirtschaftsforschung GmbH, 2001.

Hofmann, Paul. *O Vatican! A Slightly Wicked View of the Holy See.* New York: Congdon & Weed, Inc., 1984

Honan, Mark. *Lonely Planet Switzerland.* Victoria, Australia: Lonely Planet Publications, 2000.

Howard, Kathleen, ed. *Liechtenstein: The Princely Collections.* New York: The Metropolitan Museum of Art and the Prince of Liechtenstein Foundation, 1985.

Hudson, Grace L. *Monaco.* World Bibliographical Series. Oxford: Clio Press, 1991.

Lawson, Kristan, et al. *Weird Europe: A Guide to Bizarre, Macabre, and Just Plain Weird Sights.* New York: St. Martin's Press, 1999.

Logan, Leanne and Geert Cole. *Lonely Planet Belgium & Luxembourg.* Melbourne, Australia: Lonely Planet Publications, 2001.

Lombardi, Matt and Holly S. Smith, eds. *Fodor's Belgium and Luxembourg.* New York: Random House, 2001.

Macadam, Alta. *Blue Guide: Rome.* New York: W.W. Norton, 2000.

Meier, Regula A. *Liechtenstein.* World Bibliographical Series. Oxford: Clio Press, 1993.

Mikes, George. *Switzerland for Beginners.* London: André Deutsch, 1975.

Morell, Antoni. *Boris I, rei d'Andorra.* Barcelona: La Morgana, 1984.

Nagel's Travel Guides. *Six Little States of Europe.* New York: McGraw-Hill, 1964.

Office of National Economy. *Liechtenstein in Figures*. Vaduz, 2000.

Orsi, Robert A. and Norman Harrison. *The Papal States*. New York: HBJ Press, 1980.

Owen, Charles. *The Maltese Islands*. New York: Frederick A. Praeger, 1969.

Popper, Nathaniel V. *Let's Go Austria and Switzerland*. New York: St. Martin's Press, 2000.

Price, Glanville. *An Encyclopedia of the Languages of Europe*. Oxford: Blackwell Publishers, 2000.

Rogatnick, Joseph H. "Little States in a World of Powers—A study of the conduct of foreign affairs by Andorra, Liechtenstein, Monaco and San Marino." Unpublished thesis: University of Pennsylvania, 1976.

Ross, Geoffry Aquilina. *Blue Guide: Malta and Gozo*. New York: W.W. Norton, 2000.

Schaelder, Emil. *Franz Josef II*. Vaduz: Buch und Verlagsdruckerei, 1960.

Seth, Donald. *Let's Visit Malta*. London: Burke Publishing, 1978.

Steves, Rick and G. Openshaw. *Rick Steves' Rome 2001*. Emeryville, CA: Avalon Travel Publishing, 2001.

Svendsen, Christina and Daniel Beraca Visel, ed. *Let's Go Rome 2000*. New York: St. Martin's Press, 2000.

Taylor, Barry. *Andorra*. World Bibliographical Series. Oxford: Clio Press, 1993.

Thorallsson, Baldur, ed. *The Role of Small States in the EU*. Aldershot, England: Ashgate, 2000.

United Nations Deptartment of Public Information. *Image and Reality: Questions and Answers about the United Nations*. New York: United Nations, 1999.

Van Itallie, Nancy. *Fodor's The Netherlands, Belgium, Luxembourg*. New York: Random House, 1999.

Walsh, Michael J. *Vatican City State*. World Bibliographical Series. Oxford: Clio Press, 1983.

Willoweit, Dietmar. Liechtenstein, fürstliches Haus und staatliche Ordnung. Vaduz: Verlag der Liechtensteinischen Akademischen Gesellschaft, 1988.

World Book, Inc. *World Book Encyclopedia 1993*. Chicago: World Book Inc., 1993.

World Tourism Organization. *Yearbook of Tourism Statistics*. Madrid: World Tourism Organization, 2003.

Statistical Sources:

U.S. Central Intelligence Agency: *The World Factbook, 2003*; *Liechtenstein in Figures, 2003*; *Scientific Report on the Mobility of Cross-border Workers within the EEA*; *Worldmark Encyclopedia of Nations*; *Europa World Yearbook*; *Yearbook of Tourism Statistics*

Internet Statistical Sources:

Monster.lu (May 2004); www.vatican.va (May 2004); www.omniway.sm (May 2004).

Index

Index